Cover Story

THE NBA AND MODERN BASKETBALL AS TOLD THROUGH ITS MOST ICONIC MAGAZINE COVERS

Alex Wong

TRIUMPH
BOOKS

This book is available in quantity at special discounts for your group or organization. For further information, contact:

Triumph Books LLC
814 North Franklin Street
Chicago, Illinois 60610
(312) 337-0747
www.triumphbooks.com

Printed in U.S.A.
ISBN: 978-1-62937-925-8
Design by Patricia Frey

To Mom and Dad. Thank you for everything.

Contents

Foreword

There was a decade-long stretch when magazine covers were among the most important things in my life. It started in 1994 with a late-night grocery shopping trip. I was living in Delaware at the time. A magazine with a neon orange logo jumped off the newsstand. It was called *SLAM*. They were the IN YOUR FACE BASKETBALL MAGAZINE. Larry Johnson of the Charlotte Hornets was on the cover.

This was new.

I pulled it off the rack and started flipping through it.

Hold up.

There was a whole *section* on sneakers?

I wanted in.

I bought it and started hitting up the editors on the masthead while waiting for the next issue to come out. I published my first piece with *SLAM* less than a year later. I moved to New York and became their senior editor two years later. I was *SLAM*'s third editor-in-chief three years after joining the magazine.

All because a magazine cover caught my eye when I was out looking for Life cereal and kalamata olives late one night.

It changed my entire life.

A decade and a half later I look back at my time at *SLAM* in terms of covers. My first cover story was Allen Iverson's SOUL ON ICE cover. My first cover shoot was when Jonathan Mannion shot Kevin Garnett at his home in Minnesota. I still remember KG playing an advance copy of Mobb Deep's *Murda Muzik* on repeat so he could memorize the lyrics. My first issue as editor-in-chief was when Chris Webber and Jason Williams appeared on the cover with the caption DOUBLE PLATINUM. It was meant to be a split cover with Stephon Marbury and Keith Van Horn on the East Coast but we scrapped it after the New Jersey Nets got off to such an abysmal start to the season. (I still hear about the GENERATION NETS/CHAMPS BY 2001 cover line by the way, which was kinda, sorta vindicated when the Nets finally made the Finals in 2002.)

The *SLAM* covers were as important to the players as they were to the readers. It wasn't like being named to an All-Star team or getting a signature shoe, but it was close (no NBA player ever got a *SLAM* cover bonus written in their contract... to my knowledge). Gary Payton didn't talk to me because it wasn't a cover story. Antoine Walker asked to be on the cover so many times I ended up giving him a "Cover Story" headline (though he didn't make the cover for the story).

We treated magazine covers like posters. An ice sculptor in San Antonio made a throne for Tim Duncan. Someone in New York created a broken backboard and rim for Kenyon Martin. We put Shaq and Kobe on the cover before their first title. I remember wanting them to point at their ring finger on the cover. Shaq did it. And the Lakers won three in a row. Thank you, Diesel.

At their best, magazine covers are talked about years after the pages inside are forgotten. Remembered or not, all of them were of a time and for a time. Once accepted, they were an invitation that could lead you anywhere.

—**Russ Bengtson**
Editor-in-Chief, SLAM
1999-2004

PART 1

A Star Is Born

INTRO/
North Carolina
Is No. 1

I grew up when _Sports Illustrated_ covers captured an entire era of sports. The cover photos celebrated the best athletes in the world, or sometimes exposed us to the darker side of sports. The cover stories became the definitive text on all things sports. _SLAM_ came and invented a new way of publishing a sports magazine, creating a community of the world's most hardcore basketball fans. _Rolling Stone_ inspired their photography. _The Source_ inspired their voice. _Vibe_ inspired their photo layouts. Publications like _Sports Illustrated for Women_, _Source Sports_, and _ESPN the Magazine_ debuted on newsstands toward the end of the 1990s. I remember so many of these magazines piling up along the windowsill in our family home's kitchen.

These magazines are the main characters of this book.

I set out to cover a period between 1984 to 2003. This book isn't a complete documentation of an entire era, but instead it is a selection of cover stories that I hope together can provide a snapshot of a golden age of publishing and a period of transformative growth for the sport of basketball.

The magazine covers selected for this book mattered.

Most of them still matter today.

The writers, editors, creative directors, photographers, publishers, fact-checkers, assistants, sales reps, and everyone else involved in putting together a magazine (and if there's anything I've learned from writing this book, it's that every issue takes a village) are the people who spent the time and effort making these magazine covers matter. I conducted over 100 interviews with these people who were involved firsthand and also talked to those who helped shape the cover stories and their larger themes.

A *Sports Illustrated* managing editor told me during my research that he couldn't imagine the cover not being the most enjoyable part of putting a magazine together. I felt this same kind of passion during all the interviews I conducted for this book. A lot of fond memories were shared with me. Some embarrassing ones too. Once you start talking to enough people about magazine covers, you realize the beauty in how two people can work on the same cover but have completely opposite feelings about them. Every magazine cover is perceived in a particular way by the general public, but those feelings aren't always shared by the people who created them.

This book isn't just a collection of cover stories. The chapters ahead explore how a series of decisions influenced an entire era of publishing and shaped the basketball narratives of a whole generation (or two) of players. This book is about understanding how these magazine covers shaped an entire era. That's the true power of magazine covers.

Every chapter is centered around a specific magazine cover, and in some cases, several covers exploring a larger idea. Together, you will read about a period of modern basketball which is near and dear to my heart.

I've divided the book into four different sections.

The first section is called *A Star Is Born*, referencing a 1984 *Sports Illustrated* cover featuring Michael Jordan.

This section will explore *Sports Illustrated* through the lens of Jordan's career with the Chicago Bulls, which included three championships, a one-year baseball interlude, and another three championships. When did *Sports Illustrated* become the highest honor for any athlete in the world? What is the cover jinx? Who was the first basketball phenom to appear on the cover? How did so many of Jordan's defining moments end up on the cover? Why did one cover line end his relationship with *Sports Illustrated?* What happened when Dennis Rodman took a *Sports Illustrated* writer on a four-day, three-state trip? What happens when the most famous athlete in the world decides to stop talking to your magazine?

The second section, titled *The In Your Face Basketball Magazine*, references *SLAM*'s slogan.

This section is an in-depth look at *SLAM*'s golden era. We will explore how a one-page newsletter named *The Source* and a rookie named Shaquille O'Neal set the blueprint for selling hip-hop on newsstands and inspired the most influential basketball publication ever. This section will tell the behind-the-scenes stories of some of the most iconic *SLAM* covers of all-time, including the 1996 Draft class cover, Jonathan Mannion's cover shoot with Stephon Marbury and Kevin Garnett, and the defining cover photo of Allen Iverson's career, along with other *SLAM* covers you might have never thought about.

The third section is called *Generation Next*, referencing a new publishing age and a new basketball era at the end of the 1990s.

In this section, we will look at how the 1996 USA Basketball women's national team sparked a women's sports magazine publishing boom. We will explore the search for the next Jordan, both on the court and on the newsstand. We'll look at a new crop of magazines, including *Source Sports*, *ESPN the Magazine*, and *Dime*. We'll find out how Steve Francis and Beyoncé ended up on a cover together. Finally, we'll explore how *Sports Illustrated* and *SLAM* put a high school phenom named LeBron James on their respective covers.

The final section is a postscript to the era covered in this book. It will feature a series of cover stories in the period after 2003 and ask whether magazine covers still matter anymore.

Magazine covers are unique social documents that create both an immediate and long-term emotional impact. I hope this book will do the same.

Here's our first cover story.

ON THE COVER of *Sports Illustrated*'s November 30, 1981, college basketball preview issue are four starters from the North Carolina men's basketball team. They are Sam Perkins, Matt Doherty, Jimmy Black, and James Worthy, standing left to right wearing matching Carolina-blue colored jerseys and white Converse sneakers. Head coach Dean Smith stands in the foreground of the picture, sketching out a play. The cover line says NORTH CAROLINA IS NO. 1. DEAN SMITH AND HIS HIGH-STEPPING HEELS.

The cover photo is missing one person from the starting lineup.

His name was Michael Jordan and he was a freshman who averaged 29.2 points, 11.6 rebounds, and 10.1 assists in his senior season at Laney High School.

Freshman players at North Carolina were not allowed to talk to reporters until they appeared in a regular season game. Smith used this reasoning to reject *Sports Illustrated*'s request to invite Jordan to the cover shoot.

The decision to put the Tar Heels on the cover as the preseason number one team in the country belonged to college basketball editor and North Carolina alum Larry Keith.

"I did not rank them in my top-20 the previous year, and they ended up in the national championship game," he explained. "I had ignored the team that turned out to be the second-best in the country in my effort to be completely objective. I didn't want to make the same mistake again."

Keith had a personal relationship with Smith dating back to his days working as the sports editor of the school's paper.

"I remember being on the phone with him because he knew me, and I explained to him from a professional perspective how ridiculous the magazine cover would look with just four starters," he said. "I also tried to talk to him about it personally. Dean was polite about it, but he was firm in his position. None of the arguments I made were successful."

The freshman starter who didn't make the *Sports Illustrated* cover hit the game-winning jumper in the national championship game several months later.

In 2000, when Keith celebrated 30 years working at the magazine, he received a congratulatory note from Smith.

"You now have my permission," he wrote, "to place Michael Jordan on the *Sports Illustrated* cover."

A Star Is
BORN

It's hard to pinpoint when the *Sports Illustrated* cover became the highest honor for any athlete.

But it certainly wasn't the 1950s.

The first issue of *Sports Illustrated*, dated August 16, 1954, featured a photo of Milwaukee Braves third baseman Eddie Mathews batting at Milwaukee County Stadium.

This traditional sports cover was rare during the magazine's first decade. You will find cover stories about Montauk fishing, the African safari, and Swiss skiing if you flip through the early issues of *Sports Illustrated* today. The athletes who did make the cover were scuba divers, archery champions, and Kippax Fearnought, the English bulldog who won the 1955 Westminster Kennel Club Dog Show's Best in Show award. The covers start to make more sense when you flip through the inside of the magazine and find print advertisements of Burberry coats and diamond rings sandwiched between stories on horse shows and antique car rallies. *Sports Illustrated* was a white-collar, upper-middle-class lifestyle magazine. A sports fan subscribing to the magazine was more likely to find an eight-page story on America's best trout fishing spots than a preview of the upcoming football season. The magazine lost $33 million in its first decade. Half of the magazine's initial readers cancelled their subscriptions.

The *Sports Illustrated* we are familiar with today started in 1960, when André Laguerre became the magazine's managing editor. He correctly shifted the publication's focus toward covering major professional sports after recognizing pro football's growing popularity. *Sports Illustrated* hired the best photographers and assembled the most talented group of sportswriters in the country. They provided definitive behind-the-scenes coverage from the week's major sporting events. Editors in the 1950s had to send color plates to an engraver up to six weeks before the issue hit newsstands. The covers were more timely a decade later and reflected the annual sports calendar: The Super Bowl cover in January, the NBA and NHL in February, the NCAA tournament in March and April, the NBA and NHL playoffs in May and June, baseball in the summer, college and pro football in the fall, and The Sportsman of the Year issue to cap off each year. *Sports Illustrated* became a profitable business and the last word on all things sports. The magazine's weekly circulation—the number of issues distributed each week—increased from 450,000 at its inception to 2.2 million by 1979. They had an overall readership of 16 million.

"It is authoritative, fearless, powerful. Whatever else may be said about a sporting event, there's a large segment of the public that waits anxiously to see what *Sports Illustrated* says about it," wrote Ronald Green of *The Charlotte News* in 1979. "In its field, it is uncontested in quality, content, style. Its editors are imaginative and demanding. Its writers and photographers are, in their fields, the equals of the superstars that are their subjects."

The covers celebrated the most significant moments in sports. Vince Lombardi's Super Bowl II win. Hank Aaron's record-setting 715th home run. The Team USA Olympic hockey team beating the Soviet Union at the 1980 Winter Olympics.

The *Sports Illustrated* cover became the highest honor for any athlete. But not for everyone.

Skier Jill Kinmont hit a tree during a practice run and was paralyzed from the neck down in the same week she appeared on the cover in 1955. Sixteen-year-old U.S. figure skating champion Laurence Owen was killed in a plane crash en route to the world championships in Prague a week after appearing on a 1961 cover. After players went into slumps, suffered career-altering injuries, or suffered horrific tragedies after appearing on the cover, the idea of a cover jinx gained momentum.

Others simply disappeared from the spotlight after appearing on the cover.

Rick Mount was the first basketball phenom to make the cover of *Sports Illustrated*, appearing on the magazine's February 14, 1966, issue, standing in front of a barn in Boone County, Indiana. The sheepish grin on his face matched only by his perfectly shaped haircut, highlighted by the spit-curl dangling on his forehead. He looked like the American Dream. The cover line introduced him to a national audience as the BRIGHTEST STAR IN HIGH SCHOOL BASKETBALL. A sign on the outskirts of Lebanon, Indiana, said HOME OF RICK MOUNT, MR. BASKETBALL. The stories of Mount's sweet-shooting stroke became folklore in his hometown. He once showed up to the Fourth of July carnival and won so many teddy bears shooting free throws at a carnival game that the operators posted a sign allowing only a maximum of two bears per shooter the following year. Mount spent five hours every day working on his pull-up jumper. He would put a coat hanger over his bed in the evening and toss rolled-up stockings into his makeshift basket.

His high school career was legendary. Mount once scored 57 points against Crawfordsville High School. The school took advantage of his popularity and held the game at nearby Butler University, making enough money from the 10,000 fans who packed the stands to buy a new school bus. The kid who drove a '57 Chevy convertible and enjoyed rabbit-hunting in his downtime was able to choose from more than 500 college recruitment letters after averaging 33.1 points in his final two seasons in high school. Mount chose Purdue University in nearby Lafayette, Indiana, and lived up to his *Sports Illustrated* cover in college. He scored 61 points in one game against Iowa, averaged 35.4 points one year, and made everyone wonder whether he would have broken every single NCAA scoring record if the three-point line had existed. Mount signed with the Indiana Pacers of the American Basketball Association after the Los Angeles Lakers drafted him in 1970 and would later tell friends it was the worst decision of his career.

Pacers head coach Bob Leonard snapped at Mount on the first day of training camp when he launched a 25-foot jumper during a scrimmage. "You're not at Purdue anymore," Leonard said. He pinned Mount to the bench for his below-average defense. The brightest star from Lebanon became an ABA journeyman. He was traded from Indiana to Dallas to Kentucky to Utah before moving to Memphis, where a separated shoulder ended his career in 1975. You've probably never heard of Mount because he averaged 11.8 points and shot 31.7 percent from beyond the arc as a pro and never played in the NBA. They erased him from the sign on the outskirts of his hometown too.

It now reads LEBANON, INDIANA, POPULATION 12,156, A GOOD PLACE TO LIVE.

The *Sports Illustrated* cover was either the highest honor in sports or the biggest curse, depending on who you asked.

Mount wasn't the only player from his era to go from high school phenom to forgotten pro. He was simply the only player from his era named the best high school basketball player in the country on the cover of *Sports Illustrated*. The jinx continued in retirement, when Mount's outdoors shop went bankrupt after four years, forcing him to sell his house to pay off debts. He applied to be a head coach for Central Catholic High and was rejected because the school required him to have a college degree. His son Rich became a high school star in Lebanon and played in the same gym as his father 20 years later with a similar shooting stroke. Mount couldn't even enjoy those games. He told *Sports Illustrated* in 1986 how much he loathed running into some of his old classmates in the stands.

"Now a guy will come up and say, 'Hey, good to see you!' It almost makes me think, 'I don't need that guy,'" Mount said. "He was there giving me the finger when *Sports Illustrated* was taking my picture at the high school. They wanted me to go to a reunion. I said, 'I'll never go to your reunion, not the way you treated me.'"

Mike Peterson arrived in the next decade as the KANSAS SCHOOLBOY MARVEL wearing a red-and-black striped tank top and cut-off jean shorts on the cover of *Sports Illustrated*'s August 9, 1971, issue. He was a multi-sport phenom from Yates Center, Kansas, who led his high school to championships in four sports, including football and basketball.

You've probably never heard of him either.

Peterson graduated from Kansas City Teachers College and pursued a pro baseball career, signing with the Gulf States League's Seguin Toros in 1976. Peterson batted .218 and finished with zero home runs in 55 games and retired. Peterson was a 44-year-old warehouse coordinator in 1998 when he told *Sports Illustrated* about how the cover changed his life. He was at a basketball camp in Colorado when the magazine hit newsstands in 1971. "If they did well, they asked why they weren't on a cover," he recalled. "It was as if I was supposed to be the world's greatest athlete."

The cover followed him the rest of his life.

Was the *Sports Illustrated* cover jinxing the phenoms?

Probably not.

Athletes usually appeared on the cover after a period of sustained success which propelled them into the national spotlight. Their post-cover performance drop-off can be explained as a regression to the mean. This regression was even more extreme for phenoms. Most high school stars go to college and disappear. Most college stars never make it to the pros. Most NBA rookies don't end up as stars.

So it was fair to question whether we were watching the beginning or the end of a basketball phenom's rise when Alexander Wolff was assigned to write a *Sports Illustrated* cover story about Michael Jordan in 1984.

Wolff grew up in Princeton, New Jersey. He devoured every newspaper and magazine in the house while his father filled out the Puns and Anagrams puzzles in *The New York Times*. Wolff got his first byline at a local newspaper in the Mercer County, New Jersey, area called *The Trenton Times*. He attended Princeton University and traveled with close friend Chuck Wielgus across the country after his junior year. They joined pick-up games along the way and documented their experiences in the 1980 book *The In Your Face Basketball Book*. Wolff landed a fact-checker position with *Sports Illustrated* after his graduation. He joined the college basketball beat in 1982 and covered Jordan's sophomore season, when he was a first-team All-American. Wolff still remembers watching him single-handedly defeat Len Bias and the Maryland Terrapins at Cole Field House in his junior year. The *Sports Illustrated* writer wasn't surprised when Jordan became a national story in the first month of his NBA career.

"This was a guy who had been on this path," Wolff said, "and it was going to continue on that trajectory."

It wasn't just the way Jordan filled up the box score. He was an entertainer on the floor. A highlight-reel play appeared on *SportsCenter* every night. His Air Jordan sneakers were a pop-culture phenomenon. Jordan had a magnetic smile and an undeniable charisma. The Chicago Bulls improved their record to 7–2 after he scored 45 points in a win over San Antonio during the third week of the season. It was a remarkable accomplishment for a team that played in front of half-empty home crowds and missed the playoffs for three straight seasons prior to his arrival. Thanks to Jordan, the Bulls—who were scheduled for a single national television game during the season—were now a feature attraction at Chicago Stadium and on the road, even prompting long-time basketball fan and actor Jack Nicholson to give up his courtside Lakers seat on a Friday night early in the season and instead make the trip across town to watch Jordan play against the lowly Clippers.

Jordan's stardom surprised many people in 1984, including his own team. He was a consolation prize on the day of the NBA draft. General manager Rod Thorn wanted a starting center, but Akeem Olajuwon and Sam Bowie were off the board by the time he was on the clock with the number three pick. He settled on picking Jordan—considered to be the best player still available—after entertaining trade offers for the draft pick up to the final minute, telling reporters after: "We wish he were seven feet, but he isn't."

Thorn received a call from assistant coach Bill Blair after the first day of training camp a few months later. "Boy, you didn't make a mistake this year," he shouted excitedly. The rookie guard dominated one-on-one drills and took off from the free-throw line for a dunk during a scrimmage. After just one day at camp, everyone knew Jordan was the best player on the Bulls.

He became a *Sports Illustrated*–cover-worthy national story.

Wolff's cover story is an incredible portrait of the best basketball player of his generation at the very beginning of his career. Jordan lived in a suburban townhouse, did his own house cleaning, drove his Chevy Blazer around the city, enjoyed bowling, and watched stock-car racing. The magazine inset photos showed Jordan playing mini-putt golf and driving go-karts with teammates Rod Higgins and Orlando Woolridge.

"Michael was just a kid who said all these things that don't compute at all with the person we've come to know," Wolff said. "He was so innocent."

His goal was to make one All-Star appearance in his career.

It was a different time.

Did Wolff know at the time he was profiling the most popular cover subject in *Sports Illustrated* history?

Probably not.

One clue is in how he despised the cover line.

Jordan appeared on the cover of *Sports Illustrated*'s December 10, 1984, issue, flying in mid-air over Sidney Moncrief and Mike Dunleavy of the Milwaukee Bucks in his red-black-and-white road uniform. The cover line read A STAR IS BORN.

"I thought it was clichéd," Wolff recalled. "But worse than that, it was kind of soft. And if there was anything about Michael and the way he was putting his stamp on the league, soft was not it. I mentioned to my editor that RAGING BULL would be more keeping with how he was laying waste to defenses. No less clichéd, but more accurate."

It turned out to be a perfect cover line, taking the long view and correctly predicting a basketball phenom's impending stardom.

YOUR SNEAKERS or Your Life

The *Sports Illustrated* cover was the most powerful image in sports for many years.

The managing editor reviewed the table of contents each week and solicited feedback from the editorial team before choosing a cover story and selecting a cover photo and a caption to provide proper context. The magazine's deadline was Monday evening. The magazine was sent to eight printing facilities across the country once everything was finalized. A new copy of *Sports Illustrated* arrived in mailboxes across the country every Thursday.

Occasionally things would go awry.

Canadian sprinter Ben Johnson broke his own world record in 1988 in the 100-meter dash at the Summer Olympics in Seoul, crossing the finish line in a world record of 9.79 seconds. The race took place in front of 70,000 fans at Olympic Stadium and was viewed by two billion people worldwide. He was selected as *Sports Illustrated*'s cover story for their October 3, 1988, issue. The cover photo showed Johnson sprinting to the finish line. A perfect shot of the fastest man in the world. The caption said WHOOSH!

When it appeared Johnson had tested positive for a banned substance after the race, the magazine scrambled to change its cover story just as the issue was being prepared for the printers. There was a responsibility every week for *Sports Illustrated* to uphold their status as the most important sports magazine on the newsstand. Several writers woke up at four in the morning in Korea to report on the new developments. Another flew back to Canada, where a press conference was scheduled for Johnson to speak. The International Olympic Committee held a meeting and stripped Johnson of his gold medal. *Sports Illustrated* had changed their cover story from a celebration of the world's greatest sprinter to an investigative feature on the most prominent drug scandal from the Olympics within 12 hours of the news. The cover line was changed to BUSTED!

Mark Mulvoy was the person in charge. He grew up as the oldest brother in a large Dorchester, Massachusetts, household. Mulvoy showed up as a kid to Boston Garden and found ushers to sneak him into hockey and basketball games. An aspiring sportswriter from an early age, he wrote for Boston College's student newspaper and worked for *The Boston Globe* before joining *Sports Illustrated* in 1965 as a baseball writer. Mulvoy would later join the pro hockey beat and help with the magazine's golf coverage. He grew tired of traveling across the world covering sports as a father of four kids and was promoted to assistant managing editor in 1981. Mulvoy became *Sports Illustrated*'s managing editor in 1984 and shaped the national sports conversation every week.

"I could do anything with the cover because it never impacted the bottom line," he explained. "Three million subscribers got the magazine no matter who the hell we put on the cover."

No cover subject drew in a bigger national audience than Michael Jordan. He appeared on the *Sports Illustrated* cover 23 times in Mulvoy's first decade as managing editor.

"There was just something about him," Mulvoy explained. "He resonated with people. You could only put Karl Malone on the cover once because he didn't have Michael's charisma."

A basketball player being the most popular *Sports Illustrated* cover subject was unprecedented. The sport appeared about as often on the cover as yachts in the magazine's first decade. Basketball-related cover stories were mostly informational in the 1960s after the publication became pro-sports focused. The stories included "Secrets of the Shuffle Offense in Basketball," "The UCLA Press: How to Beat It," and "The Case for the 12-foot Basket." Pro basketball was still not very high on the magazine's hierarchy even after *Sports Illustrated* introduced more personality-driven covers of Julius Erving, Larry Bird, and Magic Johnson to a national audience in the 1970s.

The *Sports Illustrated* cover reflected the current national sports conversation. The absence of pro basketball covers reflected the NBA's standing in the overall sports landscape. "We were behind baseball, football, and college sports," explained Rick Welts, the NBA's director of national promotions. "We were not a well-run or well-respected league. We were the first league tainted with widespread accusations of drug use by its players. I thought I had the easiest job in the world and I would just go out and talk to companies about investing marketing dollars. It was hard to even get an appointment." Magic Johnson's 42-point, 15-rebound, seven-assist performance in Game 6 of the 1980 NBA Finals was broadcast on tape delay. CBS ran old episodes of *Dallas* and *The Dukes of Hazzard* instead of the series-clinching game.

This was the NBA's place among the major professional sports at the start of the decade. The league was a public relations nightmare. Their championship games were an afterthought.

David Stern is widely credited with turning the league around. He ran the business and legal affairs department and later became the commissioner in 1984. Stern started an in-house production team in 1982 named NBA Entertainment and hired Paul Gilbert, who launched a genius promotional campaign called *NBA Action, it's Fan-tastic!* with television spots featuring celebrities like Elton John, Oprah Winfrey, and Gary Shandling shouting out the tagline while attending games in New York and Los Angeles. A drug agreement was negotiated by Stern with the players union in 1983 to permanently dismiss any player who was either convicted of or plead guilty to a crime involving the use or distribution of heroin and cocaine. The league promoted their players in hopes of attracting fans with more recognizable stars. Jordan landed right in their laps and became the number one story in sports after he was selected third overall in 1984. He made the All-Star team in his rookie season, scored an all-time playoff record 63 points against the Boston Celtics, won back-to-back Slam Dunk Contests, led the league in scoring, and became the face of the NBA.

So did *Sports Illustrated* simply cover Jordan's stardom or did they contribute to it?

"We played a great role," Mulvoy said. "We celebrated Michael. Our advertising team celebrated Michael. We had Gatorade and Nike ads in every issue. When you're on the cover like three or four times a year, that's a hundred million people picking up the magazine. The images stick with you."

Stern's vision for the NBA was coming to life toward the end of the decade. The league signed a four-year, $600 million deal with NBC after 17 years working with CBS as their broadcasting partner. Stern correctly predicted the home video market boom, selling championship team videos and driving their product to a growing national audience. When NBA Entertainment released their first superstar-driven home video documentary in 1989, titled *Michael Jordan: Come Fly With Me*, *Sports Illustrated* offered the home video as a promotional tie-in to subscribers. Jordan's endorsers paid six-figure sums to advertise in the magazine. Reporters questioned *Sports Illustrated*'s ability to remain objective.

"I can understand why some people would say that, but I can tell you there was no relationship between us and anyone editorially," Mulvoy said. "There was a separation of church and state. Our only partner was our readers. I never saw one of those ads or promos before they were done. That was the marketing department's responsibility. I couldn't care less about those home videos. I still haven't watched a single one of them."

The magazine certainly didn't shy away from criticizing anyone, including Jordan.

Sports Illustrated writer Rick Telander came across several local articles in 1990 detailing the rise in violence over sneakers and athletic apparel in Chicago. Teenagers were being mugged and killed. The kids weren't after the shoes. They were after a social status marker. He pitched an investigative feature on this growing trend. *Sports Illustrated* asked a group of reporters to compile articles related to any sneaker-related violence in their respective cities. Telander realized this was a more problematic issue than he initially thought after seeing the number of articles which landed on his desk. He examined the problem using the perspectives of buyers and sellers and reported on the story for two weeks. Telander directed his criticism toward the sneaker companies who marketed their products as luxury items to kids who couldn't afford to purchase them. He realized seeing so many of the killings over Air Jordan sneakers there was one more person he needed to track down to complete the story as the deadline neared.

Telander had a relationship with Jordan dating back to his rookie season.

"He was delightful. But he was also a sarcastic wise-ass," he recalled. "I remember going to his place. He had a little pool table down in the basement. We were playing eight ball, and I had a little run going. I needed one more ball to win. He starts taunting me. He got really serious and kept saying, 'The house never loses. The house never loses.' The next thing I know, his tongue was hanging out. He made the next couple of shots and won."

Telander sat down with Jordan at the team's practice facility in Deerfield, Illinois, and handed him a newspaper clip about the murder of a 15-year-old named Michael Eugene Thomas. The ninth-grader from Maryland was killed by 17-year-old James David Martin, charged with first-degree murder after allegedly taking Thomas' Air Jordans and leaving his barefoot body in the woods.

"He looked really sad," Telander recalled. "Michael had this ability to compartmentalize things, but when he read it, it really affected him. The shoe was called Air Jordan, and kids were being killed for it."

Jordan asked if this was an isolated incident.

Telander handed him more clips.

Their conversation became the centerpiece of Telander's cover story, which appeared inside the May 14, 1990, issue of *Sports Illustrated*. On the cover was an illustrated photo of a man pressing the barrel of his revolver against the back of another man wearing a satin Washington Redskins sports jacket with a pair of Air Jordans dangling on his shoulder. The main cover line read YOUR SNEAKERS OR YOUR LIFE. A second, smaller cover line in the upper right-hand corner asked: SNEAKERS AND TEAM JACKETS ARE HOT, SOMETIMES TOO HOT. KIDS ARE BEING MUGGED, EVEN KILLED, FOR THEM. WHO'S AT FAULT?

The New York Times and *The Los Angeles Times* covered the story, as did *Advertising Age*. Their editor, Fred Danzig, wrote: "In the past advertisers would use hyperbole to sell a product without looking at social consequences—they felt that wasn't their role. It may now be time for the advertising business to reassess its moral position." *Sports Illustrated* helped bring the topic into the national spotlight, even if the sneaker industry hasn't changed in the decades since.

Telander didn't think his story idea would be approved, considering the feature's criticism of sneaker companies, the same brands who contributed to the magazine's $300 million advertising revenue per year.

"You couldn't piss off your advertisers week-after-week," he explained. "But you also couldn't cater to them. It was a thin line."

Mulvoy gave him the go-ahead.

"He was a fearless guy," Telander said. "He stood up for his writers and what he believed was right. I can't tell you how important that support was."

Sports Illustrated won the National Magazine Award for General Excellence in 1989 and 1990, becoming the first publication with 1 million-plus circulation to win the award for two years running.

"We stood on our own two feet and didn't answer to anybody," Mulvoy said. "We did what we thought was the right thing journalistically. We held people accountable and became the conscience of sports."

Mulvoy also placed an emphasis on the magazine's photography to communicate the news each week. After taking over as managing editor, he oversaw *Sports Illustrated*'s first full redesign since the early 1960s. Mulvoy thought the photo layouts inside the magazine were a bunch of "mumble jumble," and hired creative director Steve Hoffman, who studied design and photography at the California Institute of the Arts and was previously an associate art director at *New West* magazine, to lead the redesign. "The magazine didn't look sophisticated," Hoffman explained. "The design wasn't giving you the same feeling as the writing and photography."

The redesigned *Sports Illustrated* made its official debut in December of 1986. The issue featured a new logo typeface and more room on the cover for cover lines and secondary photos. The type inside the magazine was also overhauled. Story photos were given full-page spreads for emphasis. Mulvoy was meticulous with not just the placement of photos, but the photo choices themselves. He wanted the cover photos to properly highlight his photographers and address the problem of readers receiving an issue several days after a sporting event had taken place.

"The news was already three or four days old by the time we delivered it," Mulvoy explained. "We had to find ways to deliver it in different ways. Sometimes a picture would say a thousand words. We had so many great photographers. How could you not celebrate their genius by giving them the space?"

Jordan didn't just appear on the *Sports Illustrated* cover, he played a part in crafting their cover stories and even the occasional photo. On the day of the 1988 Slam Dunk Contest, Walter Iooss Jr. (who is responsible for some of the most iconic photos in *Sports Illustrated* history) approached Jordan and asked if there was a way he could help the photographer get the best shot of him. The defending slam-dunk champion agreed, promising to put a finger on his knee and point in the direction he would be running toward the basket before every dunk. Just moments before he took off from near the free-throw line inside Chicago Stadium for one of the most iconic dunks in NBA history, Jordan tapped his knee and motioned for Iooss to move to his right. The photographer, who was positioned against the stanchion behind the basket, did just that and was in a perfect position to capture the definitive photo of the dunk.

The frequency of Jordan's cover appearances increased at the start of the 1990s, as the magazine documented the most successful part of his NBA career. He made the cover for three straight weeks in 1991 as he led the Bulls to their first championship, sweeping the Detroit Pistons in the Eastern Conference Finals and beating the Los Angeles Lakers in five NBA Finals games. Jordan also appeared on the magazine's year-end cover as their 1991 Sportsman of the Year. He appeared on the cover four more times in 1992 in a year where he won an Olympic gold medal with The Dream Team in Barcelona, Spain, and led the Bulls to their second consecutive NBA championship. Jordan would be a *Sports Illustrated* cover subject three more times as the Bulls completed their three-peat in 1993.

No one was celebrated more on the *Sports Illustrated* cover.

There were action photos of him with his signature tongue hanging out, driving to the basket for a slam dunk, and celebrating with a victory cigar in the locker room after a championship. Jordan even appeared as a hologram in 1991, when the magazine scheduled a cover shoot with a holographic artist to showcase the many dimensions of their most popular cover subject.

Jordan stood in the visitor's locker room at the America West Arena in Phoenix on the cover of *Sports Illustrated*'s June 28, 1993, issue, moments after clinching his third championship with a Game 6 win over the Suns. Clutching the Larry O'Brien championship trophy in his hand, standing next to teammate Scottie Pippen with a wry grin on his face, the player considered by some as the greatest basketball player of all time could not have looked happier.

But the cover photo did not tell the whole story. In the opening words to *Sports Illustrated: The Covers*, a coffee table book compiling half a century's worth of the magazine's covers, managing editor Terry McDonell described the covers as snapshots of a particular era. "Put them all together in a collection like this, though," McDonell said, explaining the format of the book, which lays out the covers by year in a grid format, "and something wonderful happens: Those weeks add up to eras, and the snapshots become a panorama of the changing landscape of sport."

The *Sport Illustrated* cover was the most powerful image in sports, and across an entire era, the cover photos of Jordan provided a glimpse into his stardom. But they were still only snapshots.

The best player in basketball was about to walk away in the prime of his career.

The DESIRE Isn't There

As Michael Jordan entered the second decade of his NBA career, a transformation took place. He had gone from a wide-eyed rookie who told *Sports Illustrated* he wanted to make an All-Star team someday to the best basketball player in the league. He went from the best individual scorer, a high-flying dunker who couldn't win in the playoffs, to a three-time NBA champion.

But those weren't the only transformations.

The fame turned Jordan from a fun-loving kid who invited reporters to his basement to play pool into someone who just wanted to reclaim his private life as he became the most popular athlete in the world. From newspapers to television networks to magazines, everyone wanted a story. Famous athletes of past eras didn't have to deal with the rapid growth of media coverage in the 1990s. This was the price of fame. Jordan talked about the demands he was facing every day in a 1989 *GQ* interview. Describing a recurring nightmare he was having, Jordan predicted how the next part of his career would unfold.

"They're nightmares of something terrible happening to me that would destroy a lot of people's dreams or conceptions of me," he said. "That's the biggest nightmare I live every day. What if I make a mistake? How might that be viewed? Everybody feels it's easy to be Michael Jordan with all the good things happening to me, but the things that most scare me are the bad things—the things that would tear down Michael Jordan's image. That's the biggest fear I face."

After Jordan won his first NBA championship in 1991, *Chicago Tribune* reporter Sam Smith started the process of changing the star's public image with his book *The Jordan Rules*. Smith's behind-the-scenes look at the Chicago Bulls painted a much different portrait of Jordan than the clean-cut celebrity pitchman with a glowing smile and a perfect Q-Rating the public came to love. He ridiculed teammates who couldn't match his competitive streak, viewed Phil Jackson's triangle offense as a way to prevent him from winning another scoring title, and referred to teammate Will Perdue as "Will Vanderbilt" because he didn't deserve to be named after a Big Ten school. Jordan would physically bully his teammates, punching Perdue in practice once after getting hit with a screen and asking "Why the hell don't you ever set a pick like that during a game?"

Reporters crafted stories around Jordan's rise for nearly a decade. They focused on his team's inability to get past the Detroit Pistons in the playoffs. The 1991 championship ended those narratives. *The Jordan Rules* became a pivot point for the media to start honing in on his personal life.

Jack McCallum joined *Sports Illustrated*'s pro basketball beat in 1984 and had a more personal and intimate relationship with Jordan than any other reporter. McCallum grew up in Mays Landing, New Jersey, graduating from Lehigh University with a master's degree in English Literature. He worked at four newspapers before joining *Sports Illustrated* in 1981. "I was the long man in baseball," he said. "I was the guy they would call last minute and say, 'Hey, a story fell through, can you get up to Penn State this weekend?'" McCallum was assigned to the pro basketball beat in 1984 after developing a knack for writing niche feature stories on subjects like softball pitcher extraordinaire Ty Stofflet, who allegedly threw 104 miles per hour, and Clair Bee, a basketball coach who wrote 23 novels.

"It wasn't like, 'Oh, Jack is so great,'" he explained. "It was more like, 'He's been pretty good at other stuff. Let's try him.' Pro football, college football, and major league baseball were huge. Hockey was bigger. So it wasn't like they gave me a prime beat. I just happened to come along. It was a delicious accident of timing."

The 1980s was a golden age for NBA writers. They traveled with teams, dined with coaches, shared drinks with players at the hotel bar, built personal relationships, and gained exclusive access to players around the league.

"There was just a different way players dealt with the media," McCallum said. "There was this implicit relationship of accepting each other. The players understood the role of the national media in helping to expand the popularity of the game."

No one understood it better than Jordan, who always made time for *Sports Illustrated* during the first decade of his career.

"He would criticize other players. He would break down his own game," McCallum recalled. "He was just a kid who loved being on the cover."

Even after Jordan became the most famous athlete in the world, he maintained a strong relationship with McCallum. But there was a considerable difference in how he viewed all the media attention. Being on the cover of *Sports Illustrated* and every other magazine on the newsstand stopped being fun. When McCallum met Jordan for breakfast a week after the Bulls won the 1991 NBA Finals, the MVP arrived late after an alarm clock malfunction. "I know I'm tired of looking at you," Jordan said to McCallum when he arrived at the restaurant, "and you must be tired of looking at me." He conducted the interview and rushed off to play 18 holes of golf in the afternoon.

"I saw the frustration he felt," McCallum recalled. "He was worn down."

MANY DEFINING IMAGES from the Bulls' three-peat live on today. They include Jordan's acrobatic up-and-under layup against the Los Angeles Lakers in the 1991 NBA Finals, where he switched hands in mid-air to complete the play; his shrug after hitting six three-pointers in the first half of Game 1 of the 1992 NBA Finals against the Portland Trail Blazers; the team's comeback in the 1993 Eastern Conference Finals from down two games to none to the New York Knicks, including a Game 5 win at Madison Square Garden when Knicks forward Charles Smith improbably missed multiple attempts at the basket to win the game at the end of the fourth quarter; and John Paxson's jumper in Game 6 of the 1993 NBA Finals to clinch the team's third championship.

Another lasting memory of the three-peat took place before Game 1 of the 1993 NBA Finals against the Phoenix Suns, when Jordan called close friend and NBC reporter Ahmad Rashad on his way to the arena. He wanted to do a sit-down interview before the game. The media had prodded him about his personal life for three years and honed in on his gambling. There were six-figure golf bets he paid to business associates and bail bondsmen and a book from San Diego entertainment executive Richard Aquinas, *Michael & Me: Our Gambling Addiction... My*

Cry For Help! According to Aquinas, Jordan lost over a million dollars in golf bets over the years.

Reporters wondered if he had a gambling problem after *The New York Times* spotted Jordan at an Atlantic City casino at two in the morning before Game 2 of the 1993 Eastern Conference Finals. The questions led to a media boycott, which ended when Jordan, wearing sunglasses indoors, told Rashad and the millions watching at home there wasn't a gambling problem.

"I just felt like it was unfair that I was considered a criminal for doing something that is not illegal," he said. "I enjoy it. It's a hobby. If I had a problem, I'd be starving. I'd be hocking this watch, my championship rings. I'd sell my house, my wife would have left me or she would have been starving. I do not have a problem."

It was a strange scene for a player who was about to cement his status as one of the greatest basketball players of all-time with a third straight championship.

THE 1990S ARE REMEMBERED TODAY as the decade of the disgraced celebrity. *Vanity Fair*'s David Kamp named it "The Tabloid Decade." The media embraced any coverage of murder, tragedy, gossip, and scandal. The infamous O.J. Simpson White Bronco chase interrupted a 1994 NBA Finals broadcast and was viewed by 95 million people on television. His murder trial became a celebrity event. The Bill Clinton–Monica Lewinsky scandal swept the nation. The shootings of rappers Notorious B.I.G. and 2Pac Shakur ignited conspiracy theories about their deaths. Princess Diana's tragic death in 1997 put in context the media coverage of the decade. Diana and her companion Dodi Fayed were killed in a car crash while trying to evade the paparazzi.

The intensifying coverage of Jordan's personal life took a darker turn in the summer after his third championship. Police officers in McColl, South Carolina, discovered the body of his father, James Jordan, on August 3, 1993, several weeks after he had gone missing. The last contact anyone had with him was when he pulled over on US Highway 74 to take a nap. The media would soon learn two 18-year-old teens had spotted his red Lexus on the side of the road and shot him to death while he slept.

Jordan released a statement three weeks later about his father's death and condemned media members for linking the killing to his gambling.

"During this tragic ordeal, the vast majority of the media reports approached the situation with dignity, sensitivity, and respect for human decency," he wrote. "Unfortunately, a few engaged in baseless speculation and sensationalism. These few should cause us all to pause and examine our conscience and our basic human values. My dad taught me to carry myself with love and respect for all. The wisdom of his principles will help me rise above any thoughtless insensitivity and unfounded speculation."

The best basketball player in the world retired in the prime of his career two months later.

The question remains today.

Why?

Jordan stepped out of his black Mercedes and into the team's practice facility in Deerfield, Illinois, on October 6, 1993. He wore a tan-colored suit and sat down behind a table draped in red, facing a standing-room-only crowd of media members with his wife Juanita by his side.

"The desire isn't there," Jordan said. "When I lose the sense of motivation and the sense to prove something as a basketball player, it's time for me to move away from the game. It's not because I don't love the game. I always will. I just feel that I have reached the pinnacle of my career."

The timing of the retirement made it hard for many people to accept the explanation at face value. He was less than four months removed from averaging 41.0 points, 8.5 rebounds, and 6.3 assists in the NBA Finals and winning the Most Valuable Player Award in the series.

Why?

Was it his father's death?

"I would have made the same decision with my father around," Jordan said.

Would he consider returning to the NBA one day?

"Five years down the line," Jordan said, "if that urge comes back, if the Bulls would have me, if David Stern lets me back in the league, I may come back."

He took reporter questions for 40 minutes but did not address the league's ongoing investigation into whether he violated any rules as a result of his gambling.

McCallum watched the entire scene unfold in person.

"I was more shocked than surprised," he said. "I was shocked because it happened right before the start of training camp. But I can't say I was really astonished by the decision."

Many people honed in on Jordan's strange response to the question about a potential comeback.

Why did he refer to needing Stern's permission to return?

Was it a meaningless phrase or a slip-of-the-tongue?

People landed on what they believed to be a credible theory: Jordan received a secret gambling suspension from the league, which was now being disguised as a retirement announcement.

It was reflective of a decade where every morsel of information could be turned into a sensational headline.

Sports Illustrated wanted a cover story about the retirement.

McCallum knew immediately he wasn't going to get away with writing a standard feature remembering the best moments of Jordan's career.

"I had to write it with every shred of doubt because you didn't know what was going to come out later," he explained. "I couldn't write, 'This has nothing to do with his gambling.' I couldn't write, 'This has everything to do with his gambling.' I didn't know."

McCallum called the commissioner.

"I remember having a conversation with David," he recalled. "I was obligated to raise the question of whether Michael's gambling and the shady characters he hung around with played a role in this. He just blew my head off."

Stern screamed at McCallum over the phone for even suggesting the idea. The commissioner had grown the NBA from having Finals games broadcast on tape delay to being one of the most popular leagues around the globe. With Magic Johnson and Larry Bird now retired, would Stern really allow his most marketable player to walk away as well?

"I still don't know," McCallum said. "But my feeling is David would not have wanted him out of the league. He was a bottom-line guy, and the idea the league would be better off without Michael was utter nonsense."

The cover of *Sports Illustrated*'s October 18, 1993, issue featured a photo of Jordan walking off the court, with his back turned to the camera. The cover line simply asked WHY?

The league wrapped up its investigation into Jordan two days after his retirement, absolving him of any wrongdoing.

People still ask the question today.

Why?

BAG IT, Michael!

Eighteen thousand fans packed Sportsman's Park in St. Louis, Missouri, on August 19, 1951, to watch the St. Louis Browns play the Detroit Tigers in a doubleheader celebrating the 50th birthday of Major League Baseball's American League. Browns owner Bill Veeck was known for his quirky promotional ideas and didn't disappoint on this momentous day. He hired acrobats, a baseball clown to perform, a band to play drums at home plate, and gave free beer to every adult in the stadium.

There was one more surprise.

A large cake was wheeled out to the field before the game.

Jumping out of the cake wearing a Browns jersey in pointy shoes and a hat was 3'7" Eddie Gaedel. He walked to the plate in the first inning with three toy bats. Manager Zack Taylor presented the umpires with an official copy of Gaedel's contract as submitted to the league on Veeck's instruction when they tried to stop the spectacle. The game was interrupted for 15 minutes while the umpires called the league office. After it was decided Veeck had properly followed the rules, Gaedel was finally allowed to step into the batter's box. He trotted to first base after taking four straight balls from pitcher Bob Cain and was replaced by a pinch-runner.

It was his only major league at-bat.

His contract was voided by the league two days later.

It remains one of the biggest sideshow stories in baseball history today. Now imagine this.

A month after the best basketball player in the world walked away in the prime of his career, he started showing up to the batting cage at Comiskey Park, home of the Chicago White Sox. The last time he played baseball was on the high school team in his senior year when he quit to concentrate on basketball. His baseball résumé consisted of a Most Valuable Player Award with his Wilmington Little League team at age 12 and two city championships in the Babe Ruth League as a teenager. At age 30, he decided to try and become a major league baseball player.

Was this another sideshow?

The baseball world certainly seemed to think so after the White Sox signed Michael Jordan to a minor league contract with an invite to spring training just four months after his retirement. Seattle Mariners starting pitcher Randy Johnson told reporters: "I'd like to see how much air time he'd get on one of my inside pitches. He has a press conference every day, and all he's doing is hitting 80 miles-per-hour fastballs." Pittsburgh Pirates shortstop Jay Bell rejected his wife's request to get an autographed baseball from Jordan: "I told her I would not and I will not. I could see getting him to sign a basketball, but he hasn't earned the right to sign a baseball. I'll be surprised if he hits over .100 in spring training." Even White Sox general manager Ron Schueler placed the odds of Jordan making the majors at a million to one.

Baseball America managing editor Jim Callis was one of the few people excited to see the news. He was preparing to put Cleveland

Indians outfielder Manny Ramirez on the cover of the magazine's AL Central prospects issue when the most famous athlete in the world decided to join his sport.

"We asked ourselves, 'What are people going to be more interested in, Michael Jordan or Manny Ramirez?'" Callis recalled. "It was a pretty easy decision, to be honest. Michael Jordan helped sell magazines."

When the February 21, 1994, issue of *Baseball America* arrived on newsstands, the cover featured Jordan in the black-pinstriped uniform of the White Sox, wearing the number 23. The main cover line said: SCOUTING REPORT: MICHAEL JORDAN. A second cover line below asked: CAN HIS AIRNESS MAKE IT IN BASEBALL?

Baseball America writer Mark Ruda's cover story was a one-of-a-kind scouting report cobbled through interviews with Jordan's junior varsity baseball coach, Rick Watkins; baseball prospect turned NBA pro Danny Ainge; and analysis of Jordan's baseball swing through a review of a 1993 celebrity home run derby featuring Bill Murray, Tom Selleck, and Jim Belushi.

The magazine's readers thought it was a sideshow as well. *Baseball America* printed a letter from J.M. Popovich of Kensington, Maryland, in their next issue.

"I expected *USA Today* and *ESPN* and *CNN* to work themselves into a sensational tizzy over Michael Jordan's publicity stunt," Popovich wrote. "I expected sportswriters from every newspaper to write the requisite column. I expected television stations to broadcast Jordan's feeble swings as their top sports story. I even expected to see a column about Jordan in *Baseball America*.

"But I never expected a magazine I believed had the integrity of the game as its primary editorial guide would put Jordan on its cover.

By honoring Jordan, who is playing baseball to fill up his free time and to keep his fame, *Baseball America* has denigrated every professional baseball player. You have cheapened not only the game but your own reputation as a serious baseball journal."

Mark Mulvoy agreed with those sentiments. At the *Sports Illustrated* office, he referred to Jordan as a modern-day version of Gaedel. The managing editor of the most-read sports magazine on newsstands would make those feelings very clear with his cover photo choice for *Sports Illustrated*'s March 14, 1994, issue. The front of the magazine featured the most unflattering cover photo of Jordan's career. He's flailing his baseball bat hopelessly at a pitch that has sailed well past him, with an exasperated expression on his face. The cover line said: BAG IT, MICHAEL! JORDAN AND THE WHITE SOX ARE EMBARRASSING BASEBALL. The cover would change *Sports Illustrated*'s relationship with their most popular cover subject forever.

Jordan told reporters a few days after the cover became a national headline: "I haven't read it. I probably won't read it. I can't see how I'm hurting the game. I'm enjoying myself. It's a professional game. It should be a game that everyone has an opportunity to play."

He never talked to *Sports Illustrated* again.

WHEN STEVE WULF ARRIVED at Sarasota, Florida, to write about Jordan's spring training debut, he had no idea it would be the most talked-about cover story in *Sports Illustrated* history. Wulf grew up in Troy, New York. After graduating from Hamilton College in 1972, he drove his Chevy Malibu across the Northeast in search of a journalism career, visiting every newspaper until he landed a sports editor position at *The Evening Sun* in Norwich, New York. Wulf became a horse-racing writer at the *Fort Lauderdale News* before working the copy desk for *The Boston Globe* and the *Boston Herald-American*. In 1977, he joined *Sports Illustrated* as a fact-checker and quickly became one of the magazine's best writers. He was one of the best baseball writers in the industry and was known to profile his feature subjects with both a human touch and occasionally a quirky sense of humor.

Today, Wulf remembers finishing a story on Dorothy Hamill before arriving at spring training. Hamill became America's Sweetheart in the 1970s after winning a figure skating gold medal at the 1976 Winter Olympics. Barbie-style dolls in her image flew off the shelves. Her signature short and sassy bobbed hairstyle was a national sensation and became known as the Hamill Wedge. Wulf profiled Hamill's second career as the owner of a popular traveling theatrical ice-skating show, *Ice Capades*, which had declared bankruptcy. The former Olympian was working to revive the show and rescue the jobs of the people involved.

Wulf wonders today if going from writing about a superstar's altruistic second career to watching a superstar's attempt at landing a job in spring training which people thought he didn't deserve impacted the approach to his cover story. He watched Jordan strike out twice in an intrasquad game against his teammates, commit a two-out error in the outfield, and then take extra batting practice every morning, and felt sorry for him. Wulf watched the White Sox sell Air Jordan merchandise outside the stadium and wondered if it was all a marketing ploy. He saw no indication Jordan was anywhere near close to becoming a major leaguer.

The cover story painted the picture of someone who didn't belong at spring training. "Perhaps Michael will wake up one morning with Steve Garvey's arms and an urge to tie flies," Wulf wrote. "A much more likely scenario, however, is that he will simply wake up and realize he can't play major league baseball. And the sooner he wakes up to the White Sox's exploitation of his quest, the better." Today, the *Sports Illustrated* writer says his story might have gone a bit too far.

"In hindsight," Wulf said, "I was a little too snarky."

He doesn't however feel responsible for ending the magazine's relationship with Jordan.

"The tone of my story certainly did not match the cover," Wulf continued. "I remember having a discussion with Mark, and I told him it was unfair. He just smiled. Mark was the guy in charge, and he let his feelings about Michael dictate what the cover was. It wasn't the story. It was the cover that did it. My story wasn't all that much different than anybody else who was writing about Michael at the time."

Jordan had given *Sports Illustrated* so much of his time over the years for sit-down interviews and cover shoots. The cover felt like a betrayal of his trust. The sport of baseball was also a shared interest with his father, who played semi-pro growing up and encouraged his son to pursue a pro baseball career in their final conversation together before his tragic death.

The White Sox demoted Jordan to Double-A after he finished with a .150 batting average in spring training. Instead of disappearing into retirement again, he surprised everyone and accepted the demotion.

General manager and president of the Birmingham Barons Bill Hardekopf still remembers sitting in his office at seven in the morning when the White Sox called to confirm Jordan's arrival. He looked outside his office window at the team's stadium parking lot an hour later and saw a stream of cars flooding in. A line formed at the ticket office. The office phones started to ring and didn't stop until midnight.

Hardekopf had a local technician come to the office at one point to install six additional phone lines. Opening day was seven days away and everyone wanted a ticket.

"We had a team of 15 people," he recalled. "I told everyone that day, 'The visibility of our organization and the city has changed dramatically. This is going to change the history of the franchise.'"

The people who bought opening day tickets were disappointed a week later. Jordan was still in Chicago with the White Sox participating in an exhibition game and would arrive a day late. The following day, Jordan went 0-for-3 and struck out twice in his first game as a professional baseball player, starting in right field against the Chattanooga Lookouts.

This wasn't like any other minor league debut. One hundred thirty media members were credentialed, the stadium's banquet hall was rearranged into a press conference room for Jordan's postgame interviews, and thousands of fans waited in the stadium parking lot after the game to catch a glimpse of the most famous athlete in the world. They had correctly guessed who the Porsche with the MJ vanity license plate belonged to.

This also wasn't like any other minor league season. The Barons traveled to road games on a $350,000 luxury bus which Jordan purchased for the team. Popular country music singer Kenny Rogers dropped by during the season with a 15-person entourage. Charles Barkley threw baseballs into the crowd while doing radio play-by-play. Chris Chelios of the Chicago Blackhawks took batting practice with Jordan. A person posing as Scottie Pippen almost made it to the clubhouse before security escorted him off the premises. Barons media relations manager Chris Pika said it was like watching Elvis leave the building every single night. The team set a single-season attendance record with 467,867 fans at The Hoover Met.

Was Jordan getting better as a baseball player?

The answer appeared to be yes after a 13-game hitting streak early in the season. But Jordan went into a two-month slump once opposing pitchers adjusted their game plan and started throwing him off-speed pitches, which he had trouble hitting. He spent every day taking extra batting practice with hitting coach Mike Barnett.

"I've never seen a person with his work ethic," he said. "He would hit every day until his hands were bleeding. It was not a publicity stunt."

Barnett is convinced Jordan could have made the majors the following year even though the right fielder finished the season with an underwhelming .202 batting average in 127 games.

"His best ball was a routine fly ball to left when he first started," he said. "By the end of the season, he was hitting balls out of the ballpark every day in batting practice. His arm strength improved. His defense was getting better."

But the people in Birmingham remember Jordan for more than just what he did on the field. They saw someone who rediscovered the joy of competing and playing sports again.

Barnett still remembers when outfielders Kevin Coughlin and Scott Tedder challenged Jordan to a pick-up basketball game on the team bus. A few hours later he was Jordan's teammate at a local court, where a four-on-four game ensued.

"We beat them," Barnett recalled. "And when I say we beat them, I mean whenever we needed a basket, we gave it to Michael, and he scored."

Another pick-up game took place afterward, where Jordan played against local high school kids as hundreds of people gathered to watch the best basketball player in the world outside their apartment complex.

"This one kid scores a couple of baskets against Michael and he goes, 'Man, you ain't that good,'" Barnett recalled. "Michael says, 'Excuse me?' The kid goes, 'Man, you used to be my idol. You ain't that good.' And I tell you, the kid never got the ball off his fingertips again. So we get to game point, and Michael tells him, 'Here's what I'm going to do. I'm going to fake left, crossover, go right, and I'm going to jam on you. You ready for that?' And he did exactly that. He slammed the ball, it hit the kid in the face, and he said, 'That'll teach you to never underestimate your opponent.' He ran off the court, jumped in his car, and went to the airport to pick up his wife."

Jordan granted a 13-minute sit-down interview in Birmingham to radio broadcaster Curt Bloom when he wasn't talking to the country's most popular national sports magazine. "It set the pace for the rest of my career," Bloom said. "It gave me the confidence to interview anybody. I was never intimidated or overwhelmed by the moment after." Jordan appreciated the people in Birmingham who helped make his experience as normal as the most famous athlete in the world joining a minor league baseball team for a season could.

Hardekopf remembers approaching him with a request toward the end of the season.

"We had a policy when Michael was here," he recalled. "Nobody asked him for favors. You couldn't go and ask for an autographed bat or baseball. During our final homestand of the year, I thanked him for how gracious he had been and said, 'We've never asked you for anything, but can I ask you for one thing?' He said, 'Whatever you need, I'll do.'

"He showed up to our annual staff appreciation party the next day and took a picture with every person. He took one with me, my wife, and my kids. My youngest daughter was four at the time. I remember Michael picked her up and put her in his arms. That's still the best family Christmas card we've ever had. He did that with every family."

Jordan just wanted to be happy again in Birmingham.

Jonathan Nelson, a first-year, full-time employee with the Barons, was the last person in line for a photo that day. He spent the season as a jack-of-all-trades guy with the team. Nelson worked the ticket office, poured beer in the stands, parked cars in the stadium lot, cleaned up the stadium after home games, and even filled in as the public address announcer.

Nelson was thrilled to know the most famous athlete in the world recognized what he was doing.

"He looked at me and said, 'Come on up here,'" Nelson recalled. "He goes, 'Man, why are you always smiling?' I said, 'I'm just happy to be here. I just enjoy my job.' He said, 'Man, I need to hear why you're always so happy. Every time I see you, you're smiling.'"

Jordan spent a season in Birmingham away from the national spotlight and made everyone around him feel special.

Sports Illustrated had a chance to tell this story when Wulf flew to Birmingham in August to write a follow-up feature on Jordan's baseball pursuit.

"Michael didn't play that day, but I watched him in batting practice and was blown away by how much progress he made," he recalled. "He was a different player than the one I saw in spring training. He looked like he belonged. His batting average was a nature of his inexperience. It wasn't the nature of his ability to play baseball."

Would a more positive second story have ended Jordan's feud with the magazine?

We'll never know.

Sports Illustrated never published it.

"I was adamant about it," Wulf said, "but Mark didn't want to apologize."

Mulvoy says he doesn't remember reading Wulf's follow-up story.

"I wouldn't have printed it anyway," he added. "If you get in the business of trying to make up to people, you're in the wrong business."

Mulvoy retired two years later and lives with his wife, Patricia, in Florida today.

Jack McCallum has suggested the idea of pairing Mulvoy and Jordan on a golf course together to end the feud.

"I've talked about it with him about 50 times," McCallum said. "I go down to Florida every year to play golf with him, and it comes up every year. I think Mark should probably let it go a little bit, but he gets as fired up as Michael does. Their personalities are closer than they might think."

Mulvoy is proud of what he achieved as managing editor of *Sports Illustrated*.

"I took a great magazine," he said, "and didn't fuck it up."

But what about the cover that ended the magazine's relationship with their most popular cover subject?

"I stand by it," he said. "I stand by all the covers I did with Michael Jordan on them. Michael should be a big boy and say, 'My God, they glorified the shit out of me for 20 years.' Did he ever call and say thank you for the covers, which made everyone a shitload of money? No. But he didn't like one cover? Big deal.

"What he was doing with baseball was a sham. The White Sox brought him in to sell out a couple of games. He couldn't hit me. More power to Michael for trying, but don't turn off the world for 25 years just because you didn't like the cover. What about the other 35 covers or whatever number it was? Nike wasn't bothered by the cover. Gatorade wasn't bothered by the cover. Nobody except Michael was. It was typical Michael. It was his ego."

Rare BIRD

The only four-day, three-state reporting trip in *Sports Illustrated* history to include an impromptu last-minute trip to Las Vegas and a macaw parrot started on a Thursday night inside a popular hangout in the Beverly Hills neighborhood of Los Angeles, California, called Sanctuary. A few hours earlier, the San Antonio Spurs eliminated the Los Angeles Lakers from the playoffs in Game 6 of the 1995 Western Conference semifinals. Spurs forward Dennis Rodman spotted *Sports Illustrated* writer Michael Silver as he walked off the court.

"Come on, bro," he said. "Let's fucking go."

After graduating from UC Berkeley in 1988, Silver joined *Newsday* as a summer intern. He covered the San Francisco 49ers at *The Sacramento Union* before joining the *Santa Rosa Press Democrat*. "I was growing disenchanted with the older and more established writers," Silver said. "I self-promoted a lot and wasn't subtle about it. I was always trying to push for bigger and better things for myself. They were not vibing with me. I was reassessing whether I wanted to stay in the business when I got the miracle call from *Sports Illustrated* in 1994."

A year later, the magazine needed someone who could keep up with the 34-year-old power forward with red-and-orange hair who dated Madonna, listened to Pearl Jam, wore Oakley sunglasses and plaid flannel pants to games, started the season serving a three-game suspension after throwing a bag of ice at his head coach's face, and loved to party.

Their pro football writer seemed like the right choice.

Silver regularly hung out with football players and coaches until the sun came up. "I would go out with guys until three in the morning," he explained. "I wouldn't get a single tangible thing for my story, but three years later, I would be able to walk into a locker room and talk to them after an important game."

A 12-passenger limo whisked a group including Rodman and Silver from the Great Western Forum to Beverly Hills. Silver watched celebrities inside Sanctuary line up to greet Rodman. He was the center of attention. A Hollywood agent pitched Rodman the idea of becoming a movie villain in an upcoming Quentin Tarantino–directed picture. It was four in the morning when Silver found himself standing outside the club listening to the Spurs forward explain his break-up with Madonna to the bouncer.

"I thought I could party with this guy, but I had no idea what I was in for," Silver said. "I was applying my 'I'm in my 20s, I'm from Northern California, I drink a bunch of beers with the dudes' standards. We got to the club and were immediately on the Goldschlager and Jagermeister."

The most memorable reporting trip of Silver's career was just getting started as he raced toward the airport a few hours later to catch a flight to San Antonio.

RODMAN WAS AN INTROVERT growing up in the Oak Cliff neighborhood of Dallas, Texas, with his sisters, Debra and Kim, both All-American college basketball players. His father, Philander, left the family and relocated to the Philippines when he was three. Rodman developed a rebellious streak. He drifted across several jobs before working as a janitor at the Dallas/Fort Worth Airport after quitting high school basketball. Rodman stole 15 watches one evening from the airport gift shop and was jailed for a night. His mother, Shirley, kicked him out of the house.

Rodman played on the Cooke County College basketball team in Gainesville, Texas, for a semester before leaving due to poor grades. He blossomed into the country's best rebounder at Southeastern Oklahoma State, averaging 24.4 points and 17.8 rebounds as a senior. Rodman was selected by the Detroit Pistons in the second round in 1986 and became a critical part of two championship teams with his rebounding and defensive presence.

One evening in February of 1993, Rodman dropped off what appeared to be a suicide note to a close friend before leaving for a late-night workout. The cops found him asleep in his pickup truck with a loaded rifle later that night. His personal and professional life was a mess. Rodman was heartbroken after losing custody of his daughter Alexis in a divorce settlement with his ex-wife Annie. He was also upset at his team for parting ways with head coach Chuck Daly, a personal friend and father figure. Friends and family members were concerned for Rodman's mental well-being after the incident. The Pistons forward assured everyone he was fine. He wasn't contemplating suicide but was symbolically killing his old public persona to show the world who he truly was.

The Spurs traded for Rodman several months later before the start of the following season. He decided it was time for a new look. Rodman showed up to his first public appearance with his new team with a brand-new blonde hairdo inspired by Wesley Snipes' blonde-haired character Simon Phoenix from the 1993 science fiction action film *Demolition Man*. He received a standing ovation from the fans.

SILVER ARRIVED IN SAN ANTONIO for day two of his reporting trip nursing a hangover. Rodman, meanwhile, was at the practice facility going through rebounding drills as if the previous night didn't happen. The two would end up in Las Vegas by the end of the night, thanks to Dwight Manley.

A renowned coin collector from Orange County, California, Manley was in Las Vegas for a bachelor party in the summer of 1993 when he first met Rodman at a craps table. In the months leading up to his trade to the Spurs, Rodman had put up a "For Sale" sign at his Bloomfield Hills, Michigan, home and stayed at The Mirage in Las Vegas for the entire summer, blowing through $35,000 playing craps.

"I invited him to a George Carlin show," Manley recalled. "The next day, we hung out and hired some entertainers for the bachelor party. It was a good time. We swapped numbers before saying our goodbyes."

The two quickly became close friends, visiting each other during the season, and occasionally returning to Las Vegas together. The Spurs had a few days off before the Western Conference Finals, so Manley asked Rodman if he wanted to party. The answer, as always, was a resounding yes. Hours after landing in San Antonio for his second day of reporting, Silver was running through the airport trying to make a flight to Las Vegas. The group landed at ten in the evening and immediately headed to the craps table, calling it a night just before sunrise.

Manley's hotel phone rang at five in the morning.

It was Spurs head coach Bob Hill.

He wanted Rodman back in San Antonio in the afternoon for a Saturday film session.

Hill's relationship with Rodman got off to a rocky start in the preseason after he replaced John Lucas as head coach. He suspended Rodman for three games after he arrived late to practice, skipped several team meetings, and threw a bag of ice in his direction during a preseason game.

The feud continued throughout the season and into the playoffs.

After Rodman was benched in the second half of a Game 3 loss in the second round against the Lakers, he refused to join his teammates in the huddle, sitting by himself with a towel over his head near the bench. Hill sent his starting power forward to the locker room for the remainder of the game and didn't play him in Game 4. "I'm getting punished for some stupid reason," Rodman said. "It didn't hurt me at all. I can play or not play." Hill responded: "I would always listen very closely to Dennis, and then, probably, whatever he says, the opposite is true." The war of words continued when Hill said he hoped Rodman had learned his lesson. "Learned my lesson?" Rodman told the media. "I'm 34 years old. I'm a grown man. I know what I'm doing. So, no, I haven't learned my lesson." Hill managed to get in the last word, saying, "It's all part of our existence here. Dennis is just playing a little game there. He's trying to keep himself in a position of power. That's what he's about."

Rodman did not want to go back to San Antonio but common sense prevailed after some pleading by Manley and teammate Jack Haley and a flight home was booked for noon. Silver was still waiting for a sit-down interview with Rodman as the third day of his reporting trip started.

"Mike came up to me and said, 'What do I do?'" Manley recalled. "I said, 'Go with Dennis, and you sit with him on the way back because I'm going back to California.' He told me the next day it was the best advice ever."

During a one-hour layover in Houston, Silver and Rodman watched Hakeem Olajuwon's Rockets beat Charles Barkley's Phoenix Suns in Game 7 of their second round series. The *Sports Illustrated* writer finally landed his interview when they sat together on the connecting flight back home.

Silver got Rodman to open up about everything, including his suicidal thoughts ("Sometimes I dream about just taking a gun and blowing my head off."), murder fantasies ("Yeah, I'd kill somebody… in my mind. All of a sudden I lose control of what I'm doing. I'm in a torture chamber, and I've got to fight my way out. I definitely come out with a vengeance."), celebrity status ("They hide behind their money, fame, and success. Then all of a sudden they have no opinion, or they're afraid to voice it because they're afraid someone will take away what they've got."), his sexuality ("I visualize being with another man. Everybody visualizes being gay. They think, 'Should I do it or not?' The reason they can't is because they think it's unethical. They think it's a sin. Hell, you're not bad if you're gay, and it doesn't make you any less of a person.") and Madonna ("She wanted to get married. She wanted to have my baby. She said, 'Be in a hotel room in Las Vegas on this specific day so you can get me pregnant.' She had ways of making you feel like you're King Tut, but she also wanted to cuddle and be held.").

Rodman landed in San Antonio and joined his team for a film session and dinner afterward. He met up with Silver in the evening to show the *Sports Illustrated* writer one of his favorite local gay bars before they both retreated to Rodman's place. After spending the night writing in the guest room, Silver filed his story to his *Sports Illustrated* editor just before his Sunday morning deadline.

SILVER WOKE UP THE FOLLOWING DAY, walked downstairs past 15 exotic birds, two German shepherds, and found photographer John McDonough setting up in Rodman's kitchen.

McDonough graduated from Arizona State University with a photojournalism degree and worked for *SPORT, The Los Angeles Times,* and the *Arizona Republic* before joining *Sports Illustrated* as a photographer in 1982. He met Rodman two years earlier for the first time at a photoshoot in San Antonio.

"Dennis didn't have much money then," he recalled. "Here I am, a photographer, and here he is, a multi-millionaire, and I was buying him meals. We ended up hanging out for a few days. I remember telling him, 'I'm not going to sit around and judge whatever issues or problems you have. I just want to know who you are.' That's how our friendship started."

McDonough had asked the Spurs forward for ideas a few days before the photoshoot. "Dennis told me, 'We're not taking a picture of me in my uniform again,'" he recalled. "So now I'm driving in my rental car to his place, and I've got absolutely no idea what I was going to do."

Rodman finally came downstairs to greet McDonough and asked if he could be photographed naked on the *Sports Illustrated* cover.

"We ended up making a few calls to the editors and were told it wasn't going to work," McDonough said. "Dennis was a little disappointed. I'm looking at the skylight coming through the front entryway, and it started to go. I'm starting to worry because there wasn't time to set up any lights. Dennis comes back to us and says, 'Okay, how about I wear hot pants and a tank top?' I'm like, 'Yeah, that's fine, that's great.'"

McDonough sat Rodman in a chair and placed one of his macaw parrots on his arm for dramatic effect.

"The bird was getting fussy and started to bite him," he recalled. "I was shooting as many photos as I could."

Rodman went upstairs for a wardrobe change and came back wearing a pair of jeans with a rip in the crotch, exposing his privates.

"I was just laughing at this point," McDonough said. "I couldn't believe what was happening. It was a stressful day, but I managed to pull a rabbit out of my hat."

The second part of the photoshoot took place on a red leather zebra-skin couch where the Spurs forward sprawled out in a position where McDonough could shoot the pictures without exposing his subject's crotch.

Silver watched the entire three-hour photoshoot unfold while going back and forth with his editors fighting to keep every detail of his cover story in print. He was not convinced the feature would run.

"To my understanding, it was batted around a lot," Silver said. "It would have been a tough decision. It was 1995, it was *Sports Illustrated*, and we had an old, white readership. The photos themselves were risqué by their standards."

To his surprise, a photo of Rodman wearing a shiny tank top, metallic hot pants, and a rhinestone dog collar, while seated in a leopard-print patterned chair with a parrot in his arm appeared on the cover of the May 29, 1995, issue of *Sports Illustrated*. The cover line read RARE BIRD in red and yellow, matching the parrot and Rodman's hair dye.

It became one of *Sports Illustrated*'s best-selling May issues ever.

Shortly after the cover hit newsstands, the Spurs lost in six games to the Rockets in the Western Conference Finals. San Antonio weighed the pros and cons of having Rodman on their roster moving forward and eventually traded him to the Chicago Bulls in exchange for center Will Perdue in the off-season.

THE *SPORTS ILLUSTRATED* COVER STORY elevated Rodman to a different kind of celebrity status. He partied with Hollywood A-listers including Leonardo DiCaprio, Chris Rock, and Courtney Love. Rodman modeled a G-string for supermodel Cindy Crawford on *MTV,* and starred in the action-comedy film *Double Team* with Jean-Claude Van Damme. Manley became Rodman's agent and used the *Sports Illustrated* cover story's popularity to land him a book deal. Silver was Manley's first choice to write the book, but he couldn't convince his *Sports Illustrated* editors to give him time off. Manley and Rodman narrowed their list down to Jeremy Schapp and Tim Keown, who ended up writing the book. *Bad As I Wanna Be* was a 1996 *New York Times* best-seller. Rodman orchestrated a book signing stunt by showing up at a Barnes & Noble in New York wearing a wedding dress a day after telling late-night talk-show host David Letterman he was getting married.

Silver—who ended up writing Rodman's follow-up book *Walk on the Wild Side* a year later—saw another side of Rodman beyond the controversial stunts in public.

He saw someone who openly questioned masculine stereotypes in sports, spoke about the dangers of drug use, wore t-shirts supporting same-sex marriage to the arena during a time when homophobia was common among athletes and society at-large, and colored an AIDS awareness ribbon into the back of his head for a nationally televised playoff game.

"He had this huge groundswell of support by a wave of people who felt marginalized and misunderstood," Silver said. "They felt like they had been cast in the freak bin too. I saw people react to him. They tore their hearts out and thanked him. He was their guiding light."

THE *SPORTS ILLUSTRATED* COVER EMBODIED the qualities of a perfect magazine cover. The magazine picked the right writer and photographer to capture their cover subject's essence, and profiled their cover subject at an ideal time in his career. Even Phil Taylor, the magazine's lead basketball writer at the time, admits Silver was the right choice to write the most talked-about basketball profile of the year.

"When I read Silver's story, I was jealous to a degree," Taylor said. "But I also realized it probably would not have gone that way for me if I hung out with Dennis. I was a bit more buttoned-up and not as flamboyant. I get the feeling Dennis would have dropped me off at the hotel after the first night and said goodbye."

A year after Rodman's controversial *Sports Illustrated* cover, Taylor pitched his own feature idea on the power forward making an impression in his first year with the Bulls. "Everyone had written about his eccentricity," Taylor explained. "I told my editors, 'How about just a real hard basketball story about him?' His rebounding just stood out. It looked to me sometimes like he had this sixth sense of where the ball was going."

Before a game against the Miami Heat, Taylor found Rodman sitting by himself in the locker room. As Taylor walked over, Rodman started breaking down film from the previous night's game against the Atlanta

Hawks. "It was interesting because every time I talked to Dennis, he was a different person," Taylor said. "No two interviews were at all alike. It was consistent in that if I tried to talk to him about on-the-court stuff, he would get all weird on me. But when I tried to talk to him about the things he was doing off the court, he would invariably shift into talking about setting screens and the X's and O's of basketball. He was just so into what he was doing this time it was almost like he didn't realize he was being interviewed."

Rodman took the remote and gave Taylor a step-by-step walk-through of his process, fast-forwarding to find a possession during the Hawks game where Scottie Pippen shot a three-pointer from the top of the arc. He stopped the tape and pointed to the other players on the court, fighting in the low post for rebounding position. When he pressed play again, Taylor watched as Rodman slid past everyone to the right side of the basket, perfectly anticipating the carom off the rim for an offensive rebound. He fast-forwarded to another Pippen miss from the same spot and then a later miss from Michael Jordan, also at the top of the key.

"Anytime I see Scottie or Michael shoot from the top of the key," Rodman explained to Taylor, "I know the ball will come off the rim to the right."

On every possession he showed Taylor, Rodman was the only person on the court who knew precisely where the ball was going. He had spent hours in the gym rebounding for Pippen and Jordan to study the trajectory of their jumpers from every spot on the court. Taylor was blown away by the meticulousness with which Rodman approached his rebounding. "I definitely came away with a greater appreciation for what he did," he said.

On the cover of the March 4, 1996, issue of *Sports Illustrated* was a photo of Rodman soaring to snatch a rebound away from an opposing defender with the cover line: THE BEST REBOUNDER EVER? DENNIS RODMAN REVEALS THE SECRETS OF HIS INSIDE GAME.

While every cover story tried to replicate Silver's blueprint, Taylor managed to find a new angle to share with a national audience. Meanwhile, other magazines like *Rolling Stone*—who depicted Rodman as the devil on the cover, photoshopping the red-haired power forward with his tongue sticking out with a pair of devil horns—and *GQ*—who asked Rodman to pose naked next to scantily clad model Rebecca Romijn on the cover—tried to recreate the magic of the *Sports Illustrated* cover and fell well short. The moment had passed.

SPORTS ILLUSTRATED ALSO TRIED TO RECREATE the magic in 1999, when they asked Silver to write a feature on Derek Jeter. The 25-year-old New York Yankees shortstop had a recent high-profile fling with singer Mariah Carey and was known for his love of the city's nightlife as one of the most eligible bachelors in the Big Apple. It had the makings of another memorable cover story.

But Jeter had been trained to portray a much different image to *Sports Illustrated*.

"We were in his apartment, and he's telling me how he's a homebody," Silver said. "Meanwhile, there's one chair, a television, a bed, and a refrigerator with nothing in it. I spent days with him, and he didn't take me partying."

He called *Sports Illustrated* baseball writer Tom Verducci.

"I asked him, 'If I write a story about how Derek Jeter just likes to chill at the crib, am I going to be the biggest idiot in the world?'" Silver recalled. "Tom said, 'Absolutely. You cannot do that.'"

A photo of Jeter running mid-stride to catch a fly ball at Yankees Stadium appeared on the cover of *Sports Illustrated*'s June 21, 1999, issue. The cover line said GOOD FIELD. GOOD HIT. GOOD GUY. WHY DEREK JETER IS SO EASY TO ROOT FOR.

Silver's story explored the Yankees shortstop's relationship with the city of New York. The most controversial part of the feature was an interaction between Jeter and a Circuit City employee, who heckled Jeter as he was shopping for a videocassette recorder in the store.

Silver still remembers a moment he shared with Rodman on their connecting flight home from Houston to San Antonio after a Friday evening in Las Vegas.

"Dennis asked me what my next story was going to be when we landed," he recalled. "I told him, 'Believe it or not, it's this NASCAR thing.' He said, 'Aw bro, that's going to be so fucking boring. It's never going to get better than me. You're never going to get someone who is this weird, this good, this open, and this funny. So enjoy this.'"

He was right.

Silver never found another cover subject like him again.

DON'T BAG IT, Michael

Phil Taylor arrived for a preseason game at the Carver Arena in Peoria, Illinois, on October 13, 1995, with two assignments. The first was to write a cover story about the Chicago Bulls. The second was to convince Michael Jordan to talk to *Sports Illustrated* again.

The Flushing, New York, native grew up dreaming of writing for the magazine. "It was *the* sports publication," he said. "I read it from cover to cover every week. Even as an 11-year-old, I knew the quality of writing was above anything else that I read in sports. They were everything to me."

Taylor graduated from Amherst College with a Bachelor of Arts degree in 1982. He earned a master's degree in communications from Stanford the following year and worked at the *Miami Herald*, winning an Associated Press Sports Editors Award for feature writing. Taylor worked for the *San Jose Mercury News* and *The National* before joining *Sports Illustrated* in 1990. Jack McCallum left the pro basketball beat in 1993, moving to a new role editing the "Scorecard" section of the magazine. Taylor replaced him and had the unfortunate timing of joining the beat a month after Jordan's retirement.

The first year on the NBA beat was challenging for another reason.

"Everywhere I went, people would ask me, 'Where's Jack?'" Taylor recalled. "I remember going to Houston to do a story on Rudy

Tomjanovich. He asked me, and I told him I was the guy now. He said, 'Well, that's great, so is Jack coming back?' He was so popular on the beat. Everyone loved him. It was a hard act to follow because people were disappointed that I was showing up instead."

The number of NBA-related *Sports Illustrated* covers diminished immediately after Jordan's retirement.

"In the overall *Sports Illustrated* hierarchy, basketball was not very high," Taylor explained. "They didn't take it as seriously as some of the other sports like the NFL, college football, and major league baseball. Michael was the exception. If it had anything to do with him, it was a big deal, but they didn't care about the rest of the NBA all that much."

In Jordan's first year of retirement, the NBA was featured on the *Sports Illustrated* cover only four times during the 1993-94 season. San Antonio Spurs center David Robinson appeared as MR. MVP in March of 1994 while Seattle Supersonics guard Gary Payton and New York Knicks guard John Starks appeared on separate covers in May. During the 1994 NBA Finals between the Houston Rockets and New York Knicks, the NBA shared a cover with the NHL on the June 20, 1994, cover with the cover line WHY THE NHL'S HOT AND THE NBA'S NOT. The story honed in on a ratings decline in the NBA thanks to Jordan's absence.

Before the start of the 1994–95 season, head coach Phil Jackson approached Jordan after his baseball season in Birmingham ended about a potential return. The Bulls won 55 games in his absence but lost to the Knicks in the second round. Jordan was non-committal but left the door open for a potential return later in the season. Major league baseball players were still on strike in March of 1995. Jordan announced his retirement from baseball instead of accepting an invite to spring training as a replacement player with just a month left in the NBA regular season. He dropped by the team's practice facility in Deerfield, Illinois, throughout the season, and the visits became more frequent. Jordan announced his return on March 18, 1995, with a two-word fax from agent David Falk which said, "I'm Back." He was in the starting lineup the following day at Market Square Arena in Indianapolis, Indiana.

"There wasn't this kind of anticipation before for any other game," Taylor said. "The surprise and mystery of it made it feel different. I remember thinking, 'I've never been at an event where it seemed like the media was as excited as the fans.' We were all like, 'What do you think it will be like?' You didn't know if he was going to come out and shoot airballs or score 50 points."

Wearing the number 45, Jordan shot 7-for-28 from the field, scoring 19 points in an overtime loss to the Pacers. It was the highest-rated NBA regular season game since 1973. Jordan hit a game-winning jumper at the buzzer in his fourth game back against the Atlanta Hawks. He scored 55 points in a win over the Knicks at Madison Square Garden three days later. The Bulls went 13-4 after Jordan's return but lost to an Orlando Magic team led by Shaquille O'Neal and Anfernee Hardaway in six games in the second round.

Sports Illustrated managing editor Bill Colson decided a few months later it was time to fix the magazine's relationship with Jordan and sent Taylor to spend a week at training camp with the Bulls at the beginning of the 1995-96 season.

"The editors told me perhaps I could form a personal connection with him even if he didn't like *Sports Illustrated*," Taylor recalled. "I definitely got the sense getting Michael to talk was more important than writing a story."

Taylor was optimistic about his chances.

"There had been other athletes who had been pissed at us for one reason or another," he said. "They would ignore us for a week, at most sometimes a month. But we were too big. It was like, 'Even if we ruffle a few feathers, they'll come back. We're *Sports Illustrated.*'"

Taylor introduced himself to Jordan before a preseason game in Peoria.

"Michael asked me where Jack was, and I made some bad joke like, 'They decided to send a heavy hitter to cover you,'" he recalled. "He chuckled, and I felt like there was an opening there. So I told him our editor was willing to fly out here to figure out what could be done about the cold shoulder we were getting. He listened to the pitch and said, 'Nah, I don't want to hear that. But you tell your editor something that would help this whole thing. Tell them to hire more Black writers.' I told him I would and asked whether he would be free for a one-on-one interview later. He said, 'Not tonight. Maybe eventually, just hang around.' I didn't know if he meant hang around that night or hang around for another week, or another month."

Taylor spent a week at training camp and left without interviewing Jordan.

Today, he regrets not staying longer.

"I should have told my editors I would stay with the Bulls for as long as it took for me to get him," Taylor said. "There seemed to be enough of an opening for me to make it happen. Maybe he was just trying to see how committed I was. I'll never know."

He never got close to convincing Jordan to talk again.

"We would talk about general stuff," Taylor recalled. "I told him about my son, and he would ask, 'How's he doing? Is he a baller?' But whenever I tried to talk to him about basketball, he would say, 'Come on now. You know I don't do that.' I never had any indication he was willing to rethink things."

The Bulls became the most recognizable team in the world from 1996 to 1998. Their games were some of the most-watched television broadcasts in league history. The 1995–96 team finished with a record 72 regular season wins. Jordan led the league in scoring. He became the best player in the world again, wearing the familiar number 23. The Bulls capped off their historic season with a championship, defeating the Seattle Supersonics in six games in the NBA Finals. They would win the next two NBA titles to complete the team's second three-peat of the decade. *Sports Illustrated* put Jordan on the cover 13 times during this period, including three consecutive covers in 1998. Their most popular cover subject never agreed to a sit-down interview or a cover shoot during his second three-peat.

THE DOMINANT STORYLINE heading into the 1997-98 season was whether Jordan would retire again at the end of the season. The Bulls were on their way to a third consecutive championship but general manager Jerry Krause was convinced the team needed to embark on a rebuilding path. Taylor decided to make a case for why Jordan should play another year. It was the cover story for the magazine's February 16, 1998, issue. Taylor cringed when he saw the cover. There was a black-and-white photo of Jordan at the free-throw line. The cover line said DON'T BAG IT, MICHAEL.

"It was one more attempt to get Michael to talk to us again," Taylor said. "We were trying to say sorry. We were the bad boyfriend begging to be taken back. I was like, 'Let's keep our dignity a little bit here.'"

At the same time, *Sports Illustrated* was dealing with a new competitor on newsstands. *ESPN the Magazine* introduced themselves as a younger and hipper version of *Sports Illustrated*. Design director Darrin Perry and director of photography Nik Kleinberg brought a new-age, futuristic aesthetic to the magazine. Browsing an issue of *ESPN the Magazine* felt like flipping through an early-internet Geocities website in print. Their typography had a futuristic look. The magazine emphasized double-page photo spreads to draw the reader's attention inside. *ESPN the Magazine* won the National Magazine Award for Design in their first year.

Senior vice president and general manager of the magazine John Skipper wanted to align the publication with the digital age. The availability of information on the internet and the 24-hour news cycle created by television networks like ESPN made the idea of a magazine looking back on the week in sports feel archaic. Skipper decided on publishing the magazine every two weeks, with an emphasis on looking ahead. This strategy would also inform the magazine's cover approach.

Four athletes considered the next up-and-coming star in their respective sports appeared together in a black-and-white portrait photo on the cover of *ESPN the Magazine*'s debut issue in March of 1998. They were Alex Rodriguez, the Seattle Mariners shortstop who led the league with a .358 batting average as a 20-year-old; Eric Lindros, the Philadelphia Flyers center who led his team to the 1997 Stanley Cup Finals; Kordell Stewart, the Pittsburgh Steelers quarterback known as "Slash," who was redefining the quarterback position with his ability to play wide receiver

Don't Bag It, Michael

and running back as well; and Kobe Bryant, in his second season with the Los Angeles Lakers. The cover line simply said NEXT.

"The cover had three meanings," Skipper explained. "It was these guys are next, we are next, and we are going to write about what's coming up next as opposed to what already happened."

In the weeks leading up to their first issue, *ESPN the Magazine* editor-in-chief John Papanek, who served as *Sports Illustrated*'s managing editor for a brief period in the early 1990s, suggested *Sports Illustrated* was borrowing their design ideas. "There are certain things we were contemplating doing that *Sports Illustrated* got wind of and has co-opted," Papanek told reporters. In response, *Sports Illustrated* president Don Elliman Jr. said: "I find it amazing that they've been taking a bunch of cheap shots. Virtually every senior man they've hired came from here, so I'd love to know where they got the concept that we're ripping them off." A newsstand rivalry was brewing, and *ESPN the Magazine* would get the last laugh when they featured Jordan on the cover of their second issue. After giving *Sports Illustrated* the cold shoulder for years, he had agreed to a sit-down interview and a cover shoot with their biggest competitor. Furthermore, the cover story was written by Rick Telander—who had left *Sports Illustrated* in part because he was no longer getting access to Jordan at the magazine—and edited by Steve Wulf, who wrote the accompanying cover story to the infamous BAG IT, MICHAEL! cover in 1994.

"I haven't talked to them since they had that cover, and I'm going to hold to it," Jordan told ESPN. "What they said was totally wrong. Totally wrong. They didn't even have an understanding of the situation. I mean, if they would have at least investigated things, they would have known what I was doing. But they made their own assumption."

Sports Illustrated was no longer the magazine with exclusive access to the most famous athlete in the world.

"Michael didn't need us anymore," Taylor said. "It didn't hurt him in any way. It didn't hurt his endorsements. It didn't hurt his image. He used us to say, 'Just remember, I don't need any of this.'"

THE BULLS COMPLETED their second three-peat of the decade on June 14, 1998, inside the Delta Center in Salt Lake City, Utah. The Jazz trailed three games to two with a chance to force a series-deciding Game 7 on their home court in a rematch of the previous year's Finals, which Chicago won in six games.

Jordan came from the weak side and stripped Karl Malone in the low post with 21.8 seconds left to force a turnover with the Bulls trailing by one. He dribbled down the floor with a sixth championship on the line, drove toward the basket, pushing off forward Bryon Russell as he crossed him over just inside the three-point line, rising to hit a 20-foot jumper which gave the Bulls an 87–86 lead with 5.2 seconds left. The celebration began moments later after John Stockton missed a game-winning attempt at the buzzer. Jordan finished with 45 points.

He was the cover subject for *Sports Illustrated* and *ESPN the Magazine* a week later. *Sports Illustrated* went with the traditional approach of putting an action photo of Jordan's game-winning shot on the cover. ESPN went in a different direction.

"I've always felt a magazine cover needed to be a poster," Skipper explained. "It needed not just to tell a story, but to be visually arresting."

The magazine acknowledged Jordan's impending retirement with a cover image that captured his decade-long run of success. A photo of Jordan leaping in the air in celebration appeared on the cover against a clear white backdrop without any captions. The image stood on its own. The cover needed no words to describe the greatest basketball player in the world. It became one of the most iconic sports magazine covers of all-time.

Jordan announced his retirement on January 13, 1999, for a second time after a six-month lockout ended with a new NBA collective bargaining agreement between the players and owners.

"Mentally, I'm exhausted," he said. "I know, from a career standpoint, I've accomplished everything I could as an individual. Right now, I just don't have the mental challenges that I've had in the past to proceed as a basketball player. This is the perfect time for me to walk away from the game. And I'm at peace with that."

The last time Jordan publicly acknowledged *Sports Illustrated* came at the end of 1999, when the magazine hosted an end-of-decade event called "The 20th Century Sports Awards" at Madison Square Garden celebrating the greatest athletes in the magazine's history. Roger Bannister—featured in *Sports Illustrated*'s debut issue as the first athlete to break the four-minute mile—and legendary boxer Muhammad Ali were among those invited to the event, along with Billie Jean King, Magic Johnson, Tiger Woods, Bill Russell, Oscar Robertson, Jack Nicklaus, Arnold Palmer, Jim Brown, Pele, and Monica Seles. As the event neared, only one prominent athlete had yet to confirm their attendance. "I kept calling Michael," *Sports Illustrated* photographer Walter Iooss Jr. recalled. "I told him he couldn't pass this up. This was a once-in-a-lifetime event. He needed to be there." Jordan eventually agreed out of respect to his professional relationship with Iooss. On December 2, 1999, Jordan arrived at the awards and took his seat in the front row next to Ali. He accepted the award for Basketball's Athlete of the Century. "It's good to be back at the Garden," Jordan joked on stage. The Knicks fans in the audience booed. "I expected that," Jordan said, laughing. "That means I did my job when I came here." He thanked the fans and paid tribute to his peers. Jordan didn't mention *Sports Illustrated* or the record-breaking number of covers he received from the magazine once in his acceptance speech.

AT HIS SECOND RETIREMENT PRESS CONFERENCE, Jordan smiled and said he was 99.9 percent certain about his decision when asked about the possibility of another return. He was back for a third time after signing with the Washington Wizards two years later. McCallum was back on the pro basketball beat and proposed an interview to end the feud. Jordan put his arms around the writer who chronicled the first decade of his career. "It's not you, Jack," he said. "But I'm not doing an interview with your magazine." Jordan retired for a third and final time in 2003 and never spoke to *Sports Illustrated* again.

PART 2

The In Your Face
Basketball
Magazine

"You Wanna Hear a FRESH RHYME..."

The origin story of the most influential hip-hop magazine of all-time starts on the Harvard University campus in Cambridge, Massachusetts, where two white, Jewish kids named Dave Mays and Jon Shecter co-hosted the school's Friday night radio show *Street Beat* on 95.3FM WHRB.

Born and raised in an upper-middle-class household in Washington, D.C., Mays discovered hip-hop as a fifth grader when he heard "Rapper's Delight" for the first time. The Sugarhill Gang's 1979 hit single was the first record of its genre to hit the mainstream, opening the door for major record labels to consider the idea of selling hip-hop.

The 1980s signified an era of significant growth for the genre. Rappers were invited to perform on NBC's *Saturday Night Live* for the first time. Kurtis Blow was the first commercially successful rapper. His single "The Breaks," from his 1980 self-titled debut album, was the first-ever certified gold rap song. LL Cool J's 1985 debut studio album, *Radio*, sold over 500,000 copies within the first five months of its release. The Beastie Boys' *Licensed to Ill* became the first hip-hop record to top the Billboard charts. Run-DMC became the first rap group to sign a sneaker endorsement deal in 1986 after their hit record

"My Adidas" went viral. ABC devoted an entire primetime segment explaining this new genre of music to a national audience.

Listeners of the Friday radio show at Harvard called in regularly for upcoming albums and 12-inch singles release dates. Mays collected the names and mailing addresses of his callers, reached out to record labels for a release date schedule, and convinced local record stores to purchase $50 ads in the back of a newsletter he was putting together.

The seminal year for hip-hop is considered by many to be 1988. The debut album *Straight Outta Compton* by a Compton-based rap group named N.W.A. gave birth to the gangsta rap subgenre. Long Island–based rap group Public Enemy's second album, *It Takes a Nation of Millions to Hold Us Back*, gave rise to the concept of socially conscious rap music. Run-DMC became the first rappers to appear on the cover of *Rolling Stone*. Big Daddy Kane and Slick Rick became the genre's next mainstream stars.

It was also an important year in hip-hop history for another reason.

In August of 1988, Mays mailed a one-page yellow Xerox sheet of paper named *The Source*, which billed itself as "Boston's first and only rap newsletter," to over 1,000 of his radio show listeners. The newsletter included album dates, a list of upcoming single releases, and concert listings. The name was inspired by KRS-One, a member of the rap group Boogie Down Productions, who once rapped, "You wanna hear a fresh rhyme? You've come to the source."

Shecter saw the success of the first newsletter and joined the project. The two Harvard undergraduates used a campus Macintosh computer to lay out the first issue of *The Source* with a proper magazine cover a year later. Their first cover subject was Slick Rick. Mays and Shecter graduated the following year and moved to New York together. They opened an office and hired an editorial team. The newsletter was now a full-fledged magazine operation. *The Source* became a nationally distributed magazine with a circulation of 50,000. Shecter managed the editorial team while Mays ran point on the business side.

An entire generation of hip-hop fans read *The Source* every month, picking out songs to track down from the magazine's "Fat Tape" section, learning about up-and-coming artists from the "Unsigned Hype" column, and going to the record store to buy any album which received five mics in the "Record Report" section. Chuck D of Public Enemy referred to the magazine as the Bible of hip-hop.

But the idea of selling hip-hop wasn't mainstream yet.

N.W.A. member (and at this point the face of gangsta rap) Eazy-E appeared on the cover of the December 1990 issue of *The Source* wearing a Compton snapback hat, with black sunglasses and a bulletproof vest over a white tee, pointing the barrel of his gun toward the camera against a black backdrop. The cover line said THE GANGSTA RAPPER. VIOLENT HERO OR NEGATIVE ROLE MODEL?

The cover was indicative of the national discourse taking place over hip-hop's violent lyrics. Rappers increasingly used their music as a platform for social commentary to provide listeners with a glimpse into their personal experience of being Black. White America expressed their concern over what they perceived as the promotion of violence against authority. N.W.A's "Fuck Tha Police," a song tackling the subjects of police brutality and racial profiling, became the centerpiece of the conversation after a FBI representative sent a letter to Priority Records blaming the song for inciting violence and disrespect toward law enforcement. N.W.A. agreed to omit the song from their national tour setlist to avoid further controversy. Police officers working the show at Joe Louis Arena in Detroit, Michigan, chased the group off the stage when they surprised everyone and performed the track on the tour's final stop.

The discourse continued into the new decade, when Los Angeles–based rapper Ice-T appeared on the cover of the August 20, 1992, issue of *Rolling Stone* in a full police officer uniform, clutching a baton with both hands. The cover line said ICE-T TALKS BACK (YOU GOT A PROBLEM WITH THAT)? Ice-T's speed metal band Body Count released a track called "Cop Killer" a few months earlier. The provocative song was considered by Ice-T to be a record examining the issues with police brutality in Black neighborhoods, but this part of the message was not received by politicians around the country. President George Bush and vice-president Dan Quayle condemned the song and asked Ice-T's record label, Time Warner, to boycott the group. Ice-T eventually relented and agreed to pull the track from the group's upcoming album. Ronald Hampton, the director of the National Black Police Association, which represented over 30,000 Black police officers in the country, condemned the White House's request. "The song is not a call for murder," Hampton told reporters. "It's a rap of protest. Ice-T isn't just making this stuff up. There are no statistics to support the argument that a song can incite someone to violence."

Four Los Angeles Police Department officers were acquitted for the beating of Rodney King, a Black man, in the same year. The incident took place in March of 1991 after King was pulled over and arrested for drunk driving. The officers were acquitted on charges of assault and use of excessive force, despite substantial video evidence. Civilians expressed their outrage over yet another incident of racial profiling. The looting, protests, and demonstrations which became known as the 1992

Los Angeles Riots lasted six days, killing 63 people, and injuring thousands of others, until the California Army National Guard stepped in to restore order. The incident ignited a national conversation over police reform, which fell on deaf ears.

Advertisers were not eager to buy ads in *The Source*. The magazine did not shy away from the national conversation taking place and promoted many rappers considered by white America to be part of the *problem* on their cover. Mays remembers an invite to Nike's headquarters in Portland, Oregon, during this period to make a sales pitch.

"I flew there with a backpack full of magazines," he recalled. "When I arrived on the Nike campus, it was lily white. It was people with no connection whatsoever to hip-hop and Black culture. It was the whitest people you would run into in those days.

"They didn't get it. Even with hip-hop's influence going back to Run-DMC, the idea that sneakers were fashion and not just a functional shoe for sports activity felt wrong to them. They didn't embrace the idea. I spent a lot of time talking to ad agency executives trying to help them overcome a lot of stereotypes about Black people and hip-hop. They would say, 'Oh, these kids don't read. They don't have any money. They're just inner-city kids.'"

Corporate America was blissfully ignorant and also didn't realize upper-middle-class suburban white kids accounted for over a quarter of *The Source*'s overall readership. Mays had no idea how to get enough advertiser buy-in to turn his magazine into a sustainable business as the mainstream narrative on hip-hop's negative influence was taking shape.

THE NBA WOULD PLAY A ROLE in changing the conversation. Commissioner David Stern brainstormed a half-hour show called *NBA Inside Stuff*, which would broadcast every Saturday morning as a lead-in to the network's *NBA on NBC* broadcasts. Ahmad Rashad—a retired pro football player who joined NBC Sports in 1983—was hired to host the show. *NBA Inside Stuff* debuted in 1990 and featured a segment called "Jam Session," a weekly highlight reel set to the most popular hip-hop tracks at the time. The NBA targeted their show to an audience who grew up as part of this hip-hop generation which was now blending into the basketball space.

A new generation of basketball players was starting to embrace hip-hop's anti-establishment attitude. The UNLV Runnin' Rebels—led by Larry Johnson, Stacey Augmon, and Greg Anthony—wore all black sneakers, let their shirts hang out halfway, and played with a swagger on the court which threatened college basketball's buttoned-up approach. The Michigan Wolverines starting five of Chris Webber, Juwan Howard, Jalen Rose, Jimmy King, and Ray Jackson, who were nicknamed "The Fab Five," wore baggy shorts past their knees, blasted EPMD in the locker room before games, and celebrated by waving their arms like Naughty by Nature after obliterating their opponents. Rose remembers being vilified by the mainstream media at the time. "We were considered loud, we were considered thugs," he recalled. "It was like, 'Why are you listening to Public Enemy? Why are you listening to N.W.A.? You guys should be happy to be here playing basketball on a scholarship.' At that point, the suburbs didn't want kids dressing like me. They were trying to hide their kids from me. They were trying to hide rap music from them. The mainstream media didn't understand what we were saying and didn't care to. We were Black and they hadn't seen that before. If you look back at how I was covered, I wasn't talked about as an honor roll student in high school and a Dean's List student in college, but that's what I was, besides being a basketball player."

Rose points to the arrival of Shaquille O'Neal in the NBA as a turning point in hip-hop becoming accepted by the mainstream audience. O'Neal averaged 23.4 points, 13.9 rebounds, and 3.5 blocks in his rookie season, winning Rookie of the Year after being selected first overall by the Orlando Magic in 1992. Agent Leonard Armato took advantage of his client's popularity and landed over $30 million worth of sponsorship deals for the Magic center before he even played a single NBA game. O'Neal spent parts of his childhood in Wildflecken, West Germany, growing up with his mother, Lucille O'Neal, and stepfather, Phillip Harrison, an Army sergeant. He idolized LL Cool J, Eric B. & Rakim, and Run-DMC, performing rhymes in front of his bedroom mirror, saving up $200 at age 14 to buy his first set of turntables from a pawn shop. O'Neal appeared on *The Arsenio Hall Show* in his rookie season wearing a bright red tracksuit and made his rap debut, performing a verse off a new track titled "What's Up Doc (Can We Rock?)" alongside one of his favorite rap groups, the Fu-Schnickens, on a strobe-lit stage. Jive Records owner Clive Calder saw the performance and signed the Magic center to a record deal. *Shaq Diesel* arrived in record stores in October of 1993 and became the first rapper-athlete album to sell over 1 million copies.

"A lot of times mainstream America is comfortable with the *teddy bear* Black guy, the big, fun-loving, let your kids jump on your back type of guy. That's non-threatening," Rose said. "I was considered a city slicker. I've got gold teeth and the media was like, 'We have to watch him.' Shaq was a dominant player, but he also had a magnetic personality. Because he was so large and friendly, he was considered non-threatening."

O'Neal appeared on *Good Morning America* and *The Today Show* as part of his promotional tour and sold a more mainstream-friendly version of hip-hop to a national audience. He also appeared grinning in a perfectly-fitted Ermenegildo Zegna wool suit on *GQ*'s November 1993 cover with the cover line THE SELLING OF SHAQ. The cover story focused on O'Neal's universal marketing appeal. The *GQ* cover was a place for male fashion models until the men's fashion magazine transformed into a general-interest publication focused on pop culture, politics, and sports behind the vision of editor-in-chief Art Cooper in 1983. Michael Jordan, Magic Johnson, Pat Riley, and Isiah Thomas were among the magazine's cover subjects in the 1980s. The cover was a signifier of acceptance by a larger audience beyond sports.

THE IDEA OF SELLING HIP-HOP was starting to take shape when another magazine focusing on Black music and culture arrived on newsstands. Time Warner embarked on a joint venture in 1991 with renowned record producer Quincy Jones to publish a new magazine called *Vibe*. The publication described itself as a Black-music version of *Rolling Stone*, targeted toward the 18-to-34 age group. The magazine informed advertisers of their intentions to reach a large white audience.

The publication was in its early brainstorming phase when Mays received a call from Def Jam Records co-founder and *Vibe* partner Russell Simmons. "He called me and said, 'Hey, my friend Quincy wants to start a rap magazine, and I told him he should invest in *The Source*,'" Mays recalled. "I spent a year going back and forth with them until they finally flew us out and whisked us in a limo to this Beverly Hills mansion.

"Quincy shows up and says, 'Listen, guys, I've decided to start my own magazine instead. But I want to offer you guys $600,000 to buy out *The Source* and give you guys jobs to come work for me at my magazine.' I was pissed. Some of my other partners thought it was a lot of money, but I was like, 'Get the fuck out of here.' I was so mad. I realized they had been playing me and were just trying to pick our brains all this time to learn what made our magazine so successful."

Mays ended the partnership, but he found a silver lining to gaining a competitor when the first official issue of *Vibe* arrived on newsstands in September of 1993 with a portrait photo of West Coast rapper Snoop Doggy Dogg on the cover. "They helped open doors to advertisers," he said, "and got some of the brands to think a little bit differently." *Vibe* was a more mainstream-friendly version of *The Source*, with the backing of a corporate conglomerate. They successfully sold the idea of selling hip-hop to corporate sponsors. National brands like Nike and Coca-Cola placed ads in *Vibe*'s first issue and would eventually advertise with *The Source*.

The NBA was starting to embrace a new generation and the idea of selling hip-hop on newsstands had gone mainstream. These two factors paved the way for a new magazine merging hip-hop and basketball together in 1994.

THE IN YOUR FACE Basketball Magazine

Sports Illustrated took over a decade to figure out a blueprint for what their magazine should look like.

SLAM took one issue.

The magazine would change over time. Their voice would evolve. The magazine cover looks drastically different today. But flip through a present-day issue of *SLAM*, and it still reads pretty much the same from front to back as the very first issue, which came out almost 30 years ago.

The first issue of *SLAM* featured short-bit culture stories on Pearl Jam's near-decision to name themselves after Atlanta Hawks guard Mookie Blaylock and basketball's growing popularity in Japan. There's a dunk of the month. There's a one-page feature on high schooler Steve Wojciechowski, along with profiles of college point guard Jason Kidd, perennial NBA All-Star Charles Barkley, and New York–playground legend Joe Hammond. There are full-page photospreads of the latest sneaker releases, and a six-page photo essay on playground hoopers around the country, including a cameo from a 16-year-old Paul Pierce.

This is what *SLAM* still is today: a magazine celebrating the sport of basketball. A casual voice. An all-encompassing approach of covering high school, college, and the pro game. A magazine highlighting sneakers and athletic apparel. A personality-driven publication. A magazine that didn't tie themselves to the current news cycle.

Founder and publisher Dennis Page established a blueprint for what a modern-day basketball publication could look like from the very beginning.

"We were passionate," he said. "The feel of the magazine was like if you were playing in the playground. That's how people spoke."

Page was inside the Paramount Theater at Madison Square Garden where the 1994 Source Awards was taking place when record label executive and friend Alan Grunblatt tossed out the idea of a magazine merging basketball and hip-hop. He went home that evening and drafted up a table of contents.

A Trenton, New Jersey, native, Page studied broadcasting and film at Boston University and got his first full-time job selling ads for the alt-weekly *Boston Phoenix*. Page loved magazines. He dreamed of running his own one day. The goal was always *Rolling Stone*. Page was working for another rock 'n' roll magazine, *Circus*, in 1980 when Stanley Harris called. Harris was the founder of Harris Publications, a New York–based publisher started in 1977 with a portfolio of special-interest magazines. They had puzzle books and monthly magazines on topics ranging from gardening to guns. Page was offered a job to manage a new guitar magazine. It was a chance to run a magazine even if it wasn't *Rolling Stone*.

"I didn't know shit about playing guitars," Page said. "But I was good at the advertising and publishing business. So I said yes."

He became the publisher of *Guitar World*, which arrived on newsstands in 1980 and became the number one guitar magazine. The success of the publication earned him a lot of goodwill with Harris. Page kept searching for the next idea. He convinced Harris to start another magazine in 1987. It was called *New York Talk*.

"We launched it during a huge snowstorm and couldn't get the issue out to the newsstands," Page recalled. "It was an omen of failure."

The magazine borrowed from the concepts of *Village Voice* and the *East Village Eye* and covered the local news along with the New York film, television, and music scene. The newsstand was about taking a successful idea you liked and trying to improve upon it yourself. A lot of these publications failed, including *New York Talk*, which folded after three years.

Page's new magazine idea, inspired by his conversation with Grunblatt, was more aligned with his interests. He fell in love with basketball in sixth grade watching a high schooler named Lew Alcindor, became a high school and college hoops junkie, watched streetball legends at New York playgrounds, and joined the NBA craze during the era of Julius Erving, Larry Bird, and Magic Johnson.

But he couldn't figure out the table of contents.

"I started by building a hip-hop magazine about basketball," Page explained.

He had the two components in the wrong order.

Another lightbulb moment hit.

It would be a basketball magazine with a hip-hop voice and not the other way around.

It would look like *Vibe*.

It would read like *The Source.*

He pitched the idea to Harris, who asked him to get it on news-stands immediately.

Page needed an editor-in-chief. He called *Village Voice* editor Tom Curtis, who said no, but recommended Time Inc. writer Cory Johnson, a St. Joseph, Michigan, native who studied journalism at NYU and wrote for a bunch of magazines, including *Sports Illustrated, People,* and *TIME.*

"Tom told me this guy who makes *Guitar World* wants to start a new basketball magazine and asked me if I had any ideas for it," Johnson recalled. "I said, 'Abso-fuckng-lute-ly I have ideas.' I was in the thick of learning how magazines were made. It was what I did all day."

A meeting was set at a French bistro restaurant located in the SoHo neighborhood of Manhattan, New York, named Raoul's. Johnson sat down and pitched his vision to Page. He read a lot of Marvel comics growing up and loved how comic book writer Stan Lee would engage readers at the back of every one of them. Lee responded to fan letters and sent no-prizes—an envelope with no contents inside, which became a running joke with the readers—to anyone who wrote to him about continuity errors or typos. Johnson wanted the magazine to start by engaging their readers in the letters section.

"I presented a pretty laid-out plan," he recalled. "There would be short features in the front like *New York Magazine*'s Intelligencer section. There would be one-page profiles like *Interview* magazine. The features section would be in the style of *Vanity Fair.* The sections in the back would be devoted to angles around the business of hoops. I wanted the last page of the magazine to be a dunk of the month.

"I wanted it to feel like *Surfer* magazine. I loved that magazine so much I taught myself to surf. Their ideal was: surfing was not about the celebrities at the top of the pyramid who did it, but instead it was about the everyday experience of the sport. I always thought *Sports Illustrated* had this pyramid when it came to basketball where they didn't love the game, but instead they loved the heroes of the game. Their editors thought it was all about the stars and not about the game itself. I wanted to flip that approach upside-down. I wanted the magazine to be about the experience we all had playing the game of basketball. *Sports Illustrated* was only about Michael Jordan. I wanted us to be about the game of basketball."

There was one last thing they needed to figure out together.

A name for the magazine.

The two tossed out every basketball-related term they could think of.

Crossover.

Dribble.

Jam.

None of them felt right.

They finally landed on *SLAM*.

Johnson was hired and moonlighted as the magazine's editor-in-chief.

"I would be fact-checking a murder story for *People* and I'd get a phone call from Dennis," Johnson said. "I would hop in a taxi, race downtown to approve a layout, then race back. It was like I had moved on to my new girlfriend without telling my existing girlfriend."

Page scrambled to place ads in the magazine. Today, he credits *The Source* and *Vibe* for making his job easier back then. Page didn't have to explain what hip-hop was to advertisers. *Guitar World* art director Susan Conley designed the magazine layout. Johnson assigned stories to people he knew in the industry, including basketball writer and New York–streetball historian Vincent Mallozzi, *People* reporter Nancy Jo

Sales, and *Vibe* senior editor Bonz Malone. He also wrote a couple of stories himself and attributed them to made-up names in the masthead. "I wanted to make it look like a real magazine since it was just a couple of other guys and myself working on it," Johnson explained. "Russell Shoemaker, the senior editor in the masthead, that's me. Russell was my best friend from church. Shoemaker was my godfather's last name. I just put their names together."

Page cringes at some of the stories today, especially a *SLAM* NBA All-White Team feature where the magazine interviewed white players around the league and nominated Chris Mullin, Dan Majerle, Detlef Schrempf, Tom Gugliotta, John Stockton, and Rony Seikaly. Scott Hastings, a white power forward from Independence, Kansas, who played 11 seasons in the NBA, nominated Karl Malone, who didn't make the team. "The guy drives a diesel and raises cattle," he explained. "You don't get any whiter than that."

Fortune business writer Andy Serwer flew to Charlotte, North Carolina, and wrote the cover story on Larry Johnson. The Hornets forward was one of the most exciting young stars in the league. Selected first overall by Charlotte in 1991, Johnson won Rookie of the Year after averaging 19.2 points and 11.0 rebounds in his first season. He played an above-the-rim game and was a product of a UNLV team that embraced a hip-hop aesthetic. Johnson was a signature sneaker athlete with Converse, starring in a series of popular commercials wearing a grey wig and flower-print dress as Grandmama, an elderly woman alter-ego. He fit the profile of what *SLAM* envisioned as their ideal cover subject.

The first issue was finally ready for the newsstand.

The cover featured a photo of Johnson soaring in mid-air wearing Charlotte's famous white-and-teal jersey. The basketball in his right hand sat just above the magazine's logo. Above the logo was the magazine's slogan THE IN YOUR FACE BASKETBALL MAGAZINE. The caption said LARRY JOHNSON, LIVIN' LARGE! Cover lines filled the rest of the cover, including BARKLEY: KING WITHOUT A CROWN; KILLER BLOCKS! SHAQ, ROBINSON, MOURNING, OLAJUWON & MORE; JASON KIDD'S KRAZY MAD MOVES; KENTUCKY'S BLUE MADNESS; SLAMBOYANT SNEAKS; and SLAMADAMONTH! Every caption was a way to draw a potential reader into picking up the magazine.

Page waited to see if anyone was interested in his new project.

"That was the business at the time," he explained. "There was no internet, Instagram, or Facebook. The newsstand was the true test of whether there was a community out there who cared about your idea. We would have three issues to test whether there was an audience. If it sold, we would keep it rolling. If it didn't, then we wouldn't."

There was some concern about starting a basketball magazine immediately after Jordan retired, but they were alleviated when Harris delivered some excellent news. The newsstand sales were strong enough for *SLAM* to continue. A second issue arrived on newsstands in October of 1994, with Seattle Supersonics forward Shawn Kemp on the cover. Johnson was replaced by Tony Gervino on the masthead three months later when Shaquille O'Neal appeared on the cover of the magazine's third issue. He had accepted a job offer to become a *Vibe* senior editor.

"We sold more copies of our first issue than they did," Johnson explained. "They spent like $15 million to launch it. We spent $100,000 tops. I was called into their office, and they asked me, 'How did you do it?' I explained how the magazine worked and what our editorial focus was. They asked me if I would be interested in being a senior editor. I figured I would eventually have a shot at the editor-in-chief role, so I made the jump."

Today, he is still proud of leaving an editorial blueprint behind for his successors.

"The magazine unquestionably looked better in the years after I left," Johnson said. "But the fact it is still largely all the same ideas I brought to the table is enormously gratifying to me and tells me I got a lot of stuff right. I didn't get it right because I was a genius. I got it right because there was something wrong with the way magazines were covering sports."

IF YOU SCAN THE FIRST THREE ISSUES OF *SLAM* today, you'll notice the cover photos didn't come from original photoshoots. The photos of the early covers were licensed from the NBA. "None of the players would pose for us," Page said. "We had to buy existing photography in the very beginning." *SLAM* had a vision to one day follow the lead of *Rolling Stone.* Founder and publisher Jann Wenner was a 21-year-old UC Berkeley dropout who couldn't get anyone to take his music writing seriously in 1967 when he scraped together $7,500 from family and friends and convinced *San Francisco Chronicle* writer Ralph J. Gleason to help him put together a new magazine. The first issue of *Rolling Stone* arrived on newsstands in the same year, with John Lennon of The Beatles on the cover. The magazine debuted at the height of the hippie movement and became the definitive counterculture magazine of their era, introducing a new generation of artists, including the

Grateful Dead, Jimi Hendrix, and Janis Joplin, to the world. Wenner described *Rolling Stone* as "a publication not just about music but also about the things and attitudes that music embraces" in his first column. The magazine plucked writers from obscure places and turned them into culture-defining voices. Their photographers captured defining images of an entire generation of rock stars. The magazine's portrait photography of cover subjects set the standard for every other publication. Being selected for the *Rolling Stone* cover became the highest honor for any music artist.

"Jann broke the mold on alternative magazine publishing," Page said. "As far as I'm concerned, they changed print publishing. The way *Rolling Stone* shot their covers provided the vision for every magazine that came after them. Nobody had shot athletes that way before and we wanted to be the first. We would consider ourselves lucky if we could shoot a cover that was one-tenth as good as *Rolling Stone*."

By the time *SLAM* published their first issue, *Rolling Stone* was no longer a cultural force on the newsstand. The magazine, which was once bursting with creative energy, grew into a $250 million conglomerate in the 1980s and lost the qualities that defined them. The *Rolling Stone* cover increasingly became a landing spot for established celebrities and was no longer a birthplace for new stars. A writer who joined the magazine in 1993 compared his new job to showing up to the party just in time to see a cigarette floating in the last cocktail of the night.

SLAM's goal was to become the modern-day basketball version of *Rolling Stone*, embracing the same rebellious streak which gave birth to the rock 'n' roll magazine three decades earlier.

But they needed to find their voice first.

Scoop & A.I.

Scoop Jackson arrived at the Georgetown University campus in 1995 to watch a college sophomore named Allen Iverson. The Georgetown Hoyas guard was the Big East Defensive Player of the Year and averaged 20.4 points during his freshman year, but the second-hand accounts being described to Jackson about his summer dominance at the Kenner League was something else entirely. Iverson was scoring 50 points a game against pro players and sounded like a once-in-a-generation player. Jackson decided to see it with his own eyes. He arrived at McDonough Gymnasium with Iverson's team losing by 22 points at halftime. Jackson would later describe the second half as a part-religious, part-spiritual experience.

"I had never seen anything like it before," he recalled. "This motherfucker was nothing like what I saw in his freshman year. He had handles. He had ups. He had a jump shot. I wasn't expecting that. I walked into the gym like, 'You guys are lying. This guy is just a defensive player.' From an offensive standpoint, he just blew my mind. I was like, 'Okay, this dude I just saw is special.'"

The opposing team's first-half lead disappeared as Iverson's point total grew.

He was at 30 points…

35…

40…

45…

50…

55…

60….

Iverson led his team to a comeback win with 62 points.

Jackson saw the future of basketball.

He left the Georgetown campus with one thought:

"We have to put this kid on the *SLAM* cover."

BORN AND RAISED IN CHICAGO, ILLINOIS, Jackson started watching basketball at the age of five. "To be honest, I think my parents were worried about me," he said. "It was the most important thing in my life."

He watched the *NBA on CBS* in the dining room with his father. When his family moved to a house and installed a driveway hoop, it was the only thing Jackson did.

"I would play all day," he recalled. "It was all I ever did. I still remember just sitting in front of the television when my father was kicked out of the house when my parents got divorced in second grade. The Celtics were playing the Bucks in the Finals. My father packed his bags and said bye to me. I just waved to him and didn't even turn away from the television. I was like, 'You're not pulling me from this game.'"

After attending Luther High School South, Jackson graduated from Xavier University and obtained a master's degree from Howard

University, where he wrote for the school's student newspaper, *The Hilltop*. He started *The Agenda*, a Chicago-based newsletter described as a Black *Village Voice*. Jackson became a freelance writer covering mostly hip-hop and Black culture. Despite his love of basketball, he never wrote about it.

"I just never had the opportunity," Jackson explained. "Because of my background and because there were so few publications for someone with my background, it just never dawned on me to write about sports. Even with a master's degree, it was easier for a young brother to get writing assignments related to hip-hop and Black culture. Basketball was the most important thing in my life, but it was never an option for me to write about it."

Tony Gervino called in 1994 and asked if he was available to attend a Nike All-American camp in Deerfield, Illinois, for *SLAM*. It was Jackson's first sportswriting gig. He filed a 350-word piece and sent in a bonus 1,200-word feature on the camp.

"I wanted to prove to them I could write about basketball," Jackson explained. "It built a trust between me and Tony. He called me and said, 'The Dream Team II is in Chicago, do you think you can get Shaq for an interview?' I said, 'Let's do it.'"

The Chicago native quickly became the magazine's go-to feature writer. Every one of Jackson's *SLAM* stories became a unique documentation of basketball and the culture surrounding the sport. He brought a level of critical thinking to his writing that was different from other basketball writers, while also adding a unique creative flair to his prose. It was a hip-hop voice with a personal touch. It was social commentary and an examination of Black culture disguised as sportswriting.

"It was the first voice of its kind anywhere and certainly in sports journalism," Gervino said. "It was exciting and also literary. His writing was so evocative."

Jackson once interviewed Christian Laettner, a Duke University star who was selected third overall by the Minnesota Timberwolves in 1992, and opened the conversation by asking what being a white basketball player despised by Black fans was like.

"Once we started talking, I was like, 'Damn. We only hate on you because you are white,'" Jackson recalled. "He was like, 'You know how much you would love me if I was Black?' So guess what, if you don't like somebody strictly because of the color of their skin, that makes you a racist."

The opening paragraph of Jackson's story started like this: "I'm a racist. It's just that simple. There's no excuse, no explanation, no exaggerated, drawn-out saga to tell and no specific point of reference to justify why; I just am. I have a tendency to not like some white people simply because they are… white. My blood sometimes turns cold when it comes to dealing with affairs of humanity, being a human being, keeping it politically correct, 'acting in the best interest,' doing the right thing. Contempt is a very easy emotion to feel. Most Black folks will never say this, but they feel it inside. The only difference between me and them is that I'm just racist enough to admit it."

Jackson became the defining voice for an entire generation of basketball fans who grew up reading *SLAM*. Every single story he wrote introduced new perspectives for readers to think over. Jackson re-shaped plenty of mainstream narratives about the most popular basketball players in the world.

"My goal was to never write the same story twice," he explained. "I tried to bring a sense of creativity to the table. I wasn't ashamed of our culture and who I was as a Black man and who we were as Black people in this country, and what basketball meant to us. The approach was to be unapologetic and to not apologize for who I am and who we are as people. I wanted my writing to normalize us. It was not for white people but for us. I wanted people to be able to read stories about us without apologizing for who we are and what we do.

"We weren't trying to force ourselves to create a voice. We were trying to be as true to what we feel basketball culture was without sugarcoating it or beating around the bush. I credit Dennis and Tony. I was allowed to write without restriction. I wasn't given an opportunity. I was given a canvas."

WHILE SUBSCRIBER-BASED PUBLICATIONS LIKE *Sports Illustrated* earned revenue from over three million subscribers every week regardless of who they put on the cover, *SLAM* relied on newsstand sales and needed recognizable faces.

Dennis Page rejected Jackson's proposal to put Iverson on the cover.

A college sophomore was not going to sell any copies on newsstands.

"I was a businessman first and newsstand revenue was important to me," Page said.

Jackson was enraged.

"I told him, 'If *SLAM* is supposed to be at the forefront of basketball culture, we need to get on this,'" he recalled. "I had seen something nobody was talking about. So I told Dennis, 'If you don't do this, I'm out.' He told me, 'Motherfucker, you're not going anywhere.' He was right, I was never going to quit. He said, 'To make a point. I'll do it. Just remember, you know that writing shit, I know this publishing shit. A college basketball player on a cover isn't going to sell.'"

"I was always talking out of both sides of my mouth," Page said. "I would be like, 'You can't do that shit, it'll fuck the business up.' Then I would be like, 'We're going to do it, because it's so dope.' I was a fan just like them. I hated losing money and making bad business decisions, but I also liked breaking the rules and doing cool shit."

Jackson returned to the Georgetown campus a few days later to find Iverson for an interview.

"People always thought it was a Black school because of the basketball team," he said. "But the only Black people who went there played on the squad. It was easy to find a Black ballplayer."

Jackson stopped the first Black student he saw on campus and tracked down Iverson's dorm room moments later.

"I made the pitch to him," he recalled. "He was probably happy to see somebody who looked like him. It was rare to have a young brother come up to him as a reporter. I remember his roommate, Othella Harrington, was there too, just ironing his clothes. Allen was like, 'Oh yeah, no problem. Just come back tomorrow.'"

A phone call was waiting for Jackson when he returned the following morning.

It was head coach John Thompson.

"Who the fuck do you think you are?" he screamed on the other end of the phone.

Thompson was a towering presence at Georgetown. One of the most well-respected and influential voices in college basketball, he stood at 6'10" and ran a successful college basketball program while providing inner-city kids with an opportunity to play college basketball at a

Division I school by recruiting all-Black rosters. The program became nationally renowned in the 1980s after Thompson recruited three star centers, Patrick Ewing, Dikembe Mutombo, and Alonzo Mourning, who all went on to have successful pro careers. Thompson set very high academic standards for his players. After Mutombo missed a class during his freshman year because of a toothache, he arrived at practice later in the day and found a one-way airline ticket back to his home country of Africa sitting at his locker. He never missed another class for the rest of his college career.

The Hoyas head coach had promised Iverson's mom, Ann, he would keep her son out of trouble and was upset that a reporter tried to contact his point guard without the school's permission.

Iverson grew up in Hampton, Virginia, and was the starting quarterback and starting point guard at Bethel High School. As a 17-year-old hanging out with his high school friends at a local bowling alley, an incident took place which would alter his life. It started when, according to witnesses, a group of white kids from the nearby suburban neighborhood of Poquoson confronted Iverson and his group of Black friends. One of them called Iverson a "little boy" and used the N-word, prompting Iverson's friend Michael Simmons to blindside the kid with a punch to his face. A melee ensued. Chairs went flying and one of them hit Barbara Steele, a white woman, in the head, leaving her with six stitches around her left eye and amnesia. A video camera captured the incident on tape. Witnesses pointed the finger at Iverson as the person responsible for Steele's injuries even though the footage was blurry. He received a felony charge of maiming by mob. Iverson was convicted as an adult and received a five-year prison sentence and ended up spending four months at a correctional facility before Virginia governor Douglas Wilder granted him clemency. College basketball scholarship offers vanished after the incident. Schools did not want a convicted felon on their team. Iverson's basketball career was in jeopardy until Georgetown gave him a second chance.

Thompson wasn't going to let his point guard squander the opportunity by saying something wrong to a writer of a magazine he had never heard of.

"I was being cursed out," Jackson recalled. "At some point I was like, 'Wait a minute, I'm a grown-ass man. I'm like 30-something-years old.' So I responded. I said, 'First of all, who the fuck do you think you're talking to?' I read off my résumé. I told him I had no intention of doing anything with Iverson behind his back. I told him, 'Dude, I went to Howard. I know this area. I was already here, so I walked up to a brother, and all I wanted to do was set something up. I wasn't trying to break no rules.' He started laughing because I wouldn't stop yelling. Eventually he said, 'Alright, I like you. Here's what we're going to do. I'm going to give you the sports information director's number. I'm going to do this just for you. Let me look at the magazine and I'll tell him it's okay.' A week later I interviewed Allen over the phone."

Iverson appeared on the cover of *SLAM*'s January 1996 issue, driving to the basket in a Georgetown jersey. Page wasn't convinced the issue would sell, so he put UCLA's Ed O'Bannon, the National Player of the Year and a more recognizable cover subject, on the cover in the West Coast.

Jackson was right.

Iverson became the most influential player of his generation.

Page was also right.

It ended up being one of the worst-selling issues in *SLAM* history.

Ready or Not...
HERE THEY
COME!

The phone rang in Tony Gervino's hotel room at seven in the morning. He had flown to Orlando, Florida, the night before with Scoop Jackson and creative director Don Morris. The NBA's rookie transition program was taking place inside the Marriott World Center nearby. The program was a three-day event featuring workshops, counseling sessions, and former players as guest speakers. Incoming first-year players learned about the responsibilities of being a pro in classroom sessions. Gervino had grown tired of using the NBA Photos archive for cover photos. He flew into Orlando for a photoshoot. The plan was to put 12 rookies on the cover.

"We were getting pictures from the league and they were smiling in every photo," Gervino explained. "They were pointing at themselves. They had both hands on their hips. They had a ball under their arms. Everything was so corny."

SLAM found out about the rookie transition program through a friend who worked at Fleer, the trading card company, but they needed permission to attend the league-sanctioned event. The basketball magazine had started to develop a reputation as a snarky and obnoxious publication who would occasionally take shots at the league.

It didn't always go over well with NBA commissioner David Stern.

"He used to say he got his *SLAM* subscription in a brown paper bag," Gervino recalled. "He thought we were poking him with a stick. We were saying, 'Hey man, you can do whatever you want to do, but we're going to help make your league cool.' The league was getting younger, so the generation gap between the fans and the players was getting smaller. It wasn't like the kids were looking up to Mitch Richmond. He was trying to make Brent Barry the next John Stockton. We did a story on Brent Barry and called him Ghostface Killer."

The idea of photographing the rookies appeared dead until senior director of NBA Photos Carmin Romanelli reached out. He couldn't get the league to approve the idea but agreed to organize a clandestine photoshoot if *SLAM* flew themselves to Orlando. The team arrived and checked in under aliases at the hotel, hoping to stay under the radar. Romanelli asked *SLAM* to provide him with a list of players they wanted. Gervino huddled with Jackson and Morris to sketch out their plan.

The 12 players included Allen Iverson, Marcus Camby, Shareef Abdur-Rahim, Stephon Marbury, Kobe Bryant, and Ray Allen. It was a collection of top college prospects and high school phenoms, a gathering of players who fit *SLAM*'s aesthetic. Romanelli approved the pitch and agreed to facilitate a photoshoot the following day.

"He told us, 'You're going to get a minute and a half with them when they're walking from one building to another for lunch,'" Gervino recalled. "I woke up at seven in the morning. A league official called me and said Iverson left. I was, like, 'Motherfucker, *really?*'"

It was an ominous start to the most ambitious cover shoot in *SLAM* history.

GERVINO STILL REMEMBERS watching Bernard King score a franchise-record 60 points in person at Madison Square Garden on Christmas Day in 1984 as a die-hard New York Knicks fan growing up in Westchester County, New York. He graduated from Fairleigh Dickinson University in Teaneck, New Jersey, with a marketing and advertising degree and was an editor at a sports and fashion magazine named *SportStyle* when Dennis Page called.

"He read my magazines and liked my writing voice, so he called me in for an interview," Gervino recalled. "I had no idea what an editor-in-chief actually did. I just said, 'Look, I'm not the most stats-savvy guy, but I know enough about hip-hop and basketball to make a compelling magazine.'"

The pitch was good enough and he became the magazine's editor-in-chief. Gervino drew inspiration from some of his favorite publications in searching for an irreverent tone for *SLAM*. They included *Spy*, a New York–based monthly magazine founded in 1986 which satirized celebrity culture, and *Ego Trip*, a hip-hop magazine founded in 1992 which branded themselves as "the arrogant voice of musical truth." *SLAM* would follow the path of these magazines and be smart and knowledgable without ever taking themselves too seriously.

"I grew up reading *Sports Illustrated* and the sportswriting greats, but they were on the mountain talking down to you," Gervino explained. "It wasn't in a negative way. They were just so much more skilled. I wanted to make it a less traditional sports magazine. We were fans of the game so the first thing I wanted to do was make our voice more casual."

A ticker of assorted thoughts which ran across the bottom of the page in a section called "Noyz" was introduced in the front of the magazine. The section was written by an omnipresent voice having a one-way conversation with non-sequitur sports and pop culture punch-lines and inspired by a skateboarding magazine founded in 1992 called *Big Brother*.

"They had this column called 'The Angry Interns' where they didn't pay the interns but let them talk shit about the magazine in tiny type," Gervino explained. "I thought it was the greatest thing ever. I said, 'Wouldn't it be funny to have a counter-narrative in the magazine?' We're saying one thing in the rest of the magazine, yet, here's another voice saying so-and-so player was a dick."

"Noyz" would occasionally poke fun at players ("First of all: we love Robert Parish for a lot of reasons, but someone please stop him. Two years with the Bulls? C'mon Chief, you've had a great career, now go home before somebody makes you look like Ali when he fought Trevor Berbick.") and the league, but was mostly a place for assorted thoughts ("Just once we wanna see Dick Vitale rip someone."), and witty punch-lines ("We're all gonna miss Jon Koncak. But hey, basketball always was a non-Koncak sport.").

SLAM interacted with their readers through their "Trash Talk" letters section. They planted inside jokes for loyal subscribers and started on-going rivalries with some of the older players in the league. The magazine attracted a large group of hardcore basketball fans around the country with their attitude and playful humor.

Gervino envisioned players looking like rock stars on the front of the magazine. He points to a cover shoot with Tim Hardaway and Latrell Sprewell of the Golden State Warriors for the fifth issue, where both players appeared on the cover staring at the camera without even the slightest hint of a smile on their faces, as a turning point. It wasn't just how the players were photographed, it was also about who was being photographed.

"They weren't household names," Gervino explained. "But to us, Michael Jordan was retired and Timmy and Spree were the next big thing. They were obscure players to a national audience and we wanted to plant our flag as the anti-establishment basketball magazine."

The rookie transition program photoshoot would be another flag-planting moment for *SLAM*. A cover with the 1996 draft class would be meaningful considering these incoming rookies were the first generation of NBA players who grew up reading the magazine.

GERVINO CAN STILL REMEMBER the entire 90 seconds of the cover shoot today.

The first person who comes to his mind is Todd Fuller. The 11th pick in the draft was a North Carolina State center who was not part of Gervino's plans. Fuller saw the rookies being escorted to a brick wall backdrop for what looked like a group photo and decided to join in.

"I remember being like, 'Oh my god, we don't have room for him,'" Gervino recalled. "He was coming toward us, and I walked over, put my hand on his back, and said, 'Hey, how are you?' He was like, 'What are you guys doing there?' I was like, 'It's nothing over there. Nothing is going on over there.' No disrespect to Todd, because he's made a lot of money, but jeez, a cover with him on it would have been bad."

Fuller got the hint and left, but now there was less than a minute left. NBA photographer Nathaniel Butler stood with a large-format camera on his tripod, waiting for *SLAM* to bring their cover subjects over. "It was nerve-wracking," he said. Butler was playing through the scenarios of everything that could go wrong for a 90-second photoshoot. But he didn't have time to consider any of them. He snapped eight photos with his camera before the rookies left for lunch. Gervino breathed a sigh of relief.

The magazine had managed to pull it off.

On the cover of the magazine's 15th issue, Camby stood in his Toronto Raptors dinosaur jersey, next to Marbury, with a scowl on his face and a white towel on his shoulder. Beside them was Bryant, palming a basketball with his right arm while hiding the cast on his left wrist, and Abdur-Rahim. Allen sat in front of the four players. The rest of the cover subjects—Jermaine O'Neal, Antoine Walker, Steve Nash, John Wallace, Samaki Walker, and Kerry Kittles—appeared in the second-page foldout.

Iverson's absence is still noticeable today.

"It will always bother me that he was not there," Butler said. "He needed to be in this photo."

The cover line, referencing the 1996 hit single "Ready or Not" from the popular hip-hop group The Fugees, said READY OR NOT... HERE THEY COME!

It summarized the long-term impact of the incoming rookie class and *SLAM*'s growing presence on newsstands.

The SLAM Dome
INTERLUDE

A handful of people inside an 8th floor office on 1115 Broadway at the corner of 25th Street in Manhattan's Flatiron District were responsible for publishing the most influential basketball magazine on newsstands every month. Tony Gervino still remembers the office he shared inside this building with managing editor Anna Gebbie. "It was dark. It was dirty. There were no windows. But it was also magic," he said. "The energy in the office was great because we were doing something other people weren't doing. We were kids, and what we were doing was working."

Gervino referred to the office as the *SLAM* Dome.

"It was like Santa's workshop," he said. "I wanted people to picture the place where we made the magazine. I thought it would give us some three-dimensionality."

Every one of Gervino's memories of the *SLAM* Dome involves senior editor Russ Bengtson, who was writing for a local magazine called *Big Shout*, which covered Delaware's music and lifestyle scene, when he came across *SLAM*'s first issue on a late-night grocery store run. "I flipped through it and had no idea a magazine like that existed," he recalled. "It just hit on so many different things I was interested in." Bengtson grew up on Long Island and attended Smithtown High School before graduating from the University of Delaware. He landed a writing job at *The Oxford Tribune* after graduating as an English major. The local newspaper had an editorial staff of five people with a circulation of 1,200. Bengtson made the 45-minute drive from Delaware to Pennsylvania every morning to cover town council meetings and store openings. After picking up the *SLAM* issue, he found the magazine's fax number and sent in a couple story pitches. Bengtson wrote a 100-word story on Philadelphia 76ers center Shawn Bradley for the magazine and was hired as a senior editor in 1996.

The basketball sneaker industry was still growing by the time Bengtson joined the magazine. Michael Jordan's signature shoes remained popular with teens, while a new generation of stars, including Shaquille O'Neal and Larry Johnson, landed their own signature shoe endorsement deals. Bengtson owned his first pair of Nike sneakers in fourth grade and grew up tracking down new pairs of Air Jordans at the discount aisle at Marshalls and in thrift stores.

"I couldn't afford the pairs at Foot Locker," he explained. "When I was 15, I bought the Air Jordan 2 for $70 instead of spending $100 on the new Air Jordan 3 which just came out. The $30 difference meant the world to me at the time."

Sneakers became the gateway drug for his basketball fandom. Bengtson rooted for the Chicago Bulls and traveled to Madison Square Garden to watch Jordan play in person during high school. "I honestly can't remember if it was the Air Jordan that got me into Michael Jordan," he said, "or vice versa."

Bengtson joined *SLAM* and took ownership of the magazine's "Kicks" section.

"I would call up every single brand—Nike, Reebok, and adidas—and ask if they could send us shoes to include in the magazine," he said. "It was this thing we did that no one else was doing. I felt like once you opened one door, there were more doors behind that. You just wanted to open as many of them as possible."

Gervino was also a sneaker guy.

"We would go to the Nike employee store in Portland and just buy everything," he recalled. "I think one time Russ spent $1,500 there. We were legitimately the first two people on eBay. We had no control. Russ had a problem with collecting stuff. He was a size 9.5, which was a good sample size for sneakers. He benefited from that greatly. I was a size 14. It was much harder."

When *SLAM* was invited for a one-on-one interview with Jordan, Bengtson and Gervino spent the same amount of time preparing questions as they did discussing what sneakers they would wear to the interview.

"Those two things were equally important," Bengtson explained. "The last thing we wanted to do was get ripped on by Michael."

Nike recognized the influence of *SLAM*'s sneaker coverage and invited Bengtson to their Portland, Oregon, headquarters. He was granted exclusive access to interview the company's designers.

"It was Willy Wonka's chocolate factory, and I was the kid with the golden ticket," Bengtson said. "It opened up from there. We were covering stuff that hadn't been covered before. Sneakers were an off-the-beaten-path thing. We helped drag it into the mainstream."

Dennis Page worked at the *SLAM* Dome with Jonathan Rheingold and Ronnie Zeidel on the business side of the magazine. *SLAM* only received buy-in from urban streetwear brands like Mecca, FUBU, and Phat Farm in the very beginning. The magazine's popularity grew after the first several years on newsstands. Sneaker brands like Nike and adidas, and national sponsors like Mountain Dew, Coca-Cola, and Levi's, who rejected *SLAM*'s overtures in the beginning, were now lining up to partner with the magazine.

The players also started to understand what *SLAM* was doing. Page's editorial strategy of covering high school, college, and the pros was a stroke of genius. High school hoopers read every issue from cover to cover and eventually filled their college dorm rooms with the magazine's "SLAM UPS" posters. Making the *SLAM* cover was a personal goal by the time these players reached the NBA.

"The *Sports Illustrated* cover meant nothing to them," Zeidel said. "Their agents would call me. They would beg and offer things to be on the cover, and we would say, 'Nah. They're not deserving yet. We can't do it.' They would then ask, 'Okay, but can we get a feature then if not a cover?' The agents understood how important our cover was from a marketing perspective. If you were on the cover of *SLAM*, you were a cool motherfucker."

Jalen Rose was one of the players featured in an early issue of the magazine. "When *SLAM* was created, we felt like as players from the inner city, they represented the culture and spoke our language better than the other magazines," he explained. "When you were young, you wanted to be in *Sports Illustrated*, but you really wanted to be in *SLAM*. Being in *SLAM* made you relevant within your culture and earned you a different level of respect."

The magazine fostered their growing relationships at the arena with younger players, who delighted in catching up with *SLAM* writers in the locker room.

"Some of it was the way we grew up with them and how they grew up reading us," Bengtson explained. "Some of it was the fact we weren't talking about the same things that everyone else was. We related to players as these young hip-hop fans far better than a 50-year-old beat writer who was clocking in every day with zero interest in who the players were outside the game."

SLAM writers showed up to the arena wearing sports jerseys, baggy jeans, and Nike sneakers. "We looked like your college weed dealer," Gervino said. Traditional media members rolled their eyes.

"We got clowned by the beat writers because we weren't joining in on the scrums," Bengtson recalled. "We were there to build personal relationships. If a player came to town and we had a conversation with them, when the time came to do a story, he was gonna be mad cool because we treated him as a human being instead of tonight's news."

Rick Telander was one of the few traditional reporters who didn't share the opinions of his fellow old-school sportswriters.

"*SLAM* was saying, 'Let's just enjoy the game of basketball for what it is,'" Telander said. "You might look at it and say, 'Where are the investigative stories and where's the criticism?' And that's okay. They were about fun, and I was always happy to see it in my mailbox."

"They thought we were a joke until they got to know us," Gervino said. "We demystified sportswriting. We weren't old white guys in short-sleeve dress shirts. We elevated basketball as entertainment. We appeared to be the most obnoxious people in the magazine, but that wasn't who we were. We just played that person. We would pick on players in the magazine. It was like professional wrestling, and our villain was Reggie Miller."

The Indiana Pacers guard was a perfect foil for Gervino, a loyal New York Knicks fan, who put John Starks on the *SLAM* cover shortly after he became editor-in-chief. The Knicks took advantage of Jordan's retirement and advanced to the 1994 NBA Finals, where Starks shot 2-for-18 in a crushing Game 7 defeat against the Houston

Rockets. "I was so sure he was going to make a comeback the following season," Gervino recalled. "We did the cover shoot after practice. I went back to the office to write the cover story. He went into the worst slump of his career."

The Knicks faced the Pacers in the second round a few months later. They were winning 105–99 with 18.7 seconds left in Game 1 when one of the most improbable comebacks in sports history happened. Miller hit a three to cut the lead in half. Two Knicks players ran into each other on the ensuing inbound, allowing the Pacers guard to intercept Anthony Mason's inbound pass, dribble behind the three-point line, and tie the game with another three. The Madison Square Garden crowd was still processing what had just happened when Miller's teammate Sam Mitchell, not realizing the game was tied, intentionally fouled Starks, who went to the line and missed both free throws. Patrick Ewing collected the offensive rebound on the second miss, but Miller rebounded his putback attempt, and was fouled by Starks with 7.5 seconds remaining. Miller calmly sank two free throws to give the Pacers the lead. The Knicks were unable to get a shot attempt off before the buzzer. The Pacers won 107–105. Miller scored eight points in nine seconds and made a choking gesture at director and Knicks superfan Spike Lee sitting courtside to punctuate the entire sequence.

SLAM, or more specifically Gervino, told their readers Miller would never appear on their cover. The magazine published his high school prom photos with his sister Cheryl in an issue and took every opportunity to poke fun at the Pacers guard. David Stern saw the photos and asked *SLAM* to back off. Miller eventually appeared on the cover of the magazine's 33rd issue a few years later.

"We had a joke, and we played it out," Gervino explained. "We were like, 'Well, he's one of the best players in the league.' I felt like we were growing up."

Below the cover photo of Miller staring at the camera on the front of the magazine was the cover line THE NEW KING. The words HELL FREEZES OVER appeared on the spine of the magazine, referencing *SLAM*'s feud with the Pacers star. Over time, the spine line became a place for throwaway cover line ideas, inside jokes, and pop culture references. It would also eventually lead to one of the biggest fights at the *SLAM* Dome. "It was probably something 70 percent of our readers never noticed," Bengtson said. "But we were really proud of them. It was just as important as the cover line for us."

Cory Johnson had envisioned *SLAM* to be one of the most reader-friendly magazines on newsstands. Several years after he helped put together the very first issue, his vision was coming to life. The *SLAM* Dome was regularly filled with reader mail.

"It was my job to go through the letters," Bengtson said. "We would get letters from prison from people who were psyched to still be able to get the magazine while they were locked down. People would enclose art in their mail or draw stuff on the envelopes. It was cool to know the impact we had on people who were reading the magazine."

Gervino would respond to a handful of letters in the "Trash Talk" section every month with a playful tone.

"It was our way to have conversations with kids who thought about sports in the same way we did," he explained. "We looked at ourselves as misfits, and there were fans out there who looked at themselves the same way. Our fans watched and played basketball, but they also had a sense of humor."

SLAM figured out how to make a basketball magazine through trial-and-error.

"Honestly, if we all went to journalism school, it would have killed the magazine," Gervino said. "We would have been like, 'No, we can't put this in the magazine because it violates some journalistic principle.' Dennis gave us the freedom to screw some stuff up."

Everyone credits creative director Don Morris for his behind-the-scenes work. "He was so innovative," Page said. "He had never designed a publication before, and we just threw him into the fire. He killed it and took the magazine to the next level." The most influential basketball magazine on newsstands was designed by someone who didn't like basketball. "Don hated sports," Gervino said. "But he was also unbelievably talented. He was never overwhelmed by the moment."

Morris would draw creative inspiration for layouts from different places. Bengtson remembers a visual graphic for a Scottie Pippen feature which included a series of assault rifles. "Don was into pitbulls and guns, so a lot of that stuff ended up in the magazine," he explained. "We saw the layout and just said, 'Yeah, whatever, we'll let it go.' We got some feedback from our readers and were like, 'Yeah, that was a bad idea.' It was the first time and last time that happened."

Morris had no interest in sports, but he was a huge punk rock fan. "Don would always say, 'Did someone say Poison Idea?' and he would put it on," Gervino recalled. "He did this a lot. It was incredibly loud all the time."

But the soundtrack at the *SLAM* Dome was predominantly hip-hop.

The genre entered a golden era in 1996. Jay-Z's *Reasonable Doubt*, Nas's *It Was Written*, Mobb Deep's *Hell on Earth*, Ghostface Killah's *Ironman*, Redman's *Muddy Waters*, The Roots' *Illadelph Halflife*, Outkast's *ATLiens*,

De La Soul's *Stakes is High*, UGK's *Ridin' Dirty*, and The Fugees' *The Score* were all released during the calendar year. 2Pac Shakur released *All Eyez On Me* in February before he was killed in a Las Vegas drive-by shooting in September. His first posthumous album, *The Don Killuminati: The 7 Day Theory*, was released two months later.

"Every issue became a snapshot of what we were listening to at the time," Bengtson said. "We were so caught up in it there was one issue where all of our headlines were Outkast-related because that was all we were listening to."

When *SLAM* flew to Orlando in 1996 for their cover shoot at the NBA's rookie transition program, they also conceived an idea for a hip-hop magazine. Morris, who was tired of working on a sports magazine, suggested the idea to Gervino and Scoop Jackson. Inspired by Bruce Mau and Rem Koolhaas's architecture book *S, M, L, XL*, Morris came up with the name *XXL*. Page pitched the idea to Stanley Harris and put together an editorial team which included James Bernard, Reggie Dennis, and Robert Marriott, who had all left *The Source* after a dispute over the magazine's editorial integrity. Morris became *XXL*'s art director. Jackson moved to New York to work on the magazine. The first issue arrived on newsstands in August 1997, featuring a double cover with Jay-Z and Master P.

SLAM would hire a hip-hop photographer in the same year to define their cover vision.

Showbiz
& KG

One of the most influential hip-hop photographers of the 1990s, Jonathan Mannion grew up in Cleveland, Ohio, in a household where both of his parents were painters. "They both studied art and encouraged a certain way of seeing the world," he explained. "Most parents would say, 'I want you to be a lawyer or be a doctor.' My parents said, 'If you want to take pictures, do it and do it at the highest level.' They brought me into the art world with incredible confidence."

Mannion moved to New York after graduating from Kenyon College in Gambier, Ohio, with a bachelor's degree in psychology and studio art to pursue a career as a photographer. In 1996, he caught the attention of Adrien Vargas, the creative director for a Brooklyn rapper named Jay-Z who was looking for someone to shoot images for his debut album. A more well-known photographer named Daniel Hastings, who had shot a series of classic cover shots, including the iconic imagery of Raekwon's *Only Built 4 Cuban Linx*, was the number one choice, but Vargas became intrigued with Mannion's wealth of experience working with formal portrait photographers. The two met and Mannion offered to shoot the project for $300 less than the lowest bid. The 25-year-old photographer was hired for $1,300 without having ever shot an album cover before.

Jay-Z's debut album was titled *Heir to the Throne*, so Mannion prepared a series of Royal Family photo references for the shoot. He received a call shortly after. The title had been changed to *Reasonable Doubt*. Mannion scrapped all his plans and returned to the drawing board. He became inspired by Luc Sante's book *Evidence*, which collected black-and-white New York City Police evidence photos. He wanted the album cover to paint Jay-Z as a refined street hustler to match the portraiture being painted in his songs. Eschewing the typical gangsta rap references of silk shirts, Versace linens, and the 1983 crime drama *Scarface*, the photographer opted for a more subtle, throwback motif matching the preciseness of Jay-Z's confidence.

The cover of *Reasonable Doubt*, which was shot on the rooftop of Mannion's Manhattan apartment, featured a close-up black-and-white shot of the rapper wearing a scarf and hat, with a cigar obscuring his facial features, adding a layer of mystery to the narrator of the classic album. The photo conveyed the tone of the record and the rap artist's persona with precision.

The *SLAM* Dome was blown away by Mannion's photoshoot with Jay-Z. By 1997, it felt like a natural fit for the magazine to bring in a photographer from the hip-hop world to shoot a cover.

"The whole goal for us from the beginning was to connect hip-hop and basketball," said Russ Bengtson. "We always said, 'Why don't we make these guys look like rap stars?' We wanted these guys to look larger than life. So it made sense on a lot of levels to bring in a hip-hop photographer. If Mannion could turn Jay-Z into a mythical character, what would he be able to do with NBA players? Nobody knew who Jay-Z was when *Reasonable Doubt* came out, but those images became iconic."

They hired Mannion for a cover shoot. He was a basketball fan with a clear vision on how he wanted to photograph for *SLAM*.

"I wanted to go deeper than what NBA photographers were doing," Mannion said. "They would ask players to hold the ball under their arm and give the biggest smile possible. That was safe. It was league-approved. I wanted a 'Drop-top Benz, leaning back with your feet up on the edge' kind of personality. The ability to showcase a dynamic aspect of these players to their fans was exciting to me. I wanted to capture them not only for their basketball skills but what they represented to the culture.

"We were responsible for how these cover subjects were being perceived, and we needed to share a new layer of beauty through their intensity. *SLAM* was the Bible for this layer of storytelling. The photos had to be beautiful. There had to be a rich delivery beyond the surface of what was expected. I loved how there were statistics in sports to showcase the talent of an athlete. But averaging a triple-double or grabbing 20 rebounds in a game, that's not who they are, that was what they did. I wanted to go beyond that surface. The ability to go deeper and tell the fullness of their story is where the beauty comes from."

SLAM needed to pick cover subjects with the energy to match Mannion's approach. There was no better choice than Stephon Marbury and Kevin Garnett, two hip-hop generation kids taking the NBA by storm together.

MARBURY WAS A CONEY ISLAND KID with a signature haircut featuring a carefully shaved part in the front and a "Coney Island's Finest" tattoo on his left arm, who Tony Gervino remembers as the first player to truly embrace *SLAM*. "We had a relationship with Steph since he was 15," he said. "We were a New York publication and he was our guy." Marbury wrote the magazine's first high school diary, documenting his experience at Lincoln High School, where he was named the number one junior in the country by *The Sporting News* and received the title of Mr. New York State Basketball after his senior season. Considered by some to be the best point guard to ever come out of New York, the 6'2" Marbury honed his skills at The Garden, the outdoor basketball court within walking distance of his apartment where he grew up. He played at streetball courts around the city, from the Rucker in Harlem to The Hole in Bedford-Stuyvesant, carrying not just the burden of an entire city's expectations but the unfulfilled dreams of his older brothers.

Eric Marbury, the eldest of the four brothers, earned a scholarship at the University of Georgia and was taken by the San Diego Clippers in the sixth round in 1982 but was cut in training camp. Donnie Marbury was up next. He attended Texas A&M and led the Southwest Conference in scoring but went undrafted. The hopes of a family member starring in the NBA fell on Norman Marbury, who accepted a scholarship offer from the University of Tennessee, but watched the opportunity disappear after his SAT scores were deemed too low. He ended up playing at three junior colleges and at St. Francis University in Brooklyn before pursuing a pro career overseas.

The pressure was now on the youngest of the four brothers. Marbury averaged 18.9 points and 4.5 assists in his freshman season at Georgia Tech and declared for the 1996 draft, where he was selected fourth overall by the Milwaukee Bucks, successfully fulfilling the dreams of his older brothers. Marbury was traded on draft night to the Minnesota Timberwolves and became Garnett's teammate.

GARNETT GREW UP IN GREENVILLE, South Carolina, and played basketball at Mauldin High School in a nearby town 15 minutes from home. He got into a fight before his senior year in high school and was charged with second-degree public lynching after one of the students suffered a hairline fracture to his ankle. The charges were later dropped. Garnett decided to move to Chicago with his mother and younger sister and transferred to Farragut Academy in the city's West Side neighborhood.

The school added one of the best seniors in the country to a team already featuring Ronnie Fields, a shooting guard entering his junior season who was also considered one of the nation's best high school prospects.

Scoop Jackson remembers Garnett and Fields as local basketball celebrities. "People were in line waiting to see their games," he recalled. "Getting a ticket to a Farragut Academy game was just as special as getting a ticket to see Michael and the Bulls. They were on that level. Michael and the Bulls were universal. Kevin and Ronnie at Farragut? That was straight-up hood stuff. People on the West Side were enjoying the games, but you didn't have many white kids from the suburbs coming to see them. Public league basketball was still a thing where many white people in Chicago were scared to go to."

Farragut Academy won 27 consecutive games, finishing with a 28–2 record. Garnett scored 32 points, grabbed 14 rebounds, and added six blocks in a win over Carver in the city championship game.

The 6'11" Garnett had the shooting range of a guard, the elite athleticism of a wing player, superb passing vision, and a defensive upside that was unmatched by any other prospect in the country.

He was considered the number one high schooler in the nation. Garnett skipped college and declared for the 1995 NBA Draft after the season, becoming the first high schooler to make the prep-to-pro jump since Darryl Dawkins and Bill Willoughby in 1975. The Timberwolves took him fifth overall.

Minnesota finished the 1996–97 regular season with a franchise-record number of wins and made their first ever playoff appearance. They were led by Marbury and Garnett, who had a friendship dating back to high school, when the two racked up $80 phone bills every month chatting with each other.

A *SLAM* cover shoot was scheduled with the two young stars inside a midtown Atlanta studio before the start of the 1997–98 season.

MANNION SET UP A SIMPLE BACKDROP for the shoot to allow Marbury and Garnett to be the focal point in every photo he captured. What he remembers about the photoshoot today is the friendship between the two.

"Kevin would lean into Steph and box him out," he recalled. "They would just mess around with each other. KG put Steph in a chokehold and put gun fingers to the side of his head. They brought a playful nature to the table. There was a real camaraderie there. There was a real love that existed. I just remember seeing two people with the same mentality who were genuinely excited to be playing with each other in the league."

The cover photo wouldn't express their playfulness but instead showcase the attitude they brought to the NBA. On the October 1997 issue of *SLAM*, Marbury, with a cocky grin on his face, and Garnett, wearing a backward visor and giving a menacing stare directly into the camera, stood together on the cover. The two wore matching team-issued practice jerseys with the sleeves cut off, radiating an intentionally rebellious energy. Visible jewelry pieces appeared on their neck, a specific request by both players before the cover shoot. The picture captured a very specific moment in Marbury and Garnett's careers with precision.

"Photography is a beautiful way to have a conversation with somebody and mark the moment that will never be the same again," Mannion said. "It's a single genuine moment. Nothing that we have ever done is going to happen again in exactly the same way."

The main cover line said SHOWBIZ & KG, a play on the name of the New York–based underground rap group Showbiz & A.G. A second cover line, inspired by the hit single "If I Ruled The World (Imagine That)" from Nas's second studio album *It Was Written*, said MARBURY & GARNETT RULE THE WORLD. IMAGINE THAT.

Garnett was 21.

Marbury was 20.

At that very moment it was impossible to imagine anything else.

The Best
Point Guard
in the World
(YOU'VE NEVER HEARD OF)

There was once a time when the newsstand was a place for discovering new things.

An 11-year-old Evan Auerbach, who grew up in Hudson Valley, a town about 90 miles from Manhattan, New York, discovered hip-hop through Slick Rick's debut studio album *The Great Adventures of Slick Rick* in 1988. The rapper's storytelling prowess introduced the teenager to an entirely new genre of music.

"I was obsessed," he recalled. "I was this white Jewish kid from upstate New York where if you liked hip-hop you were an outsider. My friends listened to Nirvana and Pearl Jam. It was the opposite of the life I was living."

Auerbach ran to the grocery store at the start of every month with a pen and pad, jotting down every single release date inside *The Source*.

"It was the only way to know when new music was coming," he said. "It was also the only place where I could enjoy the music and culture that people around me were not into."

The Source introduced Auerbach, an East Coast hip-hop fan, to West Coast artists including Too $hort, DJ Quik, and MC Eiht, whose fan bases rarely extended beyond their home state in a time when the genre was mostly regional. Auerbach discovered new rappers in the "Hip-Hop Quotable" section, where the magazine picked their favorite verse of the month.

"I still remember this dude Ras Kass getting a hip-hop quotable," he recalled. "I was like, 'Who is this dude? How have I never heard of him?' He was from the West Coast. There was a whole other rap world out there I wasn't aware of. That was a real discovery point for me."

In Birmingham, England, over 3,000 miles away from where Auerbach grew up, Sammy Gunnell fell in love with basketball at the age of 10 while playing the arcade game *NBA Jam*. In a country where soccer was king and television networks rarely broadcast basketball games, he couldn't learn about the sport until a new issue of *SLAM* arrived at the corner store every month.

Gunnell collected and read the magazine religiously, discovering an entirely new world of basketball, from the pro game to the playground.

"There was something about it that was just much grimier than anything else I had read," he said. "It felt a bit daring to read it as a kid. They weren't trying to be this kind of clean-cut magazine. It felt like they were breaking the rules."

Gunnell still remembers the first time he saw a point guard named Rafer Alston on the cover of *SLAM*'s December 1997 issue.

"Reading about him introduced me to a world that I had previously been unfamiliar with," he recalled.

A NEW YORK POINT GUARD from Jamaica, Queens, Alston played at Cardozo High School before leading Ventura College to the California state junior college championship. He took a year off before joining Fresno City College, where he averaged 17.3 points and 8.6 assists as a sophomore, and transferred to Fresno State for his junior season.

The point guard was better known as "Skip to my Lou," the nickname he earned on the streetball court for his penchant to skip while he was showing off his dazzling array of dribbling moves. The stories traveled via word-of-mouth across the city. Alston was the composer of his own symphony on the playground, once embarrassing a streetballer who went by the name "Headache" with his dribble so badly, fans stopped the game and threw aspirin pills on the court. Anthony Mason, regarded as one of the toughest defensive players in the NBA, showed up to the playground once and flat-out refused to guard Alston on the opposing team. Even Stephon Marbury, who had a streetball reputation himself, admitted he got dropped by Alston's crossover once. Onlookers still remember the time Alston avoided a big man jumping to block his mid-air layup attempt by rolling the basketball down his right arm around his head and back down his other arm, making a perfect drop-off pass to his teammate for a dunk.

The legend of "Skip to my Lou" grew every time he played.

He became the most talked-about player at the Rucker.

Earning a reputation at the Rucker—the most famous streetball court in the world, located on 155th Street and Frederick Douglass Boulevard in Harlem, New York—was the highest honor for any basketball player. In its heyday, neighborhood kids lined up around the block, fighting for a seat on the bleachers for a glimpse of the action taking place inside the chain-link-fenced court, across the street from the Polo Grounds, where several New York professional baseball teams used to play.

Holcombe Rucker, a director for the New York City Department of Parks & Recreation, started a pro-am tournament at the park in 1950. The best pro players, including Wilt Chamberlain and Lew Alcindor, would show up in the summer to test themselves against the best playground hoopers in the world, giving fans who couldn't afford a ticket to watch NBA games at Madison Square Garden a chance to see the best players in the world.

The Rucker gave birth to playground legends like Joe Hammond, nicknamed "The Destroyer" for the way he would crush opposing defenses. The high-flying Harlem native famously scored 50 points in a game against Julius Erving in the 1970s. Hammond holds the Rucker single-game scoring record with 74 points. Anyone who has ever watched him calls him the best streetballer of all-time. Hammond was one of many New York streetballers who became legends in the city, along with Earl "the Goat" Manigault, whose leaping ability was so remarkable onlookers said he could pull a dollar bill off the top of the backboard and leave change, and Richard "Pee Wee" Kirkland, the man widely credited with inventing the crossover dribble.

SLAM devoted pages inside their magazine to telling the stories of these streetball legends from the very beginning. When Scoop Jackson joined the magazine, he helped expand their streetball purview beyond the five boroughs, writing features on lesser-known streetball legends like Chicago, Illinois, native Billy "The Kid" Harris, who never had a bad game according to those who watched him in the playground. Streetball became an integral part of *SLAM*'s basketball coverage every month.

"We played a big role in legitimizing streetball and what it meant to basketball culture," Jackson said. "In society, whether it's print or film, once things are documented, it is validated. We elevated streetball and gave it validation. We took it beyond just highlight clips. We rounded these people out as individuals and as cultural icons. In streetball, unless you're there, you don't have the luxury of watching full games. You don't get the depth and full scope of the player. Everybody was watching clips. Our job was to give you the full picture."

SLAM arrived on newsstands in the mid-1990s in the midst of a streetball revival. The craze had started to die down at the start of the 1980s as players started to focus on the much more lucrative pro game instead of spending their days at the park, but the Rucker was again drawing lines around the block, thanks to Greg Marius, who started a streetball tournament in 1982 called the *Entertainer's Basketball Classic*.

Marius was a member of the Disco Four when a fellow rap group named Crash Crew challenged them to a game. It grew into a tournament featuring Grandmaster Flash and the Furious Five, the Sugarhill Gang, and playground hoopers from around the city. The tournament moved to the Rucker in 1987 and became the official hang-out spot for rappers and hoopers during the summertime. Def Jam was among several record labels who sponsored the tournament. Rappers including Fat Joe and Jay-Z coached their own Rucker teams, recruiting pros like Marbury to play on them. Every game was the main event, with a play-by-play emcee talking trash on the mic to the backdrop of hip-hop booming from the speakers.

A group of modern-day streetball legends were born, including Kareem Reid, a 5'10" guard with a patented spin move known as "Best Kept Secret" at the Rucker, and God Shammgod, whose signature one-handed crossover dribble was so iconic it became a popular move in college and the pros and is today simply referred to as "The Shammgod." But no one generated more buzz than "Skip to my Lou." Alston wasn't just the next great streetball point guard from New York, he was poised to become the rare Rucker legend who would take his game to the pros.

STREETBALL WAS CELEBRATED in the neighborhoods but viewed by coaches of organized games as a selfish and undisciplined way to play basketball. It was one-on-one showcases that went against the idea of making winning plays. The story of streetball legends usually started with the glitz and glamour but often ended as cautionary tales.

For every Connie Hawkins, a New York streetball legend who won an ABA championship with the Pittsburgh Pipers and made four NBA All-Star teams in seven seasons, there are stories like Hammond's brief fling with the pro game. The Los Angeles Lakers flew Hammond cross-country for a pre-draft workout in 1971. The streetballer's reputation was enough to earn him a one-year, $50,000 contract offer from the team, even though he was a high school dropout with no experience playing at the college level. Hammond walked away from the Lakers offer. He made that amount of money playing craps on the Harlem street corners in a week. Hammond had $200,000 stashed in his apartment from selling marijuana and heroin by the time the Lakers recruited him. After serving two prison terms over drug charges, Hammond never got another chance at making the pros.

Tony Gervino wasn't sure whether Alston would be the next streetball cautionary tale or if he would make it to the NBA, but he was nonetheless intrigued with the idea of putting him on the *SLAM* cover. It was a perfect fit for the magazine. A New York point guard.

A streetball legend. A chance for the magazine to introduce someone to a national audience. But Gervino knew he needed more to convince Dennis Page to put another college player on the cover after the Allen Iverson–Ed O'Bannon cover became one of the worst-selling issues in *SLAM* history, so he pitched the bold idea of declaring Alston the best point guard in the world on the cover.

The 1990s was a golden era for point guards. Anyone from John Stockton, Gary Payton, Jason Kidd, Stephon Marbury, Allen Iverson, Kevin Johnson, Tim Hardaway, Rod Strickland, and Mark Jackson were in the best point guard in the world discussion.

Phil Taylor would have understood Page's decision to reject Gervino's cover line suggestion. In 1997, *Sports Illustrated* asked Taylor to write a cover story on the topic. He picked 16 point guards and assigned them a score from 1 to 16 across statistical categories, weighing specific stats, including assists, turnovers, rebounds, and blocks.

"That was my first primitive attempt at analytics," Taylor said.

When he added up the scores, there was a surprise at the top.

It was Cleveland Cavaliers point guard Terrell Brandon.

"When he finished first, we thought, 'Should we do this? Should we fudge things and make it somebody else?' It was an off-the-wall, unexpected choice," Taylor said. "The feeling was, 'No, it would be better to have a surprise.' I knew Terrell Brandon was not the best point guard in the league. We went with it against my better judgment."

On the cover of the February 10, 1997, issue of *Sports Illustrated* was an action photo of Brandon driving past Golden State Warriors forward Joe Smith. On the cover's left side, the main cover line in white and red said: THE BEST POINT GUARD IN THE NBA. A second cover line in white next to Brandon's sneakers said: WE RATED THE

PLAYMAKERS AND, SURPRISE, CLEVELAND'S TERRELL
BRANDON CAME OUT ON TOP.

Brandon was an above-average point guard in the league, but certainly nobody's choice as the best player at his position. The *Sports Illustrated* cover became a running joke around the league.

"I remember Dr. Jack Ramsay, who was the nicest guy, came up to me after the issue came out and said, 'Oh wow. Was that your idea?'" Taylor recalled. "I had other writers asking me if Brandon had paid me or if I was his cousin. I got a lot of shit from people about it. I had no idea it was going to be a cover story. I would have probably fought harder against it if I knew it was going to be on the cover."

Whether Gervino believed Alston was in fact the best point guard in the world didn't matter. He pitched Page the idea because it just might be provocative enough to convince people to pick the magazine up off the newsstand. Page approved the pitch.

Gervino still remembers Alston's disbelief when he arrived at Madison Square Garden for his cover shoot with photographer Nathaniel Butler. "It just seemed inconceivable to him that we were putting him on the cover," he recalled.

Alston appeared on the cover of *SLAM*'s December 1997 issue, standing at center court of the Mecca of Basketball wearing his Fresno State jersey, dribbling a ball between his legs in front of a black backdrop. The cover line to the left of the photo in bright yellow font said THE BEST POINT GUARD IN THE WORLD. But below the main cover line, it says (YOU'VE NEVER HEARD OF.) Page made a last-minute decision to add the second cover line. "You had to editorialize it," he explained. "It was reminding the reader, 'It's okay you've never even heard of this fucking guy, but we're telling you he's the guy.'"

It was one of the best-selling issues in *SLAM* history.

"It was an important moment for us," Gervino said. "We put a completely unknown player on the cover, and it sold. We could feel the power of what we were able to do. We were feeling ourselves, thinking we could put a streetball guy on the cover. For all those reasons, this cover means more to me than any of the other ones."

"It was the cover line," Jackson said. "It wasn't about who was on the cover or the photoshoot. It was us going out on a limb and saying this motherfucker is the best point guard in the world. Period. We looked at what other magazines were doing and said, 'Fuck them.' We did stuff they didn't have the balls to do. They didn't see Rafer Alston the way we saw him. We were like, 'Anytime you had a 15-year-old kid who had grown men in the NBA scared to come out and play him, that's some real shit.'"

RICK TELANDER PITCHED HIS OWN STREETBALL IDEA to *Sports Illustrated* in the same year Alston made the cover of *SLAM*. He watched *Soul in the Hole*—a documentary film following a Brooklyn streetball team called Kenny's Kings while they prepared for a summer playground tournament at The Hole in Bedford-Stuyvesant—and became intrigued with Ed "Booger" Smith, a playground legend who opened the film with the line, "If I don't make it to the NBA, I'm gonna be a drug dealer. Somehow I've gotta get me a Lexus. Whatever it takes."

Telander was familiar with the streetball scene. He read Pete Axthelm's *The City Game: Basketball from the Garden to the Playgrounds* in 1973 and pitched *Sports Illustrated* the idea of following four college players who returned home during the summer and played on streetball courts. "There were Black basketball players from New York City who were slowly being recognized by the rest of the country," he explained. "The basketball was incredible, but it was unseen and mysterious. I started hearing about all of this legendary stuff and wanted to see it." The magazine asked local reporters around the country to act as paid research assistants, helping to put together a file of streetballers from the New York, Boston, and D.C. area for Telander to review. He chose four hoopers, including James "Fly" Williams, a Brownsville, Brooklyn, streetball legend who once dunked over Moses Malone and scored 40 points in a single half while shooting cherry pits out the side of his mouth. The article, titled "They Always Go Home Again," was published in the November 12, 1973, issue of *Sports Illustrated*. Telander fell in love with the New York streetball scene, returning the following summer and detailing his experiences in the book *Heaven Is a Playground*.

He returned to New York two decades later to track down "Booger" and write another streetball feature, which appeared as the cover story for *Sports Illustrated*'s August 18, 1997, issue. It arrived on newsstands right before streetball's best-kept secret status ended.

THE ORIGIN STORY OF STREETBALL'S FORAY into the mainstream starts with Set Free Richardson, a.k.a. DJ Set Free, who grew up in the South Bronx, splitting time between New York and Philadelphia during his childhood. He idolized Eric B. and Rakim, DJ Jazzy Jeff and Will Smith, and became a DJ at the height of hip-hop's mainstream rise.

Richardson worked in the marketing department of AND1 in 1998. The basketball t-shirt brand started by three University of Pennsylvania's Wharton School graduate students was popular among teens. Hoopers from around the country sent in their streetball tapes in hopes of being featured by the brand. Richardson took one of the tapes home one evening and put it on his television screen and started playing music on his turntable set. Something strange started to happen. The kick drum of the song he was playing matched the rim-breaking dunk he saw on screen perfectly. The snare of the next track perfectly complemented a jump shot swishing through the net on the tape. Richardson messed around with the instrumentals and matched them to the streetball highlights. He went to work the following day and asked head of marketing Jeffrey Smith to send him to Florida to properly mix the footage at a music studio.

"It was the mixtape era," Richardson said. "I was like, 'Yo, I'm going to be the first person to make a video mixtape.' I knew if I produced it just like a label did a record, it would blow up."

He was right.

AND1 sent copies of Richardson's tape to basketball camps and record labels across the country. Sneaker retail store Footaction started giving away the tape for free. The first volume of the *AND1 Mixtape* went on to sell over 100,000 copies. The first three minutes of the tape featured grainy footage of a kid named "Skip to my Lou," showing off his array of dribbling skills at the Rucker to the instrumental of "One-Nine-Nine-Nine" produced by DJ Hi-Tek. The tape Richardson picked up in AND1's office kitchen area and brought home was submitted by Alston's high school coach Ron Naclerio in a bit of fortuitous timing. It became known in the streetball community as *The Skip Tape* and transformed Alston from a local streetball legend to an international star. Richardson's genius idea laid the groundwork for a popular mixtape series and a streetball tour, featuring "Skip to my Lou" and a new wave of playground hoopers from across the country, including Philip Champion, who went by "Hot Sauce" and claimed to have over a hundred streetball moves, including the "Slow Mo Cross," a series of crossovers which slowed the opposing defender's body to a crawl; Grayson "The Professor" Boucher, who earned the nickname from schooling everyone with his ball-handling; and Anthony Heyward, a Brooklyn native who earned the nickname "Half Man, Half Amazing" for regularly showing off his freakish athleticism, dunking over players twice his size.

The streetballers were the same. They were neighborhood legends who had their own personal style on the court, playing to their own rhythm, bringing fans to their feet with crowd-pleasing dunks and ankle-breaking crossovers. These people were still the pantheon of creativity on the basketball court. But it was no longer about word-of-mouth and myth-making through stories passed down from the Rucker to every park in the city.

"It was like a vacation spot that you used to go to. You love it. Nobody's there, and you can just wander around," Telander said. "Then you go back 10 years later, and suddenly there are hotels everywhere."

From Nike commercials to the *NBA Street* video game series to a skit on *Chappelle's Show* to the *AND1 Mixtape Tour* being broadcast on ESPN, streetball became a mainstream product for a mass audience. The NBA started hiring hip-hop DJs for in-game arena entertainment. The editing of the AND1 mixtape became popularized as the go-to style for sports highlights. Bill Clinton watched games at the Rucker.

"I was happy everyone could see it," Telander continued. "But when you commercialize anything, it's going to lose its innocence. It happens. You can't keep something cool a secret forever."

THE MAGAZINE PUBLISHING INDUSTRY was also starting to change by the end of the decade. The digital age was arriving and started to remove the element of discovery on newsstands, soon to be replaced by the immediate access of highlights on YouTube and social media.

But the people who remember the era of newsstand discovery are paying it forward today.

Auerbach went from collecting *The Source* as a kid to working in the music industry as an adult. He is the owner of the preeminent hip-hop archival brand *UpNorthTrips* today. His social media accounts have become the number one online source for hip-hop knowledge, where old scans of "Unsigned Hype" columns and "Hip Hop Quotable" sections appear regularly. Gunnell works as a local brewery driver, delivering beer to London pubs, and continues to visit the corner store every month for a new *SLAM* issue. He also manages an Instagram page, SLAM Archive, devoted to cataloging every single issue of the magazine from its very beginning in meticulous detail. SLAM Archive's feed is filled with images and stories from previous eras. Auerbach and Gunnell are now sharing their own magazine memories with a new generation of hip-hop and basketball fans, helping them discover a time when the newsstand mattered.

People are still discovering the legend of "Skip to my Lou" too. Alston had an 11-year NBA career after the Milwaukee Bucks selected him as a 1998 second round pick. His playground style continues to influence NBA players today.

Generation NETS

The biggest fight in *SLAM* Dome history involved three words that didn't even appear on the magazine cover, regarding a franchise nobody in the office cared about.

The New Jersey Nets started as an ABA franchise named the New Jersey Americans in 1967 who finished tied with the Kentucky Colonels for fourth place in the Eastern Division in their first season, forcing a one-game playoff with the winner advancing to the first round. The game was scheduled at the Teaneck Armory in New Jersey but there was one problem. The arena was already booked for a circus show. The team scrambled to secure a date at the home of the Eastern Hockey League's Long Island Ducks. The court was too slippery when players arrived for warm-ups at the Commack Arena. The baskets were not of equal height, there was no padding on the backboards, and there were holes on the court. The Colonels players refused to leave their locker room for the opening tip, citing the potential risk of injury. League commissioner George Mikan canceled the game, rewarding Kentucky with the win. The Nets franchise lost their first-ever playoff game 2–0 in a forfeit according to the official record books.

In 1973, the now-renamed New York Nets acquired Julius Erving in a trade with the Virginia Squires. The most electrifying individual talent in the league, Erving led the Nets to two championships. The

ABA folded in 1976 and the Nets were one of four franchises from the now-defunct league to join the NBA for the 1976–77 season. Erving sat out training camp and demanded a raise, citing an agreement he had with owner Roy Boe to renegotiate his contract if the team joined the NBA. Boe was in a financial bind, having paid a $3.2 million fee to join the league and owing another $4.8 million over a 10-year period to the New York Knicks over territorial rights. He traded Erving to the Philadelphia 76ers in exchange for $3 million cash. Erving signed a six-year, $3.5 million contract in Philadelphia and led the Sixers to a championship in 1983.

This was the franchise's NBA start. The Nets lost their franchise player and finished their first season in the league with a 22–60 record, moving to the Meadowlands in East Rutherford, New Jersey, in 1981 as an afterthought. Their lone highlight in the early years came in 1984, when the team upset Philadelphia in the first round. It was the franchise's only playoff series win of the decade. The player who led them to the second round, Micheal Ray Richardson, described by a local beat reporter as better than every point guard in the NBA except for Magic Johnson when he was sober, was banned for life in 1986 after violating the NBA's drug policy for the third time.

Optimism at the start of a new decade arrived in the form of Derrick Coleman, the first overall pick in 1990; Kenny Anderson, the second overall pick the following year; and Dražen Petrović, who the team acquired in a trade with the Portland Trail Blazers. During the 1992-93 season, the Nets recorded their first winning season in eight years, finishing with a 43-39 record. The future was bright until tragedy struck the team when Petrović died in the summer of 1993 at the age of 28 after a car accident in Denkendorf, Germany. The Nets still had Anderson and Coleman but they soon became the most dysfunctional duo in the NBA. After being benched in the fourth quarter of a blowout loss in 1994, Anderson skipped practice and was spotted by a local newspaper at the famous New York strip club Scores. Coleman shrugged off the incident when asked about it with the now-famous quote: "Whoop-de-damn-do." The Nets power forward had refused to check into a game in the final week of the regular season with the team fighting for a playoff spot and reportedly gave the Nets a blank check and told them to fill in the total amount of fines for the season after saying no to the team's guideline of wearing shirts and ties on the road. Coleman was portrayed as a crybaby on the cover of *Sports Illustrated*'s January 30, 1995, issue. The photo showed him sitting on the bench with his mouth wide open with a caption below his face saying WAAAAAAH!! The rest of the cover line said PETULANT PRIMA DONNAS LIKE NEW JERSEY'S DERRICK COLEMAN ARE BAD NEWS FOR THE NBA. The Nets were starting over again by the end of the 1995–96 season after trading Coleman to Philadelphia and Anderson to the Charlotte Hornets after he rejected a six-year, $40 million contract extension.

TONY GERVINO NEVER PAID MUCH ATTENTION to the Nets.

"They lived in the shadow of the Knicks," he said. "They weren't really a minor league team, but it was like halfway through *Space Jam* when everyone lost their powers."

It appeared the Nets were finally ready to turn the corner in 1998. They hired John Calipari to coach the team after his success with the University of Massachusetts men's basketball program. They traded for two-time NBA champion Sam Cassell and paired him in the backcourt with Kerry Kittles. Their starting frontcourt featured the perennially underrated Kendall Gill, All-NBA Rookie first teamer Keith Van Horn, and one of the league's best rebounders in Jayson Williams. *SLAM* decided to put the Nets starting lineup on the cover, along with a prediction that they would win an NBA championship within three years. The magazine wanted to get the attention of potential readers who were browsing the newsstand. A cover shoot was scheduled at the team's practice facility. The plan was almost derailed at the final minute when the team demanded for *SLAM* to include sixth-man power forward Chris Gatling on the cover.

"We were close to packing up and leaving," Gervino recalled. "We weren't putting six guys on the cover. It was the starting five, and that was it."

Team officials eventually relented on their request.

A photo of Cassell, Kittles, Gill, Van Horn, and Williams posing together in their white Nets home uniforms against a black backdrop appeared on *SLAM*'s April 1998 cover. The cover line said GENERATION NETS. CHAMPS BY 2001. COUNT ON IT. The spine of the cover was supposed to say NEW YORK'S FINEST. Bengtson suggested the spine line knowing it would draw Gervino's ire.

"I was totally down to disrespect the Knicks as much as possible," he said. "It also fit with declaring them as the best team in the world. It wasn't a big deal to me. Putting the Nets on the cover was already a little out there. What was the point of even doing it if we were going to play it safe? We might as well go all the way."

Gervino pushed back.

"It was easy to say they would be champs by 2001. That was three years away," he said. "But to call them New York's Finest? That crossed the line."

Bengtson didn't see how three words on the spine of a magazine could matter so much.

"So you're okay with calling them the best team in the world on the cover," he said, "but you didn't want to call them the best team in New York?"

The two went back and forth for an entire afternoon at the *SLAM* Dome until Dennis Page stepped in.

"I said something sharp to Dennis," Gervino recalled. "It wasn't sharp enough to be fired, but I hurt his feelings. I had to go to his office and apologize. It was a provocative spine line. I could dish it out, but I couldn't take it. I didn't want them to make fun of the Knicks. There weren't a lot of tense moments at *SLAM*. That was one of them. It was a low moment in my career. I handled it like a baby."

Bengtson eventually withdrew himself from the argument.

"Tony could have technically fired me," he said. "You learned to pick your spots."

The spine line was changed to read DERRICK COLEMAN'S WORST NIGHTMARE.

THE *SLAM* COVER WASN'T ENOUGH to turn the fortunes of the Nets franchise around. They finished the 1997–98 season with a 43–39 record, losing to the Chicago Bulls in a first round sweep. They entered the following year with expectations of being a championship contender but instead started an all-time franchise worst 3–18. Cassell sprained his ankle in the season opener and was traded. Williams broke his tibia and never played in the NBA again. Calipari was fired a month into the season, finishing with a 72–112 record in two-plus years with the franchise. The Nets missed the playoffs the next three seasons. In 2001, the year *SLAM* predicted them to win it all, they went 26–56. Their leading scorer was Stephon Marbury, whose partnership with Kevin Garnett lasted just two-and-a-half seasons in Minnesota. The Nets then traded Marbury in the summer of 2001 to the Phoenix Suns in exchange for Jason Kidd.

It was another fresh start for the Nets and *SLAM* decided to try again. They put New Jersey's starting five on the cover before the 2002 playoffs. This time it was Kidd, standing alongside power forward Kenyon Martin, center Todd MacCulloch, and two holdovers from the 1998 cover, Van Horn and Kittles.

The cover line read THE NETS. THE BEST TEAM IN THE WORLD.

The spine line?

STEPHON MARBURY'S WORST NIGHTMARE.

Kidd led them to the 2002 NBA Finals a few months later.

The Nets were swept by the Los Angeles Lakers in four games, finishing as the *second best team in the world.*

They remain the second most popular NBA team in New York today, and are still seeking their first championship since joining the league.

SOUL
On Ice

Rick Telander was catching up on several months worth of magazines on his desk in 1999 when he came across the Christmas issue of the NBA's official publication, *HOOP*. He couldn't shake the feeling that something was off about the cover featuring Allen Iverson posing in a Philadelphia 76ers home jersey with the caption PHILLY DECLARATION "I'M THE BEST GUARD IN THE NBA."

Telander studied it some more and found an issue of *The Sporting News* from the same year featuring another picture of Iverson in his team uniform from the same photoshoot. He figured out the problem by putting the two magazine covers next to each other.

The *HOOP* cover photo had been photoshopped to remove Iverson's tattoos, diamond earrings, and necklace.

A call was made to photographer Jesse Garrabrant, who took both pictures. He wasn't aware of any airbrushing. In subsequent conversations with Jan Hubbard, the vice president of editorial of *HOOP*, and Brian McIntyre, the league's senior vice president of sports communications, they told Telander a member of the editorial team touched up the photo after thinking Iverson's neck tattoo looked like a bite.

Telander wasn't buying it.

"They were protecting their image," he said. "Every league does it, but when you get caught, it's pretty embarrassing. It makes you wonder how many times they've done it before."

"They could have used somebody else if they didn't want to accept me as a whole," Iverson told reporters. "This is who I am. It kind of hurts because I've got my mother's name on my body, my grandmother's name, my kids, my fiancée. That means something to me. Airbrushing them, that's like a slap in my face."

HOOP put Iverson on the cover again a few months later.

This time his tattoos and jewelry were untouched.

Ron Berler, who became the editor-in-chief of *NBA Inside Stuff* magazine—a joint venture between Time Inc. and the NBA—in 1996, was not surprised by the airbrushing controversy. Part of Berler's responsibilities was to sit down with reps from the league office to get final approval on the magazine's ideas.

"I opened the first meeting by asking them what story ideas they had," he recalled. "They all looked at each other like, 'What?' I realized immediately they didn't want to run the magazine. They just wanted veto power and control over the stories."

The magazine selected players who resonated with the younger demographic for the cover.

"We had a pretty good handle on who was generating buzz with the youth," Berler continued. "It was impossible to ignore Iverson's impact on them."

Iverson was a one-man force in his first season as the starting point guard of a rebuilding Sixers team, scoring at least 40 points in five straight games during one stretch, and winning Rookie of the Year after averaging 23.5 points, 7.5 assists, and 2.1 steals. Iverson wasn't a global superstar like Michael Jordan or a larger-than-life force like Shaquille O'Neal. He was the David to their Goliath. Iverson's underdog mentality and his stature as the smallest guy on the floor made him relatable to millions of kids across the country. He displayed a healthy amount of disrespect to players he grew up idolizing who he now considered his competition. When Iverson sized up Jordan in his rookie season at the top of the key and unleashed his signature crossover dribble, creating enough space to make a pull-up jumper while the 33-year-old Bulls guard stammered backwards, it became a passing of the torch moment for an entire generation of basketball fans who embraced the Sixers guard as their own.

Despite his popularity with the fans, the NBA did not embrace Iverson. The league office conducted an official review on Iverson's signature crossover move during his rookie season and concluded he was in fact committing a palming violation. The league also issued a warning about the length of his game shorts, which were well below his knees. Media members questioned his criminal record and the friends he associated with, painting the image of a troublemaker with a checkered past. Berler saw the backlash but could not ignore his popularity and decided to put Iverson on the cover.

"We'd gone through his agent to get approval on the story," he recalled. "I took the train from New York to Philadelphia and went to Sixers practice to do the interview. When I got there, word came down from the league office. They wouldn't give us permission to do the story. I had to explain to Iverson that we couldn't go ahead with it. He couldn't understand the decision and the NBA's reasoning. It was hard because I didn't get it either."

THE IDEA OF WHITE AMERICA controlling the presentation of Black athletes on newsstands goes back decades to the racial segregation era and a time when allowing Black players to compete in major professional sports leagues was still a novelty.

In *Sports Illustrated* writer Frank Deford's memoir *Over Time: My Life as a Sportswriter,* he recalled a time in 1966 when he had to fight to get Los Angeles Lakers forward Elgin Baylor featured on the cover of *Sports Illustrated* because the magazine feared putting Black stars on the cover would turn off their white readership. "Owners, editors, writers, PR people, broadcasters, and advertisers excused it as being *only* commercial racism, not your traditional immoral kind, you understand. Don't take it personally," Deford wrote. "But, of course, racism is what it was, and the end result was the same Blacks suffered. They didn't get the chances they deserved." Baylor was eventually featured on the cover of the magazine's 1966-67 pro basketball preview cover. According to Michael MacCambridge's book *The Franchise: A History of Sports Illustrated Magazine,* a *Sports Illustrated* editor once described a portrait photo of Baltimore Bullets star Earl "The Pearl" Monroe, the reigning Rookie of the Year and the league's leading scorer at the time, as one of the ugliest and least appealing covers he had ever seen. In the same year Monroe appeared on the cover, *Sports Illustrated* devoted a five-part editorial feature written by Jack Olsen exploring the idea of opportunity but not quality for the Black athlete. The magazine covered Black athletes but were less thrilled to make them the face of the product they were selling.

A magazine would arrive in the 1970s in response to this. The first issue of *Black Sports* arrived on newsstands in 1971 featuring Milwaukee Bucks stars Kareem Abdul-Jabbar (then still Lew Alcindor) and Oscar

Robertson on the cover. The publisher was Allan Barron, a 30-year-old from Newark, New Jersey, who went to college in Huntsville, Alabama, and became an active member of the civil rights protests in the South. Barron didn't have a journalism background but explained the purpose of his magazine in a publisher's statement.

"*Black Sports* is dedicated to the entertainment and education of society by providing up-to-date information on the new major force: the Black athlete," he wrote. "*Black Sports* will be a four-dimensional exposure, with the fourth dimension being that certain quality of understanding that can only come from being in the same family, experiencing the same problems."

Barron expanded on his vision in an interview with the *San Francisco Examiner* after the first issue arrived on newsstands.

"America is a hero-worship type of society and in athletics it becomes clearer," he said. "Take, for example, the pro football draft: 200 out of 260 choices were Black. Now the newspapers and magazines only give what a Black athlete makes a year and his statistics. But there's more to him than just that. And if the young read the magazine they will know more about themselves through the Black athlete. The press seldom talks about the Black athlete's home life, or what it's like to be a Black man or how it is to be a winner."

When Barron pushed for the idea of a National Black Sports Hall of Fame, it was opposed by writer Dick Young in an op-ed for *The New York Daily News* in 1973.

"It is the intention of the people behind the Black Hall of Fame to do sociological good," he wrote. "They intend to support charities for youth programs, to fight drugs and such. If it helps poor kids of all types, fine, but I'm afraid it won't. It is Black oriented, and biased. A Black Sports Hall of Fame is polarization, and polarization is a mistake."

Young also challenged the idea of having a Black sports magazine.

"Suppose Time Inc. were to change the name of its athletic publication to *White Sports Illustrated*," he wrote. "There'd be a picket line thrown up around their building before the first issue hit newsstands."

Black Sports published its final issue in 1978 after limited financial success.

THE POPULARITY OF HIP-HOP AND BASKETBALL increased the representation of Black athletes and entertainers on magazine covers in the next two decades. From Dave Mays and Jon Shecter's hip-hop magazine to Quincy Jones partnering with Time Inc. on a Black culture publication to Dennis Page publishing a hip-hop-influenced basketball magazine, the newsstand was decidedly more Black. But the racial makeup of publishers and owners of the magazines remained the same, and the idea of a predominantly white masthead publishing stories featuring Black subjects raised concerns about cultural appropriation.

Harris Publications employees discussed this topic with *SLAM*'s first editor-in-chief, Cory Johnson, before the first issue hit newsstands. They were uncomfortable with the use of street slang inside the magazine. Johnson took the feedback and sat down with *Vibe* senior editor Bonz Malone, who was a senior editor on *SLAM*'s first issue masthead and one of the most respected Black voices in the industry.

"It was not lost on me the privileges I had as a white man," Johnson said. "We had this conversation about the magazine's approach, and it was not a friendly conversation. I asked Bonz, and he was cool with it.

It just seemed inauthentic to use The Queen's English to describe the game of the streets, but I also wasn't the right person to make that call. But if it was cool with Bonz, it was cool with me. But I'm still not sure today if I made the right call."

Dennis Page has considered these concerns over the years.

"There have been people along the way who have accused us of exploiting Black culture," Page said. "We had a motto from the very beginning to respect the game. That went for hip-hop and basketball. I grew up admiring and respecting Black culture. I played basketball and listened to Black music. All of my sports heroes were Black. They were Willie Mays, Lew Alcindor, Elgin Baylor, Connie Hawkins, Julius Erving, and David Thompson. I understood Black culture and never had doubts in my mind about being a white person exploiting it. I always treated the people we covered with the utmost respect, and hopefully, I hired people that were equal to me in that understanding."

Scoop Jackson credits Page for providing a platform for Black writers like himself to share stories from a Black perspective without airbrushing his point of view to corporate America.

"I always felt his heart was in the right place," Jackson said. "He was providing authentic opportunities for Black individuals to tell our stories when others weren't. There's a fine line between providing opportunity and taking advantage of a situation. I never felt like Dennis was taking advantage of a situation. He wanted the right person to tell the story, and he thought I was the right person to do it. He said, 'I can't be this white, Jewish guy who controls the narrative of American culture that at its roots is Black, but if I get the right person to tell these stories and he can make it authentic, then I can be responsible for presenting it, but I wouldn't be the one controlling it.'"

The image of Iverson being portrayed by the media and the league's attempt to airbrush his cover photo was a continuation of how Black athletes had been treated for decades.

"America first got a glimpse of what Black freedom looked like with Muhammad Ali," Jackson said. "He became a problem because white America controlled everything else, but they had no control over him. Allen represented Black freedom. He didn't answer to anybody but himself. It wasn't just about being a rebel. White America saw in him somebody who was unapologetic about who he was and what he represented."

Ali was stripped of his heavyweight title in the midst of the civil rights movement and Vietnam War protests after refusing to be drafted into the military and suspended from boxing for five years in the prime of his career. *Esquire* art director George Lois conceived an idea in 1968 of putting Ali on their magazine cover dressed as St. Sebastian, the third-century Christian martyr. The cover photo, featuring the heavyweight champion in his boxing uniform, and six arrows piercing through his torso and legs, became the defining cover image of Ali's career.

SLAM would provide a similarly defining cover image of Iverson's career during a period of time when the NBA did not want him presented on the newsstand at all.

TONY GERVINO WAS SIFTING THROUGH photo archives for cover ideas on a Friday afternoon at the *SLAM* Dome when he came across a picture of Julius Erving in his signature afro from the ABA days. It was the middle of an NBA lockout in 1998 and the editor-in-chief was desperate for ideas.

Iverson developed a reputation for being disrespectful to the previous generation of players during his rookie season after a trash-talking incident with Jordan was blown out of proportion by the media. Reporters painted a portrait of Iverson as the representation of what was wrong with the new generation entering the league. They were selfish millionaires, the classic example of too-much, too-soon, with no respect for the game's history. Gervino became intrigued with the idea of having Iverson recreate Erving's ABA photo on the cover. It was an opportunity to pay homage to a Sixers legend and to pay respects to the history of the game. He pored over every single detail of the cover after a photoshoot was scheduled.

"That's just how everything went when it came to Tony executing things for the magazine," Jackson said. "It was true to the foundation of *SLAM*. It was built on authenticity."

Gervino made sure there was a red-white-and-blue Spalding basketball for the shoot to pay homage to the ABA properly, and tracked down a sports equipment manufacturing company named Mitchell & Ness, who had recently started to license vintage jerseys, to ensure Iverson would wear a throwback jersey on the cover. Company owner Pete Capolino agreed to let *SLAM* borrow a retro Sixers uniform with Iverson's number 3 on the chest for 72 hours. There was one final detail to obsess over when Gervino arrived at a Philadelphia studio in the warehouse district to supervise the cover shoot. The magazine wanted to photograph Iverson with an afro instead of his signature cornrows to replicate Erving's look. The Sixers guard had a morning photoshoot before his *SLAM* shoot and Gervino was worried sick another publication would scoop him on this idea.

"I thought it was the greatest idea in history," he said. "It's kind of embarrassing looking back, but the fear was real at the time. I thought someone was going to steal my idea."

Iverson was scheduled to arrive at eleven in the morning but missed his flight from Washington, D.C., pushing the cover shoot to three in the afternoon. *SLAM* was still waiting for their cover subject to arrive at seven in the evening and decided to take a break.

"We smoked some weed and went to Dave & Buster's and just hung out," Gervino recalled. "They kept saying, 'He'll be there in half an hour.' Then it was, 'He'll be there in an hour.' They kept saying, 'He's going to be right there.' Eventually, we just went back to the studio and waited."

Iverson finally arrived with his signature cornrows at around midnight.

Gervino breathed a sigh of relief.

No one had scooped his idea.

Iverson spent 10 minutes with his hair stylist, put on a throwback Sixers jersey, and was ready for the cover shoot with photographer Clay Patrick McBride, who still remembers the assignment details he received from creative director Don Morris.

"He had called me and said, 'Get me some dope pictures,'" McBride recalled. "I told my friends about the shoot, and they were like, 'Yo, this guy is the baddest motherfucker there is.' I was not aware of who Allen was at all."

After spending his teenage years studying painting and art history in the South of France, McBride moved to New York in the early 1990s and earned a Bachelor of Fine Arts at the School of Visual Arts, where he developed an interest in portrait photography.

McBride had a no-nonsense approach to his work.

"I'm not going to fuck around and waste your time by asking how your kids are," he explained. "I wanted to give them what they wanted with my photos. I didn't want them to leave the barbershop with a haircut they didn't fucking want and feel like a herb."

McBride found a perfect cover subject in Iverson.

"Allen was willing to do whatever I wanted to do and wasn't stand-offish," he said. "I had him doing all these exaggerated poses, which isn't the easiest thing to do with athletes because they're so self-conscious."

It was around one in the morning when McBride finished the longest cover shoot in *SLAM* history.

The cover photo on the magazine's March 1999 issue would become the defining image of Iverson's career. Wearing a throwback Mitchell & Ness PHILA jersey with a giant neckpiece dangling just above the number 3 on his chest, Iverson stared into the camera, rocking an afro reminiscent of Erving in his prime. He wore a watch and bracelet on his left wrist and palmed a red-white-and-blue basketball on his right hand. The SOUL ON ICE cover line referenced Eldridge Cleaver's 1968 essay collection written in Folsom State Prison and considered one of the essential pieces of commentary on Black America.

"I remember thinking about it, and it was just perfect," Gervino said. "Iverson was like a literary character in the story about basketball. He came from a completely authentic place. It evoked the late 1960s and early 1970s, which is what the Dr. J photo did too. The game was on ice at the time, and we were on ice. It was three short words. It just all worked in concert. I couldn't imagine it with a different cover line."

Mitchell & Ness's throwback jerseys became the most popular fashion trend among rappers and basketball players.

"People didn't know there was a company making the jerseys," said Lynn Bloom, the company's director of authentics and archives. "The cover gave us so much exposure."

It also elevated the magazine in the eyes of the players. *SLAM* remained authentic in their approach in an era of owners versus players and the league trying to control the public image of their biggest stars. But not everyone understood the cover.

"I had lunch with a guy at *Sports Illustrated* a week later," Gervino recalled, "and he asked me, 'How did you convince Allen Iverson to wear a wig?'"

IVERSON LED THE SIXERS to the NBA Finals in 2001 and won the Most Valuable Player Award. A year later the team lost in the first round to the Boston Celtics. Head coach Larry Brown questioned Iverson's commitment to the team four days after the season ended, citing the need for his starting point guard to start showing up to practice like everyone else. Iverson took the podium afterward and was asked about his coach's comments.

"We talking about practice," he said. "Not a game. Not a game. Not a game. We talking about practice. Not a game. Not the game that I go out there and die for and play every game like it's my last. Not the game. We talking about practice, man."

The clip was played across every television network and printed in every newspaper.

The rest of Iverson's statement is forgotten today. His best friend Rahsaan Langford had been shot and killed seven months earlier and his murder trial had just started when Iverson arrived for his exit interview.

"I lost my best friend," Iverson said. "I lost him, and I lost this year. Everything is just going downhill for me, as far as just that. You know, as far as my life. And then I'm dealing with this. My best friend is dead. Dead. And we lost. And this is what I have to go through for the rest of the summer until the season is all over again."

The media's failure to provide the proper context for Iverson's frustration with the season was not a surprise to Jackson.

"America has reduced Martin Luther King Jr.'s entire career to one saying, so why would I be surprised if they would reduce everything Allen Iverson said to one word," Jackson said, referring to the civil rights activist's famous "I Have a Dream" speech. "It's what we do. This is our history. The media is smart enough to know exactly what they're doing. His best friend just died, but 'Nah, that's irrelevant to the story.'"

The practice rant became the defining soundbite of Iverson's career.

McBride photographed Iverson again a few years later and asked the Sixers guard to autograph their first cover together.

Iverson picked up a pen and stared at the cover photo.

"This is the greatest fucking picture ever taken," he said.

PART 3

Generation NEXT

CHAMIQUE

Chamique Holdsclaw was the first woman to appear on the cover of *SLAM*. The University of Tennessee forward posed for a cover photo on the front of the magazine's October 1998 issue wearing a custom New York Knicks jersey in her number 23. The cover line said IS THE NBA READY FOR CHAMIQUE HOLDSCLAW?

The cover and its provocative headline wasn't a publicity stunt ("Hey, look! We finally put a woman on the cover"), but a legitimate question posed by *SLAM*'s editorial team.

A Queens, New York, native, Holdsclaw led Christ the King Regional High to four straight New York State championships and was entering her senior year at Tennessee, having just wrapped up an undefeated 39–0 season—an NCAA record for most wins in a year—and a third straight national championship. Holdsclaw won every award in the country after averaging 25.2 points and 9.7 rebounds in the NCAA tournament, including the College Player of the Year Award, the Associated Press Women's College Basketball Player of the Year, and the USBWA Women's National Player of the Year, cementing her status as the best college basketball player in the country.

Tony Gervino received a phone call from the university after the cover shoot.

It was head coach Pat Summitt.

"Are you the fucking blockhead who almost ruined my player's eligibility?" she asked.

The photoshoot had been arranged through Holdsclaw's family, and NCAA rules prohibited their student-athletes from receiving gifts. Accepting the Knicks jersey would have been a violation of the rules. Holdsclaw was thankfully not gifted the jersey. The spine line of the issue said PLEASE PAT, DON'T HURT US.

Holdsclaw entertained the idea of one day joining the NBA in the cover story. "I don't think I'm ready for the NBA right now," she said, "but maybe one day." Holdsclaw finished her senior year at Tennessee as the all-time leading scorer and rebounder at the school and in NCAA tournament history. She was selected first overall by the WNBA's Washington Mystics in 1999. Holdsclaw didn't make the jump to the NBA, finishing her career as a six-time WNBA All-Star.

When *SLAM* ran a reader poll in their magazine years later, her cover was voted the worst cover of all-time, prompting the editors to ask: "Are our readers sexist?"

It would be another 20 years before another woman appeared on the cover of *SLAM*. In 2018, Maya Moore—a four-time WNBA champion, two-time Olympic gold medalist, and two-time NCAA champion at the time—appeared on the cover posing in her Minnesota Lynx jersey, holding a basketball with both hands. The cover line said MAYA MOORE. RECOGNIZE.

THE RECOGNITION OF WOMEN on magazine covers has been an ongoing issue since sports publications started appearing on newsstands many decades ago. Aside from the occasional cover celebrating tennis phenoms and Olympic gold medalists, women have appeared on the cover of *Sports Illustrated* over the years as secondary subjects (spouses and girlfriends who stood alongside New York Jets quarterback Joe

Namath and Olympic swimmer Mark Spitz), objectified for a straight male audience (professional model Babette March appeared on the front of the first swimsuit issue in 1964, which became the most popular annual issue of the magazine), and as tragic figures (tennis star Monica Seles after surviving a knife attack from a deranged fan during a match in Hamburg, Germany; American skater Nancy Kerrigan after she was struck with a police baton at a Detroit ice rink two days before the 1994 Olympic trials).

When *Sports Illustrated* celebrated 35 years on newsstands with a commemorative issue in 1990, the magazine reflected on their cover subjects. 181 people had appeared on the front of the magazine at least three times. Less than one percent of them were women. Three of the eight women who made the list were swimsuit issue models.

Sports Illustrated cover subject and tennis star Billie Jean King—who had just defeated Bobby Riggs in the "Battles of the Sexes" exhibition tennis match viewed by 90 million people worldwide—decided to start her own magazine in 1973 named *womenSports* to provide proper coverage of female athletes on newsstands. The magazine debuted shortly after Title IX—the amendment to the Civil Rights Act that banned gender discrimination in education—was passed in 1972. Schools across the country poured record amounts of money into their athletic programs for women to comply with the amendment. It led to historic growths in female participation in sports at the high school and college level.

Women's basketball was included as an Olympic event for the first time in 1976. The NCAA held its first Division I Women's Basketball Tournament in 1982. Louisiana Tech forward Janice Lawrence led her team to the national championship. Their story ran inside the April

5, 1982, issue of *Sports Illustrated* as a half-page sidebar at the end of a six-page cover story on the University of North Carolina's win over Georgetown in the men's national championship game.

While Michael Jordan became the most popular male athlete in the world and appeared on the *Sports Illustrated* cover at a record pace, Cheryl Miller—the USC star who led the Trojans to the 1983 NCAA championship in her freshman season and was considered the face of women's basketball in the 1980s—received a single *Sports Illustrated* cover during her entire career, sharing the front of the 1985–86 college basketball preview issue with Mark Price and Bruce Dalrymple of the Georgia Tech men's basketball team.

When the eight-team Women's Basketball League folded in 1981 after three seasons due to a lack of fan interest and financial issues, it left no options for women to play professionally in the United States. The women found scant opportunities overseas, with much smaller paychecks and without the notoriety and fame as the men, who went from college stars to becoming NBA pros who earned millions from their contracts and endorsement deals.

The pro sports landscape remained barren for female athletes at the start of the 1990s, even as overall participation in women's sports was on the rise. The newsstand was still a male-dominant place. But the golden era of women's sports coverage on newsstands was just around the corner.

IT WOULD ALL START WITH FIVE PLAYERS—Jordan, standing alongside Magic Johnson, Charles Barkley, Patrick Ewing, and Karl Malone—appearing on the cover of *Sports Illustrated*'s February 18, 1991, issue in Team USA basketball jerseys. FIBA voted in April of 1989 to remove restrictions on professional basketball players in international events. NBA players would appear at the Olympics for the first time. The five cover subjects were *Sports Illustrated*'s choice to start for the Team USA men's basketball team at the 1992 Olympics in Barcelona. The cover line named them the DREAM TEAM.

The roster, composed of the five *Sports Illustrated* cover subjects— along with Larry Bird, John Stockton, David Robinson, Clyde Drexler, Scottie Pippen, Chris Mullin, and Christian Laettner—made their debut at an Olympic qualifying tournament in Portland, Oregon, defeating Cuba by 79 points.

The Dream Team, still considered today as the greatest team ever assembled, featured 11 future Hall of Famers and went undefeated at the 1992 Olympics, winning by an average margin of 44 points in Barcelona. Their gold medal game victory over Croatia by 32 points was their lowest margin of victory.

Between a legendary scrimmage at Monte Carlo, late-night card games, table tennis tournaments at the hotel, and Barkley's decision to ignore security concerns and roam the Las Ramblas strip surrounded by fans, the men's team didn't just destroy opposing teams at the Olympics, they had fun doing it. Thousands of fans gathered at the team's hotel entrance every day, hoping to get a glimpse of the most popular basketball players in the world.

The Dream Team didn't just win the gold medal. They were *the* story of the 1992 Olympics and the perfect promotional vehicle for introducing the NBA and the game of basketball to a global audience.

David Stern was inspired by the Dream Team's overwhelming success and wanted to explore new ideas to continue expanding the game of basketball. He asked Val Ackerman to look into the potential of launching a professional women's basketball league.

After graduating in 1981 as a four-year starter on the University of Virginia basketball team, where she became one of the first women to receive an athletic scholarship, Ackerman joined a pro team in France for a year before coming home early. She joined the NBA in 1988 as a staff attorney, became a special assistant to the commissioner, and was later promoted to vice president of business affairs.

The 1992 USA Basketball women's national basketball team—who didn't have the same catchy nickname as the men and received little to no mainstream media coverage—finished with a disappointing bronze medal result in Barcelona. They lost in the semifinals to Brazil two years later at the 1994 World Championships in Sydney.

Ackerman recognized the sport of women's basketball needed a marketing push to avoid the same pitfalls from previous attempts to start a pro league. This new league needed recognizable players who were marketable to both fans and advertisers.

The Dream Team became the blueprint.

America embraced dominance in any sport. Ackerman was convinced if the women's team could win a gold medal at the upcoming 1996 Summer Olympics in Atlanta, Georgia, they would be the catalyst to drawing national interest in a new women's pro league. It became the central focus of a plan that would change the landscape of women's sports and its coverage on newsstands.

The Summer of WOMEN

The brainstorming session started among the USA Basketball officials. Dream Team Too. Dreamettes. Fab Femmes. Liberty Belles. The Hoop Troupe. The 96ers. The Golden Girls. The Chicks Who Set Picks.

USA Basketball had approved Val Ackerman's idea of sending the women's national team on a 10-month barnstorming tour in the lead-up to the 1996 Olympics in Atlanta, Georgia, in the fall of 1995 and now they wanted a nickname for the group.

The NBA viewed the team's success as a critical part of their plan to launch a new league. The women had disappointed at their previous two major tournaments. A year playing together would give them an advantage heading into the Olympics. The tour would also act as an international showcase for women's basketball.

The committee had shot down Ackerman's initial pitch.

"They didn't feel like it was necessary," she recalled. "So we worked up a budget and came up with a number of $3 million. It would include paying players and coaches, travel expenses, the cost of the actual games, and marketing. We built a revenue model through ticket sales, licensing revenues, and sponsorships. We would get television deals with ESPN and ABC. The thing would pay for itself. They reviewed the plan and eventually approved it."

Now the NBA and USA Basketball just needed to convince 11 women to take a year off and travel the world together.

The invitation didn't sound very attractive at first.

The women would be paid $50,000 for the barnstorming tour, a quarter of some of the salaries being offered by pro teams overseas. There was also the travel schedule. The plan was for the team to play 52 exhibition games, including 21 games in the United States against the top NCAA programs in the country and *Athletes in Action*, a Christian-organization women's team. There would be tours to Russia, Ukraine, China, Australia, and Canada. The players would also have to sign agreements to make a set number of public appearances at charity and media events, appear at organized autograph sessions, and make themselves available for interviews after every practice and game. Media consultants would provide seminars teaching the players about the proper etiquette of dealing with reporters. The team was also required to practice six days a week.

The best women basketball players in the world understood the potential impact of the tour on the future of the sport and agreed despite their concerns. USA Basketball announced the roster after tryouts at the United States Olympic Training Center in Colorado Springs, Colorado, in May of 1995.

The group, including Sheryl Swoopes, considered the Michael Jordan of women's basketball; Lisa Leslie, a three-time All-American and 1994 National Player of the Year at USC; and Rebecca Lobo, who had led the University of Connecticut Huskies to a 35–0 record and a national championship earlier in the year, would begin their barnstorming tour in the fall.

The women's national team won their first 21 games on tour by an average margin of 45.8 points. Tara VanDerveer, who took a year off from Stanford University to coach the team, instituted rules to keep her team engaged. They passed the ball five times before anyone could shoot. They would not run the full-court press against college opponents. VanDerveer never ran a single play or scouted a single opponent during the exhibition schedule.

The barnstorming tour was also an overwhelming success off the court. The turnout at games was encouraging. The women saw young girls in the stands who were discovering new sports heroes to root for. The mainstream media became enamored with the team in the months leading up to the Olympics in Atlanta. Point guard Teresa Edwards was featured in a *Vanity Fair* photoshoot by renowned photographer Annie Leibovitz. *Time* and *TV Guide* scheduled cover shoots with the team. Leslie and Swoopes appeared in a cover story for *Newsweek* titled "Year of the Women: Why Female Athletes Are Our Best Hope for Olympic Gold." Swoopes was also the cover subject for an issue of *New York Times Magazine* devoted to the female athlete.

Ackerman started to put together a model for a women's league as the team embarked on their pre-Olympics journey. The league would start in the summer of 1997, with eight teams and a June to August schedule. David Stern held a press conference after an NBA Board of Governors meeting in April of 1996 announcing the board's approval of Ackerman's plan to start a women's league the following summer.

The league was officially in the women's basketball business.

The Olympics were just days away in July of 1996 when Ackerman scheduled a meeting with ESPN, one of several television networks interested in broadcasting rights for the new league. On her way to the office for the meeting, she walked past a newsstand and smiled.

On the gatefold cover of *Sports Illustrated*'s July 22, 1996, Olympic preview issue was the starting five of the women's national team wearing their Team USA jerseys in various action poses, along with VanDerveer mimicking a jump-shooting motion in her dress shirt and slacks. The cover line said YOU GO, GIRLS! THE U.S. WOMEN'S BASKETBALL TEAM.

"It was validation of our decision to reintroduce women's basketball in this powerful way," Ackerman said. "The stars were aligned. The timing couldn't have been better."

She purchased several copies and brought one to Stern's office. A giant smile came over the commissioner's face. Stern walked into the conference room to meet ESPN executives and started the meeting by tossing the new issue of *Sports Illustrated* on the table. The network signed a five-year contract to broadcast women's pro basketball, beginning in 1997. NBC and Lifetime agreed to similar deals.

The women capped off their year-long run by winning all eight of their games at the Olympics, including a 24-point victory over Brazil in the gold medal game. Between the 100,000 miles they traveled around the world on their barnstorming tour and the eight games in Atlanta, the women's national team finished with a 60–0 record.

Ackerman was named WNBA president three days later. "We had a million details to work through," she recalled. "We had to select teams, find players, design uniforms, find referees, and develop schedules. We had to deal with the networks and the sponsors, we had to develop licensing, and figure out the names and logos of the teams. It was a marathon and a sprint at the same time."

The WNBA convinced the three most popular players on the gold medal–winning team—Swoopes, Leslie, and Lobo—to sign two-year contracts. The women were featured together in an award-winning marketing campaign with the slogan WE GOT NEXT and became the face of the league.

Ackerman traveled to the Great Western Forum in Inglewood, California, on June 21, 1997, to watch the first game in WNBA history. The New York Liberty defeated the Los Angeles Sparks 67–57. Tyra Banks, Magic Johnson, Penny Marshall, and Arsenio Hall were in attendance. A fan in the audience held up a THANK YOU TITLE IX sign. The NBC television broadcast of the game was the highest-rated national sporting event that weekend, outdrawing major league baseball and the PGA's Buick Classic.

Ackerman tossed up the ceremonial opening tip and sat in the stands afterward, reflecting on being in the hospital giving birth to her daughter Sally when she received the call confirming USA Basketball had approved her barnstorming tour pitch. The two-year journey had led to a gold medal for women's basketball and the launch of a new pro league.

"It was a very emotional day," Ackerman said. "It was a culmination of a couple years of work. It wasn't the best game I've ever watched, but the building was electric. There were a lot of women in the building. We finally made it."

THE 1996 OLYMPICS WASN'T JUST A WATERSHED MOMENT for women's basketball. It was a historic event for women's sports in America. The U.S. women's gymnastics team won their first team gold medal after Kerri Strug landed her final vault on an injured ankle. The U.S. women won gold in the inaugural softball tournament at the Olympics, as did the soccer team, who beat China in front of over 76,000 fans at Sanford Stadium on the University of Georgia campus in the gold medal game. The Olympics became known as *The Summer of Women.*

The success of American women athletes started an era of tremendous growth in professional women's sports and also gave rise to the idea of women's sports magazines on the newsstand.

Time Inc. launched a test issue of *Sports Illustrated Women/Sport* in the spring of 1997, distributing the magazine for free to 450,000 women subscribers of *Sports Illustrated* and 60,000 other women from their consumer database. An additional 200,000 copies were distributed to newsstands across the country, with 20,000 more copies given away at Lady Foot Locker retail locations. Swoopes wore a Houston Comets practice jersey, holding a basketball in one hand while palming her pregnant belly with the other on the test issue's cover. The cover story was a postscript of the women's national team after their gold medal win and a preview of the inaugural WNBA season. The cover line read A STAR IS BORN.

Editor-in-chief Sandra Bailey described the publication as a "magazine for every woman" in her introduction letter to the readers. The test issue included personality-driven features of female athletes, workout tips columns, and fashion-focused articles.

Sports Illustrated Women/Sport was one of many women's sports magazines that arrived as part of a post-Olympics publishing boom. They all struggled with establishing an identity on newsstands. There was a central debate in the editors' room over who the intended audience should be. Some editors believed their magazine should be tailored toward the spectator, the woman who enjoyed watching and reading about team-based sports. Others argued to create a magazine for the participant, the woman who took part in individual-based sports. *Sports Illustrated Women/Sport* tried to cater themselves to every woman instead of choosing one of those paths, and as a result, failed to attract a large enough audience.

The magazine's first official issue was published two years later in the spring of 1999, under a new name *Sports Illustrated for Women*. Time Inc.'s editor-in-chief, Norman Pearlstine, became concerned with the magazine's direction and asked Susan Casey to write a critique. Casey spent six years working as a creative director at *Outside*—a sports and adventure magazine with a 40 percent women readership—before joining Time Inc. as a development editor. She landed on the side of creating a magazine for the participant and not the spectator.

"I couldn't figure out who our readers were," Casey recalled. "The stories were limiting the range of sports that I thought women were interested in. It was the team sports that were covered in *Sports Illustrated*. While women may want to spectate sports, they were just as interested in participating in sports. It becomes this whole spectrum. My intention was for the magazine to be about any woman who is active, rather than someone who is just interested in the WNBA and women's soccer. To me, that's a pretty interesting woman. She's not just active in sports. She's active in life."

The once-again renamed *Sports Illustrated Women* became a participant-based women's sports magazine focusing on individual female athletes after Casey became the publication's editor-in-chief in 2001. The magazine profiled America's best women's football players and motorcycle racers and featured niche sports stars, including wave surfer Sarah Gerhardt, snowboarder Tara Dakides, triathlete Paula

Newby-Fraser, and first lady of drag racing Shirley Muldowney. Casey put six-time Hawaii Ironman Lokelani McMichael on the cover of her first issue running the magazine in a close-up portrait shot of her working up a mid-workout sweat.

"She was a real athlete who represented an archetypal reader for that magazine," Casey explained. "I wanted a close-up picture of her face. She's sweating and not wearing makeup. She looks intense but pleasant. It was meant to be an invitation to any woman who does any sport. We were saying, 'Any woman who is out there playing and using her body, this is a magazine for you.'"

The definition of participant sports broadened over time. *Sports Illustrated Women* covered ostrich racing and sent reporter Mary Roach to write a first-person story on attending dirt-bike school. "It was really about expanding the definition of what women's sports was," Casey said. "I wanted the magazine to be successful enough where we could make a dent in the world of women's magazines and portray this other image of women and do it in a commercially successful way so it wasn't marginalized."

The magazine had a circulation of 400,000 and a definitive editorial vision, but Time Inc. decided in 2002 it wasn't a financially viable part of their overall portfolio. *Sports Illustrated Women*'s run on the news-stands ended after just 12 issues with Casey as editor-in-chief. "It is with deep sadness that I tell you the bad news: this issue will be *Sports Illustrated Women*'s last," she wrote in the final issue. "These are tough times for a magazine, and sometimes even loyal readers aren't enough to make the numbers add up. It's my fierce hope that we'll be back some day in some form."

COLLEGE BASKETBALL ISSUE

Sports Illustrated

NOVEMBER 30, 1981 $1.50

NORTH CAROLINA IS NO.1

Dean Smith and His High-Stepping Heels

otograph by: Rich Clarkson/*Sports Illustrated*.)

(Photograph by: Manny Millan/*Sports Illustrated*.)

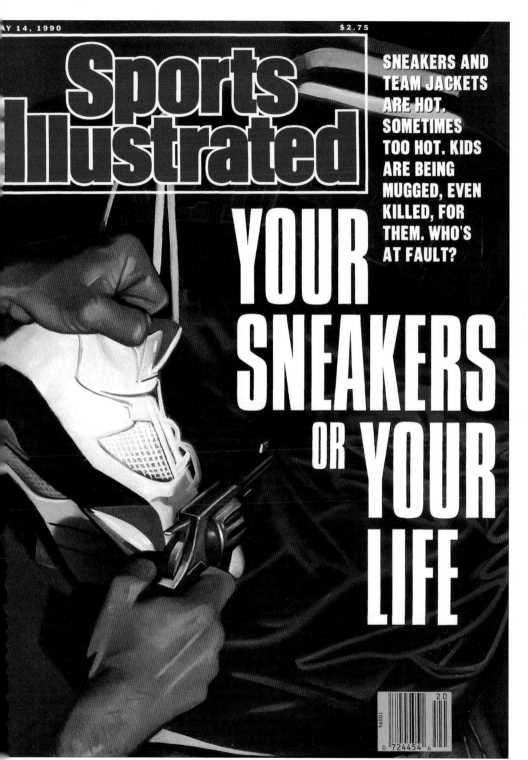

Sports Illustrated

SNEAKERS AND TEAM JACKETS ARE HOT. SOMETIMES TOO HOT. KIDS ARE BEING MUGGED, EVEN KILLED, FOR THEM. WHO'S AT FAULT?

YOUR SNEAKERS OR YOUR LIFE

otograph by: Julian Allen/*Sports Illustrated*.)

(Photograph by: Andrew D. Bernstein/*Sports Illustrated*.)

Sports Illustrated

Bag It, Michael!

Jordan and
The White Sox
Are Embarrassing
Baseball

(Photograph by: John Iacono/*Sports Illustrated*.)

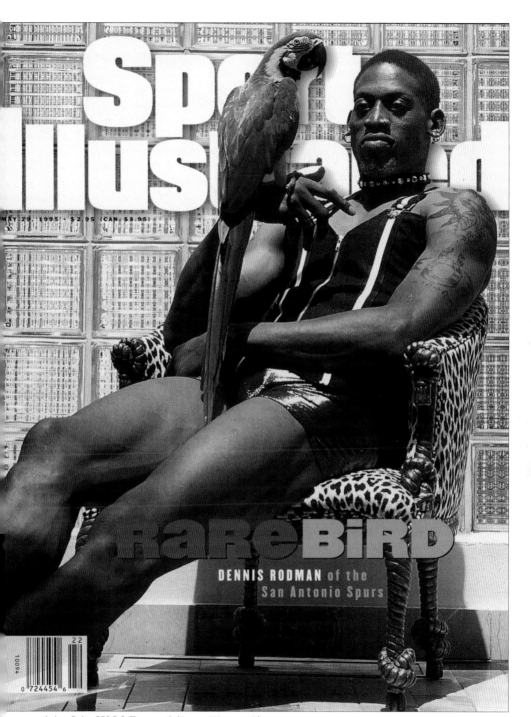

photograph by: John W. McDonough/*Sports Illustrated*.)

(Courtesy of ESPN Enterprises, Inc.)

In Effect!!
August 1988   Volume 1, No. 1
Boston's First & Only Rap Music Newsletter

Please address all comments,
inquiries, or suggestions to:
Go-Go Dave
c/o Street Beat / WHRB Radio
45 Quincy Street
Cambridge, MA 02138

THE WORD ON THE STREET? HOT PICKS!

1. **Night of the Living Bassheads**
   Public Enemy
   CBS/Def Jam
2. **Follow The Leader**
   Eric B. & Rakim
   Uni/MCA
3. **Strictly Business**
   EPMD
   Fresh
4. **Ain't No Half Steppin'**
   Big Daddy Kane
   Warner Brothers

5. **Talkin' All That Jazz**
   Stetsasonic
   Tommy Boy
6. **Straight Out The Jungle**
   Jungle Brothers
   Warlock
7. **Poison**
   Kool G. Rap
   Cold Chillin'
8. **Watch Me Now**
   Ultramagnetic MC's
   Next Plateau

9. **Let's Go**
   Kool Moe Dee
   Jive/RCA
10. **Girls I Got 'Em...**
    Superlover Cee
    DNA/Elektra
11. **Paper Thin**
    MC Lyte
    First Priority/Atlantic
12. **Chillin'**
    Chill Rob G
    Wild Pitch

SNEAK PREVIEWS

ALBUMS :

Sparky D   August 1
"Sparky D's World" B-Boy Records
45 King   August 22
"Master of the Game" Tuff City Records
JVC Force   August 1
"Doing Damage" B-Boy Records
Various   August 1
"U-Rock Posse In Effect" Urban Rock
Various   August 1
"Slammin Jams Anthology" Tuff City
Crown Rulers   August 8
"Paper Chase"   Idlers Records
The Alliance   August 15
"Bustin' Loose"   First Priority Music
Sweet Tee   August 15
"Sweet Tee"   Profile Records
Superlover Cee   August 29
"Girls I Got 'Em Locked" DNA

12-INCH SINGLES : *to be released in Aug.*
Kid'n'Play   "Gettin' Funky"
Marley Marl   "Droppin' Science"
Steady B   "Let The Hustlers Play"
Mikey D   "Out of Control"
The Real Roxanne   "Respect"
4 Ever Fresh   "I Got A Good Thing"
De La Soul   "Jenifa Taught Me"
Spoonie Gee   "You's An Old Fool"
Latee   "Wake Up"
Wee Papa Girl Rappers "Busting Loose"
Yogi Bear&Tim Scratch "It Is What It Is"

THE RAP ABOUT TOWN

Aug 11   **Big Daddy Kane, Ron-Ron**
          Club Chameleon; Lynn, MA
Aug 14   **Run-DMC, Public Enemy,**
          Jazzy Jeff and Fresh Prince,
          and EPMD
          Providence Civic Center

The Rap Report: the Inside Scoop

By Jackie Paul and David Mays
The Battle for World Supremacy featuring
the best dj's and mc's from around the
world takes place every year as part of the
New Music Seminar in New York City,
and it has got to be one of the most
exciting events in the rap world. The
finals of the contest that in the last two
years has brought dj's **Jazzy Jeff** and
Cash Money into the limelight took
place this year on July 16 at the Ritz
Theater in New York. The hosts for the
evening were **Flavor Flav**, **Biz
Markie**, and **Daddy-O**. The judges
included **Grandmaster Flash**,
**Mixmaster Ice and the Educated
Rapper**, **Cut Creator**, **Ice T**, **Jazzy
Jeff and Fresh Prince**, **Red Alert**,
and **Mr. Mixx and Marquis of the 2
Live Crew**. In the mc competition,
despite outstanding performances by
Bango from Cleveland and **MC Serch**
from New York, the title was taken by
rapper **Mikey D** of the LA Posse in
Queens. On the turntables, Philadelphia
dj's again made a strong showing, placing
two dj's, **Tat Money** and **Miz**, in the
semifinals; however, it was **DJ Scratch**
from Brooklyn who decisively won the
final over dj **All-Star Fresh** from
Holland. One of the highlights of the
night was when **Mr. Magic** of WBLS
Radio came on stage and decided he wanted
to be one of the hosts of the show. When
he was told that he could not have a mike,
he threw a cup of water on one of the
contestants and was then ejected from the
club. Another note of interest was the
unplanned battle between last year's top
mc, **Melle Mel**, and this year's winner,
Mikey D. Although the crowd
overwhelmingly picked Mikey D as the
winner, Melle Mel refused to give up his
belt. He then grabbed both belts and
walked out of the building, flexing his
muscles and daring anyone to stop him.
Once the battling was over there were
some awesome live performances by
Doug E. Fresh, **Big Daddy Kane**,
and **Public Enemy**.

MUSIC NEWS: LL Cool J and one of
his dj's have split: **Bobcat** will no longer
be part of the group....**MC Tee** is no
longer with the group Mantronix; look
out for Mantronik's new mc, **MC
Ike**....Congratulations to EPMD, as
their *Strictly Business* LP went gold...**DJ
Red Alert** has been on the Dope Jam
Tour with Boogie Down Productions so
Sammy B from the Jungle Brothers has
been doing his show on KISS FM in New
York....A second national rap record pool
has just started. In addition to **The Rap
Pool of America** (14038 Carrigan Pl.,
Houston, TX, 77083; 713-568-7582)
headed by Steve Fournier there is now the
**Put The Needle To The Record
Pool** (970 Pennsylvania #306, Denver,
CO, 80203; 303-860-0367) headed by
Honey B.

STREET BEAT   FRIDAYS   10PM-MIDNIGHT   95.3FM WHRB

ourtesy of Dave Mays)

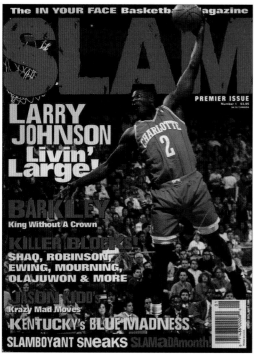

The IN YOUR FACE Basketball Magazine

SLAM

PREMIER ISSUE
Number 1 $3.95
$4.50 CANADA

LARRY
JOHNSON
Livin'
Large!

BARKLEY
King Without A Crown

KILLER BLOCKS
SHAQ, ROBINSON,
EWING, MOURNING,
OLAJUWON & MORE

Krazy Mad Moves
KENTUCKY's BLUE MADNESS
SLAMBOYANT SNeaks SLAM aDAmonth!

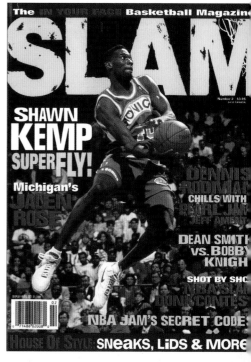

The IN YOUR FACE Basketball Magazine

SLAM

Number 2 $3.95
$4.50 CANADA

SHAWN
KEMP
SUPERFLY!

Michigan's
JALEN
ROSE

DENNIS
RODMAN

CHILLS WITH
PEARL JAM
JEFF AMENT

DEAN SMITH
VS. BOBBY
KNIGHT

SHOT BY SHO

NBA SLAM
DUNK CONTEST

NBA JAM'S SECRET CODE
HOUSE OF STYLE SNeaks, LiDS & MORE

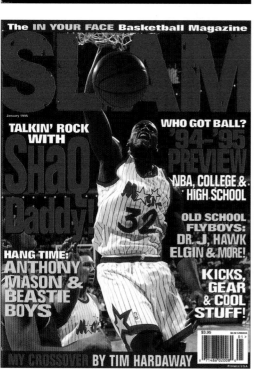

The IN YOUR FACE Basketball Magazine

SLAM

January 1995

TALKIN' ROCK
WITH
SHAQ
Daddy!

HANG TIME:
ANTHONY
MASON &
BEASTIE
BOYS

WHO GOT BALL?
'94-'95
PREVIEW
NBA, COLLEGE &
HIGH SCHOOL

OLD SCHOOL
FLYBOYS:
DR. J, HAWK
ELGIN & MORE!

KICKS,
GEAR
& COOL
STUFF!

$3.95 $4.50 CANADA
01 >

MY CROSSOVER BY TIM HARDAWAY
Printed in U.S.A.

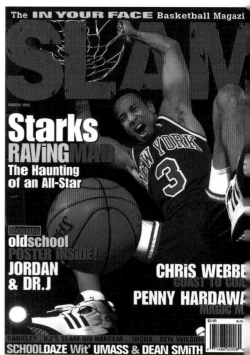

The IN YOUR FACE Basketball Magazine

SLAM

MARCH 1995

Starks
RAVING MAD
The Haunting
of an All-Star

Bonus
oldschool
POSTER INSIDE!

JORDAN
& DR.J

CHRIS WEBBE
COAST TO COA

PENNY HARDAWA
MAGIC M

$3.95 $4.50

BARKLEY, KJ's SLAM ON HAKEEM, 'NIQUE, BEN WILSON
SCHOOLDAZE Wit' UMASS & DEAN SMiTH

(Courtesy of *SLAM* Magazine)

(Courtesy of *SLAM* Magazine)

PENNY: "PUT IT **ALL** ON MY SHOULDERS." PG.

SLAM

MARCUS CAMBY ★ SHAREEF ABDUR-RAHIM ★ ANTOINE WALKER BRING DA

Ready or Not.

FEBRUARY 1997

NBA ROOKIES SET TO BLOW

$4.95 Can
$4.50
02 >
0 27172 02008 7

(Courtesy of *SLAM* Magazine)

here they come!

THE SPOT

(Courtesy of *SLAM* Magazine)

(Courtesy of *SLAM* Magazine)

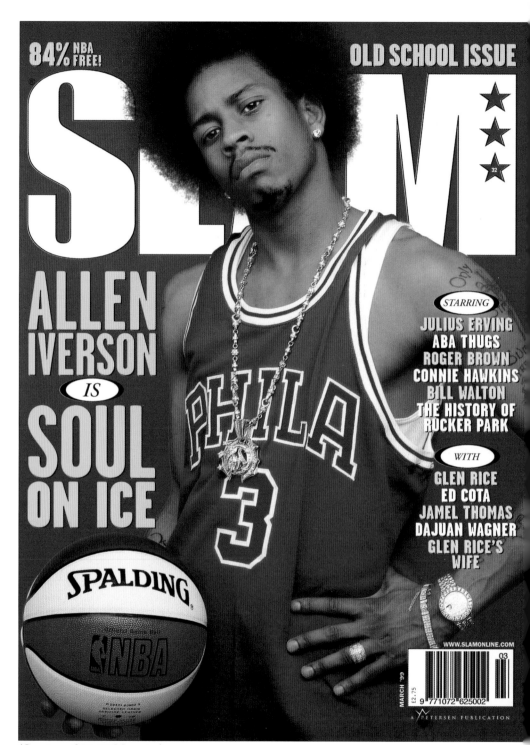

(Courtesy of *SLAM* Magazine)

(Courtesy of *SLAM* Magazine)

Sports
Illustrated

Olympic
Preview Issue

(Photograph by: Lois Greenfield/*Sports Illustrated*.)

You Go, Girls!
The U.S. Women's Basketball Team

m left: Sheryl Swoopes, Katrina McClain, Ruthie Bolton, Lisa Leslie, Teresa Edwards, coach Tara VanDerveer)

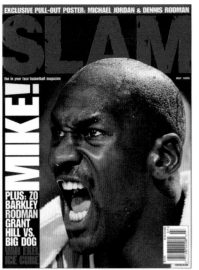

EXCLUSIVE PULL-OUT POSTER: Michael Jordan & Dennis Rodman

SLAM

the in your face basketball magazine

JULY 1995

MIKE!

PLUS: ZO
BARKLEY
RODMAN
GRANT
HILL VS.
BIG DOG
VAN EXEL
ACE CORE

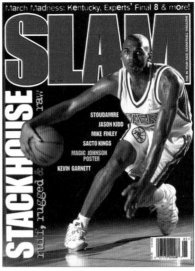

March Madness: Kentucky, Experts' Final 8 & more!

SLAM

THE IN YOUR FACE BASKETBALL MAGAZINE

STACKHOUSE raw, rugged &

STOUDAMIRE
JASON KIDD
MIKE FINLEY
SACTO KINGS
MAGIC JOHNSON
POSTER
KEVIN GARNETT

THE DEFINITIVE DR. J INTERVIEW

SLAM ★★★

JUWAN HOWARD
JASON KIDD
SPREWELL

IVERSON &
THE ROOTS

MARCH
MADNESS
PREVIEW

KOBE
BRYANT
POSTER

GRANT HILL

JUST LIKE MIKE. ONLY BETTER.

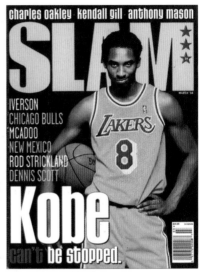

charles oakley kendall gill anthony mason

SLAM ★★★

MARCH '98

IVERSON
CHICAGO BULLS
MCADOO
NEW MEXICO
ROD STRICKLAND
DENNIS SCOTT

Kobe

can't be stopped.

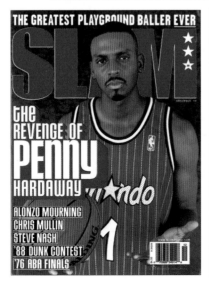

THE GREATEST PLAYGROUND BALLER EVER

SLAM ★★★

DECEMBER '99

the
REVENGE OF
PENNY
HARDAWAY

ALONZO MOURNING
CHRIS MULLIN
STEVE NASH
'88 DUNK CONTEST
'76 ABA FINALS

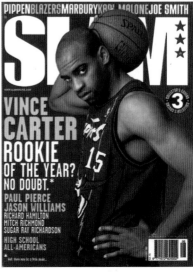

PIPPEN BLAZERS MARBURY KARL MALONE JOE SMITH

SLAM ★★★

3

**VINCE
CARTER
ROOKIE
OF THE YEAR?
NO DOUBT.***

PAUL PIERCE
JASON WILLIAMS
RICHARD HAMILTON
MITCH RICHMOND
SUGAR RAY RICHARDSON

HIGH SCHOOL
ALL-AMERICANS

(Courtesy of
SLAM Magazine)

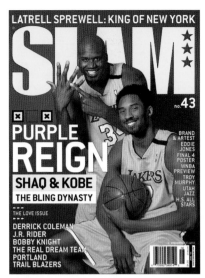

LATRELL SPREWELL: KING OF NEW YORK

SLAM

★★★

no.43

☒ ☒ ☒

PURPLE
REIGN

SHAQ & KOBE
THE BLING DYNASTY

THE LOVE ISSUE
★★★
DERRICK COLEMAN
J.R. RIDER
BOBBY KNIGHT
THE REAL DREAM TEAM
PORTLAND
TRAIL BLAZERS

BRAND
& ARTEST
EDDIE
JONES
FINAL 4
POSTER
WNBA
PREVIEW
TROY
MURPHY
UTAH
JAZZ
H.S. ALL
STARS

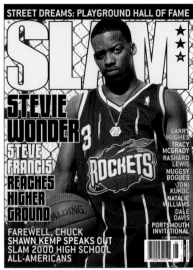

STREET DREAMS: PLAYGROUND HALL OF FAME

SLAM

★★★

STEVIE
WONDER

STEVE
FRANCIS
REACHES
HIGHER
GROUND

FAREWELL, CHUCK
SHAWN KEMP SPEAKS OUT
SLAM 2000 HIGH SCHOOL
ALL-AMERICANS

LARRY
HUGHES
TRACY
MCGRADY
RASHARD
LEWIS
MUGGSY
BOGUES
TONI
KUKOC
NATALIE
WILLIAMS
DALE
DAVIS
PORTSMOUTH
INVITATIONAL

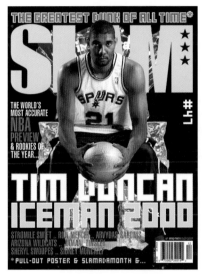

THE GREATEST DUNK OF ALL TIME

SLAM

★★★

#

THE WORLD'S
MOST ACCURATE
NBA
PREVIEW
& ROOKIES OF
THE YEAR...

TIM DUNCAN
ICEMAN 2000

STROMILE SWIFT .. RON MERCER .. ARVYDAS SABONIS
ARIZONA WILDCATS .. JAMAAL TINSLEY
SHERYL SWOOPES .. SIDNEY MONCRIEF

* PULL-OUT POSTER & SLAMADAMONTH &...

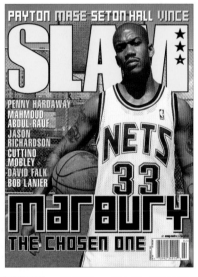

PAYTON MASE-SETON HALL VINCE

SLAM

★★★

PENNY HARDAWAY
MAHMOUD
ABDUL-RAUF
JASON
RICHARDSON
CUTTINO
MOBLEY
DAVID FALK
BOB LANIER

NETS
33

MARBURY
THE CHOSEN ONE

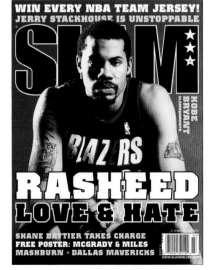

WIN EVERY NBA TEAM JERSEY!
JERRY STACKHOUSE IS UNSTOPPABLE

SLAM

★★★

KOBE
BRYANT
SLAMADAMONTH

BLAZERS

RASHEED
LOVE & HATE

SHANE BATTIER TAKES CHARGE
FREE POSTER: MCGRADY & MILES
MASHBURN × DALLAS MAVERICKS

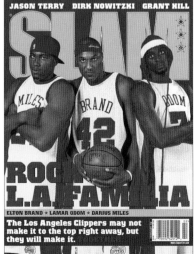

JASON TERRY   DIRK NOWITZKI   GRANT HILL

SLAM

★★★

MILES
BRAND
42
ODOM

ROOKIE
L.A. FAMILIA

ELTON BRAND • LAMAR ODOM • DARIUS MILES

The Los Angeles Clippers may not
make it to the top right away, but
they will make it.

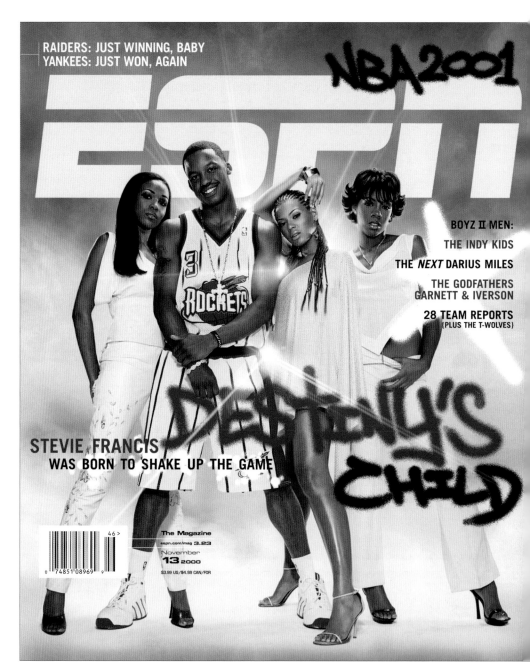

RAIDERS: JUST WINNING, BABY
YANKEES: JUST WON, AGAIN

NBA 2001

ESPN

BOYZ II MEN:
THE INDY KIDS

THE *NEXT* DARIUS MILES

THE GODFATHERS
GARNETT & IVERSON

28 TEAM REPORTS
(PLUS THE T-WOLVES)

STEVIE FRANCIS
WAS BORN TO SHAKE UP THE GAME

DESTINY'S CHILD

The Magazine
espn.com/mag **3.23**
November
13 2000
$3.99 US/$4.98 CAN/FOR

0 74851 08969 9   46 >

(Courtesy of ESPN Enterprises, Inc.)

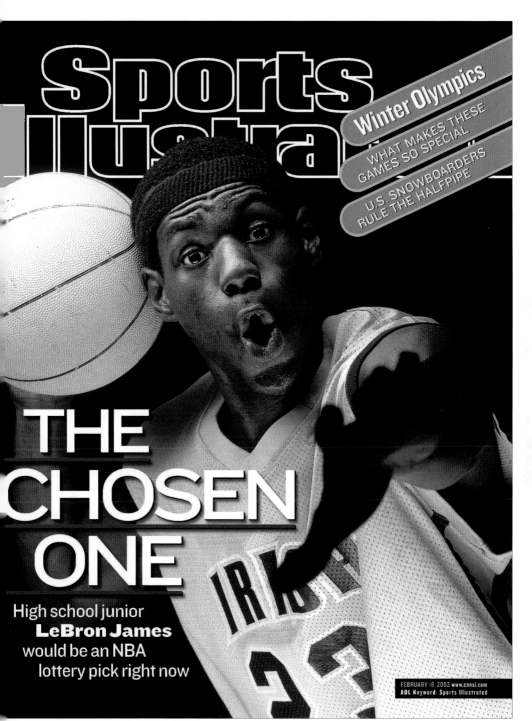

(Photograph by: Michael J. LeBrecht II/*Sports Illustrated*.)

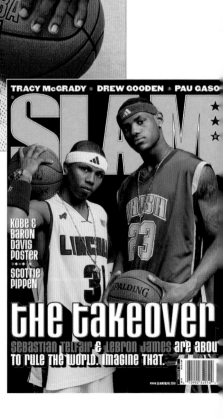

(Courtesy of *SLAM* Magazine)

Photograph by: Heinz Kluetmeier/*Sports Illustrated*.)

COLLEGE PREVIEW: **THE RETURN OF DUKE** PLUS: D

SLAM

JOEL EMBIID ★ JABARI PARKER ★ MARCUS SMART ★ ANDREW WIGGINS ★ JULIUS RANDLE ★ AARON C

Ready or not...

NOVEMBER 2014 $5.99

THE BEST ROOKIE CLA

0 72440 34914 8   11

slamonline.com

(Courtesy of *SLAM* Magazine)

ROSE ★ DEMARCUS COUSINS ★ CHAUNCEY BILLUPS

RAY ALLEN ★ MAYA MOORE ★ MONTA ELLIS

VONLEH ★ NIK STAUSKAS ★ ELFRID PAYTON ★ ZACH LAVINE ★ DOUG MCDERMOTT ★ TJ WARREN

re they come!

NCE... '03? '96?? '84???

100% ROY **TRUST US**

SLAM

JOEL
EMBIID
IS
SOUL
ON ICE

PHILA
21

SPALDING

STARRING
DEMARCUS
COUSINS
JAE CROWDER
CALEB
SWANIGAN
ANGEL
MCCOUGHTRY
POINT-GUARD
TAKEOVER
THE SPURS'
CULTURE
BRANDON
MCCOY

WITH
ALLEN
IVERSON
DR. J

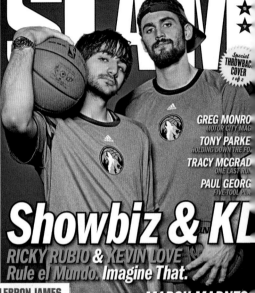

JEREMY LIN IS THE NEW KING OF NEW YORK

SLAM

Special
THROWBACK
COVER
1 of 2

GREG MONRO
MOTOR CITY MAG
TONY PARKE
HOLDING DOWN THE FO
TRACY MCGRAD
ONE LAST RUN
PAUL GEORG
FIVE-TOOL PLA

Showbiz & KL
RICKY RUBIO & KEVIN LOVE
Rule el Mundo. *Imagine That.*

MARCH MADNESS:
Carolina, Cuse, Kentucky and more

(Courtesy of *SLAM* Magazine)

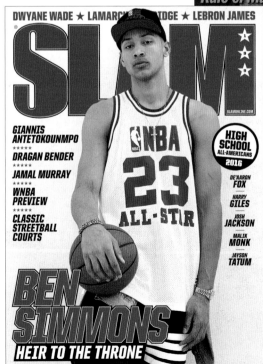

DWYANE WADE ★ LAMARCUS ALDRIDGE ★ LEBRON JAMES

SLAM

GIANNIS
ANTETOKOUNMPO
★★★★★
DRAGAN BENDER
★★★★★
JAMAL MURRAY
★★★★★
WNBA
PREVIEW
★★★★★
CLASSIC
STREETBALL
COURTS

NBA
23
ALL-STAR

**HIGH
SCHOOL
ALL-AMERICANS
2016**

DE'AARON
FOX

HARRY
GILES

JOSH
JACKSON

MALIK
MONK

JAYSON
TATUM

BEN
SIMMONS
HEIR TO THE THRONE

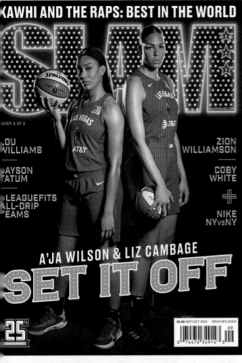

KAWHI AND THE RAPS: BEST IN THE WORLD

SLAM

COVER 3 OF 9

LOU WILLIAMS

JAYSON TATUM

LEAGUEFITS ALL-DRIP TEAMS

ZION WILLIAMSON

COBY WHITE

NIKE NYvsNY

A'JA WILSON & LIZ CAMBAGE

SET IT OFF

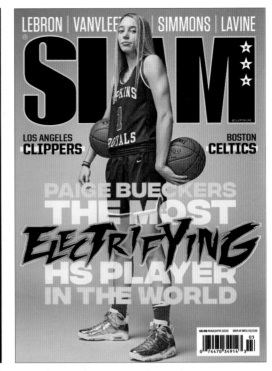

LEBRON | VANVLEET | SIMMONS | LAVINE

SLAM

LOS ANGELES CLIPPERS

BOSTON CELTICS

PAIGE BUECKERS

THE MOST ELECTRIFYING HS PLAYER IN THE WORLD

MONI BATES | JALEN GREEN | LAMELO BALL

SLAM

THE Future ISSUE

ZION

IMMANUEL QUICKLEY

ANTHONY EDWARDS

RAVEN JOHNSON

COLLIN SEXTON

CURRY BRAND MINI MAG

SABRINA IONESCU

THE NEXT QUEEN OF NY

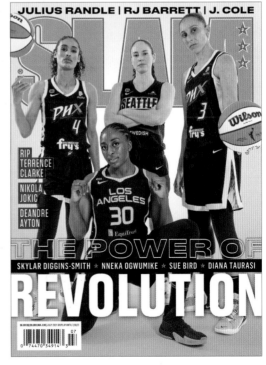

JULIUS RANDLE | RJ BARRETT | J. COLE

SLAM

RIP TERRENCE CLARKE

NIKOLA JOKIC

DEANDRE AYTON

THE POWER OF

SKYLAR DIGGINS-SMITH ★ NNEKA OGWUMIKE ★ SUE BIRD ★ DIANA TAURASI

REVOLUTION

(courtesy of *SLAM* Magazine)

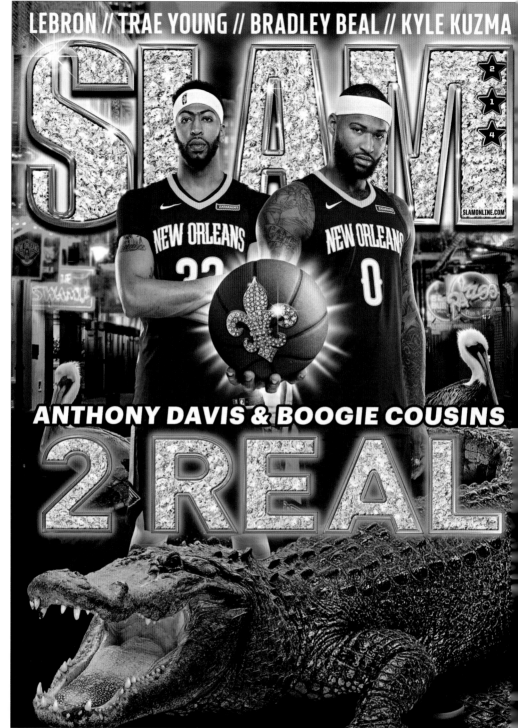

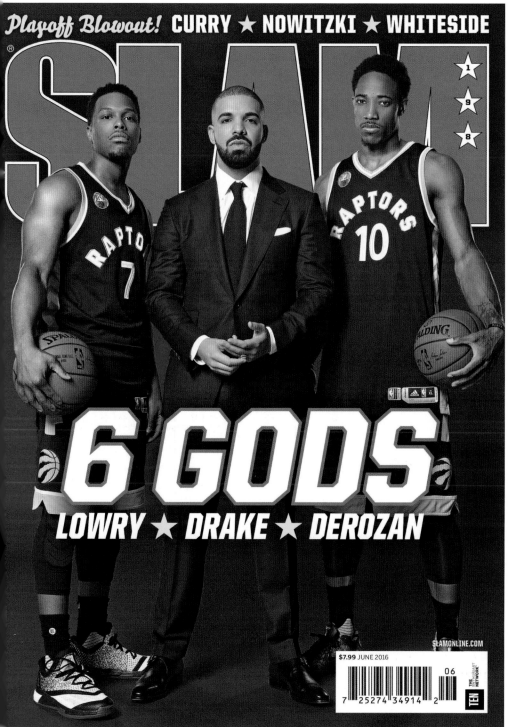

SLAM

the REMIX

no. **106**

ZACH RANDOLPH
GANGSTA BALLIN'
★★★★★

CHARLES BARKLEY
HIS GNARLIEST INTERVIEW YET
★★★★★

THE GREATEST DUNK EVER

+

MONTA ELLIS
KEVIN DURANT
LENNY COOKE

BRON
IS THE ONE

APRIL '07 $4.99 $5.99 CAN

04
0 74470 34914 3

WWW.SLAMONLINE.COM

(Courtesy of *SLAM* Magazine)

Considered a niche publication at Time Inc., the marketing team ran into challenges convincing advertisers to place ads in the magazine. The *Sports Illustrated*–related name added credibility to readers and sponsors but was also a detriment to those who viewed them as a smaller spin-off of the main publication.

Sports Illustrated took years to transform their vision and lost millions of dollars in the first decade. *Sports Illustrated Women* was given a year after Casey took over.

Many of the women's sports magazines from the post-Olympics boom didn't survive the newsstand. Conde Nast's *Women's Sports & Fitness* ended after three years in 2000. *Real Sports* started in 1998, covering women's college and pro sports, but transitioned to a digital format after five years. *Women's Basketball* launched shortly after the WNBA's debut and had a circulation of only 13,000 after five years.

The failure of these magazines led publishers to believe there was no audience for a women's sports publication.

Casey vehemently disagrees.

"The audience has always been there," she said. "I learned that at *Outside*. They're highly educated, highly affluent, and highly active. You couldn't hope for a better audience. Forty percent of our readers were women, and that was with almost no content aimed at them."

Women were once again secondary cover subjects on sports magazines at the start of a new decade after losing the unique space they had carved out on newsstands. *Sports Illustrated* featured a total of nine covers with women as the main cover subject in a five-year period after the 1996 Olympics. The Comets won four straight WNBA championships during this period but didn't receive a single *Sports Illustrated* cover during their run.

USA BASKETBALL NEVER DID END UP CHOOSING a nickname
for the 1996 Olympic gold medal team. They are simply known today
as the most influential women's basketball team of all-time. Between
their barnstorming tour, their Olympic run, and their *Sports Illustrated*
cover, these women paved the way for the next generations to grow up
and dream of playing professionally in the United States. The golden
era of women's sports magazines they inspired laid the groundwork for
greater representation of female athletes on the cover of sports magazines in the decades after.

ESPN the Magazine celebrated the WNBA's 20th anniversary season
in 2016 with a gatefold cover featuring the most influential women
from the league's first two decades, including Maya Moore, Elena Delle
Donne, Tina Charles, Chiney Ogwumike, Breanna Stewart, Skylar
Diggins, Sue Bird, Tina Thompson, Teresa Weatherspoon, Tamika
Catchings, Katie Smith, and Lobo, the lone cover subject representative
from the 1996 Olympics team. Wearing a custom-designed white-and-
silver basketball jersey, the women—photographed across six different
shoots in New York and Bristol, Connecticut—were sequenced in a
photo showing them dribbling to the basket for a layup.

One person who didn't appear on the cover was Katrina McClain,
the only player from the 1996 Olympics team who never played a single
game in the WNBA. One of the best power forwards in the country,
McClain attended the University of Georgia in 1983 and averaged 24.9
points and 12.2 rebounds in her senior year in college, winning the 1987
National Player of the Year award. Like other women's basketball stars
from her era, she had to travel overseas to find a professional career,
joining a pro team in Japan called the Kyoto Petroleum after graduating. "It was the cleanest place I've ever been to," McClain recalled. "I

loved the food. My teammates were awesome. I loved it there." After three seasons, she moved to Italy to play for a club team named Sidis Ancona for one season, followed by a stint in Spain. McClain won the gold medal with Team USA at the 1988 Olympics in Seoul and was part of the 1992 Olympics team in Barcelona who finished third. The 6'2" power forward turned down a $300,000 contract from a pro team in Hungary in 1995 to join the barnstorming tour. After the 1996 Olympics, McClain signed a $500,000 contract to play in Turkey, making her the highest-paid women's basketball player in the world. That was when the injuries started.

"I had a lot of excruciating pain in my knee," McClain said. "I flew to Virginia to get it checked out by a doctor, and she said it was a torn meniscus. My pro team asked me to come back in two weeks, and it just went downhill from there. Every time I would bend down and jump, it was painful."

She returned to the United States and signed with the Atlanta Glory of the American Basketball League. The ABL was a women's basketball league launched in the fall of 1996, immediately after the Olympics in Atlanta. The idea was conceived by Steve Hams, the vice president of a small software company in Silicon Valley; Anne Cribbs, a former Olympic swimmer and sports marketing executive; and her business partner, Gary Cavalli. The ABL was approaching its first season when they learned about the NBA's plans to launch their league in 1997.

Cavalli and Cribbs established personal relationships with members of the women's team heading into the 1996 Olympics and recruited eight of them to play in the ABL's inaugural season. They convinced

Swoopes and Leslie to join them at an introductory press conference, where the players wore ABL shirts.

"The NBA started to send messages to players about the launch of their league," Cavalli recalled. "When we sent our first contracts out to the players, that's when Lisa and Sheryl dropped out."

The league offered higher starting salaries than the WNBA and would play in the fall. Teams were strategically placed in cities with strong local college basketball fan bases. The presence of the WNBA loomed over the ABL's three-year run. They were in negotiations with Nike as a major sponsor and ESPN for television rights, but those conversations ended shortly after Stern publicly declared the NBA's intentions to start a women's pro league. Without a national television presence and a marketing budget to compete with the WNBA, the ABL folded in 1998, a month into the start of their third season. The league is largely forgotten today in the conversation about the history of women's basketball.

"I still feel great about what we accomplished. Our quality of play for the first two years was much better than the WNBA," Cribbs said. "But they had a huge impact on people's desires to go into business with us."

After Chamique Holdsclaw was taken first in the 1999 WNBA Draft, 15 of the following 16 players selected were ABL players, including Jennifer Azzi and Dawn Staley from the 1996 Olympics team.

Meanwhile, McClain's injuries continued to pile up in the ABL, forcing her to retire early.

"I told myself early in my career," she said, "if I was hurt or if I no longer loved the game, I would no longer want to be part of the game."

McClain was Team USA's second-leading scorer and top rebounder in Atlanta. Considered one of the best women's basketball players of all-time, she was inducted into the Women's Basketball Hall of Fame in 2006. McClain is immensely proud of the one magazine cover she appeared on—the 1996 *Sports Illustrated* Olympic preview issue.

"We always said, 'The men get everything, and we get nothing,'" she said. "We were like, 'Wait a minute, we do the same things they do. We play the sport they play.' So when the *Sports Illustrated* cover happened, it was like, 'Alright, we're finally getting some attention too.' Girls would always ask, 'How come we don't have anybody to look up to?' That was what the cover meant to me. It wasn't for any personal gain. It was for them and for women's basketball."

The AIR APPARENT

Seimone Augustus was a 14-year-old high school freshman in the spring of 1999 when she first appeared on a magazine cover. While she was playing at a state championship tournament, one of her teammates came across the new issue of *Sports Illustrated for Women* at Walgreens and brought it back to the team hotel. Augustus looked at a portrait photo of herself on the cover with the caption: IS SHE THE NEXT MICHAEL JORDAN?

"I couldn't even process it," she said. "I grew up watching Michael. I couldn't imagine being in the same breath as him. In terms of the torch I was being asked to carry, it was something I couldn't process at that young of an age."

Augustus was considered the most exciting women's basketball player since Cheryl Miller, with colleges recruiting her starting in fifth grade. She was already used to the spotlight but the comparison to Jordan would change the rest of her career. "The bullseye on my back was huge," she said. "Everyone was like, 'That's the girl on *Sports Illustrated*.' Everyone wanted to take their shot at me."

After the magazine cover hit newsstands, Augustus averaged 27.0 points and 10.5 rebounds at the tournament, leading Capitol High School to a runner-up finish. After the championship game, the head coach of the opposing team celebrated their victory by asking why his team didn't receive the *Sports Illustrated for Women* cover treatment instead.

"When he made that comment, that's when I realized how hard it was going to be for me," Augustus recalled. "It hit me at that very moment. Whether it was at the rec center or the park, everybody was coming for me from that day on. It changed the way I prepared for the following season."

There is still rarely a day that goes by without people reminding Augustus of the *Sports Illustrated for Women* cover. "People still send it to me on Instagram all the time," she said. "I've had a few players tell me, 'Man, I remember when you were on the cover and my dad would put it on the wall and use it as motivation for me.' Hearing those stories makes me feel good that it made an impact." Augustus looks back on the Jordan comparison fondly. "It was good for me," she said. "It gave me something to work toward. I wanted to live up to those expectations. I don't know if it would have been good for everyone."

Augustus became a high-school All-American, College Player of the Year at Louisiana State University, won four WNBA championships, and three Olympic gold medals with USA Basketball. She retired in 2021 as one of the greatest basketball players of all-time.

MICHAEL JORDAN LEFT the GAME OF BASKETBALL with a career résumé beyond comparison after retiring for a second time in 1999. With six NBA championships, a 6–0 record in the NBA Finals capped off by a series-clinching jumper over Bryon Russell, six NBA Finals Most Valuable Player Awards, 12 All-Star appearances, 10 All-NBA First Team selections, and 10 scoring titles, the 35-year-old walked away from the game of basketball as the greatest player in modern basketball history.

He single-handedly transformed the Chicago Bulls from a mediocre NBA franchise to one of the world's most recognizable sports teams.

His signature sneaker line transformed Nike from an upstart footwear and apparel company to one of the world's most profitable brands.

He was at the center of the NBA's rise from a second-rate pro league to a global phenomenon as the most famous athlete in the world.

This was what every player in the 1990s was being compared to.

The idea of being compared to a player from the previous generation wasn't a novel concept. Jordan's freakish athleticism invited comparisons to Julius Erving when he joined the NBA. He appeared on the cover of the October 29, 1984, issue of *The Sporting News* dressed in a surgical gown holding a stethoscope to a basketball with the caption THE NEXT DR. J—MICHAEL JORDAN IS READY TO OPERATE IN THE NBA. The Bulls rookie pushed back against the comparisons after the magazine hit newsstands. "I don't want to follow in his footsteps," he told reporters. "I want to make my own."

Many of the players being compared to him in the 1990s felt the same. Inglewood, California, native Harold Miner was nicknamed "Baby Jordan" for his dunking ability before he played a single NBA game. He was selected 12th overall by the Miami Heat in 1992 after averaging 26.3 points in his junior year at USC, becoming the first Pac-10 player to score 2,000 career points since Lew Alcindor. Miner grew up idolizing Jordan and played one-on-one against him as a ninth grader at Nike summer camp.

"The comparisons were flattering at first, but I'm just Harold," he told reporters after the draft. "There will never be another Michael Jordan."

Miner averaged just 9.0 points in 200 career NBA games, despite winning the same number of Slam Dunk Contests as Jordan. He told *Sports Illustrated* many years later the "Baby Jordan" nickname both helped and hurt him.

The Orlando Magic selected Michigan forward Chris Webber in 1993 with the first overall pick and traded him on draft night to the Golden State Warriors in exchange for Anfernee Hardaway (who was the number three pick in the same draft) and three future first round picks. The best high school player in the country at Treadwell High School in Memphis, Tennessee, Hardaway averaged 22.8 points, 8.5 rebounds, and 6.4 assists in his final season at Memphis State. Arkansas head coach Nolan Richardson described him as "Larry Bird, Magic Johnson, and Michael Jordan rolled together."

The 6'7" guard was chosen by 80 percent of NBA scouts as "the player most likely to captivate the imagination of basketball fans like Jordan" in an informal poll conducted shortly after draft night. Hardaway starred in the 1994 basketball film *Blue Chips* alongside Nick Nolte and his teammate Shaquille O'Neal, and received his own Nike signature shoe, the Air Penny. A series of commercials featuring a wise-cracking puppet named Lil' Penny, voiced by comedian Chris Rock, became a pop-culture phenomenon. Hardaway received two All-NBA First Team selections and made the All-Star team four times during his career, but injuries derailed his chance to become the next Jordan.

The Detroit Pistons selected Grant Hill with the third overall pick in 1994. The son of Calvin Hill, an All-Pro NFL running back, and Janet Hill, a lawyer who shared a dorm with Hillary Clinton during her freshman year at Wellesley College, the 6'8" forward didn't just draw the Jordan comparison for his ability to dominate opponents with his all-around game. Hill had a clean-cut image and a sports lineage from his father, making him a recognizable name and an ideal face of the NBA.

Hill was the star of a prestigious college basketball program, winning back-to-back NCAA championships at Duke, and was named ACC Player of the Year and a consensus first-team All-American in 1994. He appeared on the cover of *GQ*'s April 1995 issue with the cover line CAN GRANT HILL SAVE SPORTS?

Hill admitted the comparisons to Jordan made him uncomfortable before the start of his rookie year in Detroit.

"If you compare me to him, and I have a successful career but don't do the things he did, then it's considered a letdown," he told reporters. "The comparison has been the toughest adjustment I've had to make in the NBA. I really hate it. It's foolish. I mean, he's the best player ever."

Hill won Rookie of the Year and seemed destined to be the next Jordan. *SLAM* even put him on the cover with the cover line JUST LIKE MIKE. ONLY BETTER. But a lingering ankle injury derailed Hill's potential as an all-time great even though he did finish his career as a seven-time All-Star.

Jerry Stackhouse started to hear the Jordan comparisons as the leading scorer at North Carolina in his sophomore year. "It was flattering," he said. "I remember after I got drafted, a magazine had this famous photo of me taking a jumper which faded into Michael taking the same shot. I jumped high. I could dunk. I played with flair. I wore my hair bald sometimes. It was natural for me to get that comparison."

Stackhouse still remembers meeting Jordan for the first time at North Carolina. "Michael came to practice one day," he recalled. "We were just making baskets against each other. We didn't keep no score, and not one time did we ever say, 'We're gonna play to seven.' We were just out there having fun. I was sharing the floor with one of my childhood heroes." The story got passed around and made its way to reporters in Philadelphia after the Sixers drafted Stackhouse with the third overall pick in 1995. The media ran with a storyline of the rookie guard claiming he had beaten Jordan in one-on-one before their first NBA matchup against each other. The Bulls guard proceeded to score 48 points in a blowout win.

"To this day, I'm sticking to the fact I never said I beat him," Stackhouse said. "But Michael was motivated because he thought I said it. All of the stories come out after the game saying he gave me 48 points. If you go back and watch, I probably guarded him for like 10 of those points. Vernon Maxwell caught a bunch of them. Trevor Ruffin caught a bunch of them. I had a much better game when we went to Chicago, but nobody writes about that."

Stackhouse had a long and successful career in the NBA but admits today the Jordan comparisons hampered him.

"Some people still feel I didn't live up to the expectations," he said. "But I'm satisfied with who I was. I played almost two decades in the league and made a couple of All-Star teams."

IT APPEARED THE HEIR APPARENT finally arrived in 1998.

Vince Carter was selected fifth overall by Golden State and traded on draft night to the Toronto Raptors for his college teammate Antawn Jamison.

The Raptors joined the NBA as an expansion franchise in 1995 alongside the Vancouver Grizzlies. After a promising start with Damon Stoudamire, who won Rookie of the Year in the franchise's inaugural season, and Marcus Camby, the second overall pick the following year, Toronto entered the 1998 Draft as a team in the middle of a freefall. Part-owner Isiah Thomas had left the team, and Stoudamire had requested a trade and landed in Portland. The team finished their previous season with a 16–66 record. Reporters questioned whether the franchise would still be in Toronto by the end of the decade.

Carter would single-handedly turn the franchise around. The reigning Rookie of the Year averaged 25.7 points per game in his second year, reinvigorating the Raptors with his highlight-reel performances and signature dunks, leading them to a 45–37 record and the team's first-ever playoff appearance. Carter's Slam Dunk Contest performance at the 2000 All-Star Weekend remains the standard-bearer for any dunk contest participant today. The Raptors appeared on nationally televised games on NBC for the first time in franchise history and Carter became the new *it* athlete.

It was a familiar narrative. Carter was a North Carolina alum who lifted an NBA franchise into the national spotlight. He was one of the best scorers and dunkers in the league and the most popular player among the fans, leading the league in All-Star voting for three straight years. The man who had become known as "Air Canada" was also a magazine cover star. In 2000, he appeared on the cover of *Sports Illustrated*, with the cover line POSTER BOY, in reference to the posterizing he was doing to opposing defenders; *SLAM*, with the caption THE GREATEST SHOW ON EARTH; and *ESPN the Magazine*, who asked in their NBA playoff preview issue: MUST SEE VC. WILL VINCE CARTER SAVE THE PLAYOFFS?

Carter did not save the playoffs, shooting 15-for-50 and scoring a total of 58 points in a three-game first round sweep to the New York

Knicks in his second year. He would lead the Raptors to the second round a year later, where Carter exchanged 50-point games in the second round with Allen Iverson. The Sixers won in seven games after Carter missed a series-clinching shot at the buzzer. His stardom up north would fade from there. Carter was dealt to the New Jersey Nets in 2004 after a series of injuries and the mismanagement of the roster by Toronto's front office led to a trade request.

The comparisons stopped soon after. It was a relief for Carter, who told family members and the media in private conversations during his first two NBA seasons in Toronto he was tired of the storylines comparing him to Jordan. He would spend 22 seasons in the league, retiring in 2020 at the age of 43 as one of five players in NBA history to record 25,000 points, 5,000 rebounds, 4,000 assists, and 500 made three-pointers. Carter transformed from a high-flyer early in his career into one of the most respected veteran leaders in the NBA. His lasting impact on the game of basketball in Canada remains today.

A theme emerged.

The basketball world needed someone who wasn't just an entertaining dunker, a North Carolina graduate, a signature sneaker endorser, a public-friendly personality, and an all-around player on the court.

They needed someone who was willing to embrace the idea of following in Jordan's footsteps.

KOBE BRYANT SPENT A PART OF HIS CHILDHOOD in Italy while his father, Joe, played pro basketball overseas. He studied NBA game tapes and modeled his entire persona after Jordan. From his mannerisms to his signature fadeaway jumper, the similarities were hard to ignore when he arrived in the NBA in 1996 as a 17-year-old teen.

Tony Gervino remembers seeing Bryant as a high school junior at Lower Merion High School in Ardmore, Pennsylvania. "He was playing a whole different game than everyone else," he recalled. "He had a single-minded purpose. Basketball was his obsession."

Bryant declared for the 1996 NBA Draft after leading Lower Merion to their first state championship in 53 years in his senior season. He was selected by the Charlotte Hornets with the 13th pick and traded to the Los Angeles Lakers in exchange for center Vlade Divac on draft night. Bryant joined the NBA's most prestigious franchise, paired alongside Shaquille O'Neal, who signed a seven-year, $120 million deal with the team in free agency. Bryant's introverted nature, combined with his confidence, didn't make him a favorite of many teammates.

"He was an outsider from day one," Gervino said. "He was this genuine, curious kid. But he grew up in Italy, and then he comes back when he's older. He just didn't have a lot of friends."

Bryant averaged 7.6 points and played 15.5 minutes per game in a rookie season that is remembered today for how it ended.

Facing elimination on the road against the Utah Jazz in the second round, the situation got more dire for the Lakers after O'Neal fouled out in the fourth quarter. With Byron Scott out with a sprained wrist and Robert Horry ejected in the third quarter, head coach Del Harris turned to his rookie guard with the season on the line.

Bryant launched a game-winning attempt with the score tied at the end of the fourth quarter.

Airball.

He caught a pass from teammate Nick Van Exel and shot another jumper in overtime.

Airball.

Bryant pulled up with 43 seconds left from beyond the arc with the Lakers trailing by three.

Airball.

Bryant shot another three to send the game into double overtime with three seconds left.

Airball.

The Lakers' season was over.

It would be a career-ending sequence for some players. It was just another step in trying to become the greatest player of all-time for Bryant. He was back in the gym the following day, spent the entire summer in the weight room, and arrived at training camp with a new mini-afro and a new perspective. "Even though I didn't hit the shots," he told reporters, "I knew that my teammates had confidence in me to take the shots."

Bryant appeared on the cover of *SLAM*'s 24th issue at the start of his second NBA season. Wearing the iconic purple-and-gold jersey colorway of the Lakers, Bryant flashed a cocky smile toward the camera against a black backdrop. The cover line said KOBE CAN'T BE STOPPED.

"He looked at the camera with a level of confidence you don't see much," Gervino said. "It was like, 'Who the hell does this kid think he is?' The smartest people have the most to learn, and Kobe knew enough to know that he didn't know enough. That was the look of a guy who said, 'I might not be there yet, but I'll get there.'"

The confidence didn't go over well with teammates and opposing players. Some felt he acted like a superstar before he was one, carrying himself as if his stardom was preordained.

"He always had to carry himself as someone older than he was," Gervino said. "People saw him trying to behave like he belonged and saw it as inauthentic. He was just trying to fit in. He said, 'That's my north star. It's Michael Jordan.' He was honest about it. He embraced the burden of it because he wanted to be the best player ever."

Bryant was voted an All-Star starter in his second season despite still coming off the bench and averaging only 15.4 points.

The 1998 All-Star game turned into a one-on-one showdown.

Bryant and Jordan exchanged highlight-reel dunks and fadeaway jumpers, putting on a show for the Madison Square Garden crowd. Bryant totaled a team-high 18 points in 22 minutes but sat out the entire fourth quarter. Some of his teammates, including Karl Malone and David Robinson, were upset with what they viewed as a selfish display by the youngest All-Star starter in league history.

Jordan finished with 23 points and added eight assists, six rebounds, and three steals in a 135–114 victory for the East. He was named the Most Valuable Player.

The two would form a relationship that lasted throughout Bryant's career. Even in retirement, Jordan remained a close friend and mentor. In 2001, when he was asked about the Bryant comparisons, Jordan told reporters he didn't view them negatively. In fact, he admitted there were similarities to their games. "Oh, yeah," Jordan said. "I'm looking at his post-up game and the way when his jump shot isn't falling he goes to the hole, or does what he needs to get himself to the foul line. You know what I've noticed, the difference between this year and last year? He's not chasing the game as much. With that much talent, you don't need to chase it."

THE LAKERS WERE A WIN AWAY from their third straight championship in 2002 when they arrived at the Continental Airlines Arena in East Rutherford, New Jersey, for Game 4 of the Finals against the Nets. Bryant had grown into one of the best shooting guards in the league and a perfect complement on the court next to O'Neal.

He averaged 26.6 points, 5.8 rebounds, and 4.6 assists during the postseason and paid homage to the greatest athletes from past eras throughout the playoffs by wearing throwback jerseys to every game. Bryant wore the jerseys of New York Jets quarterback Joe Namath, Brooklyn Dodgers second baseman Jackie Robinson, and Edmonton Oilers center Wayne Gretzky through the first three games of the Finals. He told reporters before Game 4 he was saving the greatest athlete of all-time for last. A few days later, Bryant strolled into the arena in a throwback red-and-white Jordan Bulls jersey. The Lakers clinched their third consecutive title that evening. Bryant celebrated with a victory cigar in his mouth in the visitor's locker room a few hours later, wearing a Bulls warm-up jacket over his throwback Jordan jersey. He was a three-time champion with a perfect record in the Finals.

The comparison wrote itself.

The SLAM Dome
INTERLUDE 2

Tony Gervino surprised everyone in 1999 when he accepted an offer to become the vice president of editorial for *NBA Inside Stuff* and *HOOP* magazine. "I figured they were bringing me in because they wanted to do what *SLAM* was doing," he said. The decision didn't sit well with Dennis Page. "I was personally hurt," he said. "I loved Tony. But he went for the check. They paid him a lot of money and I couldn't compete with them." Russ Bengtson became *SLAM*'s editor-in-chief. "I remember walking home with Don Morris one day, and he said, 'You know they're going to offer you the position, right?'" he recalled. "I was like, 'Man. I don't know if I can do this.' I was 27 at the time and hadn't been doing national media stuff for that long. Don told me, 'You'll figure it out. You can do this.' That was important to me."

The magazine also needed a new managing editor after Anna Gebbie left in the same year. Susan Price Thomas was a copy editor at *Twist*, a teen magazine, when she saw the job posting in *The New York Times*. "I loved my job," she said. "But I was sick of finding new ways to describe glittery nail polish or write about what to do when you get in a fight with your BFF."

A Long Island native and New York Knicks fan, Thomas graduated from NYU with a journalism degree and landed an internship at *The Sally Jessy Raphael Show* before joining the publishing industry. She applied for the job and landed an interview at the *SLAM* Dome.

"I called my brother-in-law and said, 'Dude, what am I supposed to do?'" Thomas recalled. "I thought they were going to grill me about college basketball, which I knew nothing about. He was like, 'You can fake your way through it.' I showed up in a suit and got hired the next day. They didn't ask me a single college basketball question."

By the time Thomas joined the magazine, the editorial team had moved into a corner office, where the *SLAM* covers started above the door and went around the entire room, creating a collage beginning with Larry Johnson's photo on the front of the first issue. Sneaker boxes were everywhere, stacked to the point where they approached the ceilings. Press credentials hung on the wall as badges of honor. Stacks of reader mail were scattered across every desk. Basketball memorabilia surrounded the room. This was the new *SLAM* Dome.

"It wasn't a work environment for everyone," Thomas recalled. "It was loud and frantic. You had no privacy. It looked like a teenage boy's bedroom, and it was not spacious."

The managing editor's job was all-encompassing. Thomas assigned features to writers, scheduled photoshoots with players and teams, coordinated with photographers, and made sure a new *SLAM* issue arrived on newsstands every four weeks. "She was the point god," Page said. "You could have the most amazing photos and stories, but the managing editor is the glue."

Thomas got an up-close look at the magazine's growing relationship with the players when she attended a Stephon Marbury cover shoot in 2001.

"We wanted to recreate EPMD's *Unfinished Business* album cover with him at the court near where he grew up in Brooklyn," she recalled. "We were waiting for him, and suddenly we started to hear the bass from far away. It started getting closer to us. Steph showed up with two Bentleys and had his daughter with him. He gave the whole day to us. People started coming down from their buildings to see him. They weren't asking for autographs. It was like, 'Steph is back. Let's catch up with him.' At one point, I see him just sitting on the park bench. He's changing his daughter's diaper in his Nets uniform. We finished in the morning, and Steph just pulled out a wad of cash and told our intern to get Nathan's for everybody. The kid came back with 1,000 bags of everything possible."

SLAM's readership was growing but like every magazine at the start of the millennium, there was a new audience they needed to figure out.

The online audience.

The digital transition began with Lang Whitaker, who grew up in Atlanta, Georgia, and wrote for the alternative weekly *Creative Loafing* when he discovered *SLAM* in a grocery store. Whitaker played high school basketball and was an Atlanta Hawks fan during the Dominique Wilkins era. He started freelancing for *SLAM* before moving to New York and joining the magazine full-time as their online editor in 2000.

"When I started, we had one column on the website," Whitaker recalled. "It was a column written by an entry-level scout named Stephen Silas which we ran several times a year. We started to set up cover galleries and a few different things, but I realized we had to give people something to come back to every day."

Whitaker found a newspaper directory and published a daily round-up of articles every Monday to Friday called "The Links." "We didn't advertise it. It was just word of mouth," he said. "This was pretty early on. There wasn't even a comment section. We had college students grab notes for us from games. I would interview players and include some questions and answers. I would post something and get emails from Mark Cuban and Ernie Johnson half an hour later. It just kept growing and growing." Whitaker ended up doing "The Links" for seven years. The readership grew and laid the groundwork to usher the magazine into the digital age.

Whitaker also has the most talked-about locker room interaction in *SLAM* history. He was working on a Rasheed Wallace cover story in 2001 and needed to interview him. Whitaker spent an entire day tracking down the Portland Trail Blazers forward when the team arrived in New York for a game.

"I went to morning shootaround in Manhattan and Sheed said, 'Nah, let's talk later,'" he recalled. "I go to the Garden pregame and he says, 'Nah, after the game.' I told him, 'I need 15 minutes because [it's] a cover story.' He gets a technical during the game, and I'm like, 'This doesn't bode well.' I'm standing in front of his locker after the game and he's getting dressed. He turns around and someone starts to ask him a question. He says, 'No, no.' He points to me and says, 'I'm only talking to him.' At this point I'm like, 'Sheed, these guys are on deadline.' He says, 'No. I'm only talking to you.' I go, 'Soooo, you guys were down five in the first half and came back in the second half. How were you guys able to do it?' He answered me and everyone was able to get a quote and we did our interview."

The magazine had plenty of fun at the arena, but the week before the magazine's deadline was always a stressful time at the *SLAM* Dome. "We would each read a story as the copy was being laid out, and then we would go through three passes of each page once it was laid out," Bengtson recalled. "By the time it hit newsstands, we would be like, 'Oh my god. I never want to see it again.' Sometimes you would be like, 'Damn, I wish someone else could read this fucking thing and get it ready for print.'"

Arguments would take place between the editors and the creative director over layouts. Discussions would take place over headlines and spine lines. Bengtson was always bothered by the number of cover lines that would fill the magazine cover. "Sometimes I would ask Dennis, 'Can we please just make the cover look good?'" he recalled. "He would say, 'No. We need the cover lines for the newsstand.' I remain convinced if you strip off all the names and left only the cover line about the actual cover subject, it would have been negligible how many fewer issues we sold. I just didn't think we were selling any more copies by putting Travis Best's name on the cover. If people wanted to see what was inside the magazine, they could just flip to the table of contents."

"It's like what clickbait is today. You got the customer with your cover lines," Page said. "Did we go overboard with the cover lines? Absolutely. But the cover lines sometimes meant the difference between breaking even or losing money."

A perfect example of the cover line debate happened when Bengtson decided to put San Antonio Spurs forward Tim Duncan on the cover in 2000. A U.S. Virgin Islands native, Duncan was selected first overall in 1997 after being named National College Player of the Year at Wake Forest University. He averaged 27.4 points and 14.0 rebounds in the 1999 NBA Finals, leading the Spurs to their first title and winning the Finals Most Valuable Player Award at age 23.

SLAM decided to pay homage to San Antonio legend George Gervin and reference Duncan's stoic public persona with an "Iceman" theme on the cover. Melissa Brennan, who replaced Don Morris as the magazine's creative director, tracked down an ice sculptor in San Antonio to carve out a throne for the cover shoot. The cover lines completely erased the ice throne effect when the issue hit newsstands.

"We went through so much trouble finding a sculptor and a freezer to keep the throne in," Bengtson said, "and it was ruined."

The photo was taken by Atiba Jefferson, who grew up in Colorado Springs, Colorado, where he developed an interest in photography in high school and fell in love with capturing the skateboarding movement. When *SLAM* called in 2000 and asked him to shoot Phoenix Suns guard Jason Kidd for the cover, Jefferson was living in California and pursuing his dream of becoming a professional photographer. "I took what I knew from skateboarding and brought it to basketball," he explained. "I wanted to give it a different look."

SLAM asked Jefferson to shoot a cover with Houston Rockets star Steve Francis a few months later. "I was so stoked," he said. "I did the shoot and sent the film to *SLAM*. A couple of weeks passed, and I didn't hear anything from them. They called me and were like, 'Where's the film?' It had gotten lost. I was so devastated."

Jefferson had shipped the film in a flat FedEx box and the photos were accidentally thrown out. The magazine was running up against the deadline without a cover photo. Thankfully a reshoot was rescheduled at the very last minute and Francis appeared on the cover after all. Jefferson was helping out photographer Andrew Bernstein at the time. "I told Andy, 'This is gonna be my last job. I lost the film. They're never going to ask me to shoot again,'" he recalled. "He looked at me and said,

'What's wrong with you? Trust me. This stuff happens to everyone. It's not your fault.'" Bernstein was right. Jefferson went on to shoot many of *SLAM*'s classic covers in the 2000s.

An official photographer for the NBA since 1986, Bernstein was a student at the Art Center College of Design when he was introduced to *Sports Illustrated* photographer Lane Stewart, who hired him as an assistant when the magazine decided to shoot a double-page spread photo of the Los Angeles Lakers for a 1981 issue.

"They wanted to shoot it in a classroom," Bernstein recalled. "Lane wasn't an action photographer. He was the guy back in the day who did all the portrait shoots. So we would have these big production shoots all the time. I spent two days in a studio building a classroom setting on a soundstage."

The Los Angeles–based photographer soon became a regular at Lakers games and got his first *Sports Illustrated* cover in 1985 when an action photo he took of Kareem Abdul-Jabbar made it to the front of the magazine. The *Sports Illustrated* cover was also the highest honor for photographers.

"That was the moment I felt like I had arrived," Bernstein said.

He built relationships with Lakers greats across several eras and captured the franchise's most significant moments.

Bernstein was an obvious choice for *SLAM* when Bengtson decided to put Shaquille O'Neal and Kobe Bryant on the cover of their 2000 playoff preview issue. After three straight embarrassing playoff exits, including Bryant's four airballs against the Utah Jazz and back-to-back sweeps to end the season, the Lakers were wrapping up a 67–15 record in the regular season. They were consensus championship favorites in their first season under head coach Phil Jackson. Bengtson wanted

O'Neal and Bryant to predict a championship for the Lakers on the cover by pointing to their ring fingers.

"The magazine was going to be off the newsstands in a month. You just needed people to be like 'Oh shit!' for that month," he said. "Even if we were completely wrong, it didn't matter. You just needed to catch people for that one moment on newsstands when they're browsing. If it makes them pick it up and buy it to see what the hell we were talking about, that's what we wanted to do."

The cover shoot took place on a game day. "I had to coach them up a bit," Bernstein recalled. "I told them, 'Guys, this is going to predict you guys to get the ring. So we've got to make it realistic.' Russ wanted both guys to do it, which seemed hokey to me, but Shaq had no qualms about it. He always liked to ham it up. So he did it. It was a quick shoot."

The two Lakers stars appeared on the cover of *SLAM*'s 43rd issue. O'Neal pointed at his empty ring finger while Bryant stood alongside with a grin on his face. The cover line said PURPLE REIGN. SHAQ & KOBE. THE BLING DYNASTY. They would win the next three championships.

"It's my favorite cover ever," Bengtson said. "The photo is just so perfect. Kobe had such an easy-going smile. Shaq too. He's got his hand spread out with a giant smile on his face. It was more like a shit-eating grin. He knew they were coming. You could tell he wanted to do that. It's also my favorite cover because it was a prediction that came true."

The other NBA team in Los Angeles would get their own cover two years later. The Los Angeles Clippers didn't just live in the shadow of the Lakers. They were considered one of the worst franchises in sports. The team's entire postseason résumé consisted of three first round exits dating back to 1984, when they moved from San Diego. Bengtson decided to put Elton Brand, Lamar Odom, and Darius Miles on the cover in 2002.

"We wanted to be ahead of the game," he explained. "We didn't know how long they were going to be together. Were they going to win a championship that season? No. But they were exciting, and they were at the intersection of hip-hop, basketball, and fashion. Those were the guys we wanted to get for the cover."

The trio arrived at the cover shoot with the idea of swapping their jerseys with one another, wearing them backward and untucked to show each other's names on the front.

"Elton was more of a consummate old-school pro back then," Bengtson said. "I feel like him swapping jerseys with Lamar and Darius made him a Clipper for real. That wasn't just a moment for the magazine. It was a sign of who these guys were and who they wanted to be. That's what *SLAM* did better than anyone. We showed these guys as who they really were. The best way was to say yes to them wearing a durag and an untucked jersey. They wouldn't have been able to do that with an official NBA publication."

Brand, Odom, and Miles appeared on the front of *SLAM*'s 57th issue with the cover line ROCK L.A. FAMILIA. THE LOS ANGELES CLIPPERS MIGHT NOT MAKE IT TO THE TOP RIGHT AWAY, BUT THEY WILL MAKE IT. TOGETHER. When the Clippers finally won a playoff round in 2006, Brand was the lone cover subject still with the team.

There was no place basketball writers wanted to work at more than the *SLAM* Dome. Ben Osborne dreamed of being a sportswriter at the age of 13 and was the sports editor of George Washington University's school newspaper. He interned for *The Washington Post* in his senior year, fact-checking stories for now-famous national sports media personalities including Tony Kornheiser, Michael Wilbon, J.A. Adande, and Rachel Nichols. Osborne walked into the *SLAM* Dome in 1997 as a summer intern transcribing interviews for the magazine and was hired as a full-time editor two months later.

"It was a pressure-packed environment," Osborne said. "But I've also never felt more seen or rewarded in my life for something I cared about."

A rite of passage for every person at *SLAM* was to have an Allen Iverson cover shoot story to tell. Osborne's initiation took place in 2000, when he drove in a rental car with photographer Clay Patrick McBride to the Philadelphia 76ers' facility for a shoot.

"We had scheduled a shoot with him after practice," Osborne recalled. "Clay got set up, and we're sitting in the lobby. Practice ends. And he walks right past us. He didn't even look at us, got in his car, and drove away. He just didn't feel like doing it."

McBride returned to Philadelphia a few days later and was given five minutes to shoot Iverson before the game.

"He was walking out to the court when his publicist grabbed him," he recalled. "She told me, 'You have five minutes,' and she wasn't kidding. She told me, 'Four minutes. Three minutes. Two minutes.' I got the shoot done. It was like that with Allen most of the time."

The newsstand has always been a place for borrowing and sampling other people's ideas in hopes of making a better version of someone else's magazine. "When I launched *Guitar World*, it was a *Guitar Player* knockoff," Page said. "It was sampling. I used to rip out pages from a magazine and say we were going to bite this. There was no pride or shame. We were going to evolve it."

SLAM was so successful they tried to borrow from themselves. An NFL magazine called *BLITZ* arrived on newsstands in 1995 with Deion Sanders on the cover. New York Mets pitcher Bill Pulsipher appeared on the cover of *HARDBALL*'s first issue the following year. They were billed as the "In Your Face" football and baseball magazines respectively. It was Page's idea to replicate *SLAM*'s success across every other sport.

"They were horrible on every level," Page said. "We couldn't get any advertising, and it didn't sell on newsstands at all. None of them worked. We couldn't even launch the hockey one because of trademarks for a magazine name we wanted. There was no culture behind the other sports to make it work."

The newsstand became more crowded at the start of a new decade, but *SLAM* didn't view the new magazines as their competition. *Source Sports*, a sports magazine started by *The Source*, marketed themselves to the same audience, but their editorial approach expanded beyond just hoops. *ESPN the Magazine* wasn't a competitor either. "They were a 3 million subscriber magazine," Osborne explained. "In our heyday, we sold 200,000 copies on newsstands."

A basketball magazine named *Dime*, which debuted in 2001, also focused on basketball and culture and considered themselves a potential competitor to *SLAM*.

Josh Gotthelf was one of *Dime*'s co-founders. "We considered ourselves to be graduates of *SLAM*," he explained. "They had pull-out posters. Their slogan was the in your face magazine. We said, 'That's great when you're a teen, but we want to pick up our audience as they entered their twenties.'"

The idea for *Dime* started after Patrick Cassidy was laid off from a digital basketball website. "It was the classic early dot com story," he explained. "We blew through things too quickly. One day, our CEO came in and said, 'We're out of money. Thanks for everything.'" Cassidy grew up in Philadelphia and graduated from Boston College with a degree in English and political science. He spent the first two months of unemployment brainstorming a basketball magazine idea with Gotthelf, and two of his close friends, Matt O'Neill, and Jed Berger. "*SLAM* was the Bible," Cassidy said, "but we wanted something slightly older."

Dime looked outside of traditional sports magazines for inspiration. They were fans of a music and culture magazine called *Fader*, which debuted in 1999. Their cover photos were especially appealing, featuring close-up portrait shots with minimal cover lines, creating a clean and aesthetically pleasing look on newsstands. The creative director of the magazine was Jeff Staple, who started a creative agency in New York.

"We took the general visual vocabulary of music magazines and applied a graphic design feel to a subject matter that didn't usually get that treatment," Staple explained.

He received a call from *Dime*. They wanted him to apply the same concepts to a basketball magazine.

Photographer Gary Land arranged a cover shoot with Iverson on the rooftop of a building for the magazine's first issue. In the cover photo, the Sixers guard stood mid-dribbling motion, staring at the camera in a black bandana with a matching tank top and basketball shorts which fell well below his knees. Staple produced a magazine cover with Iverson's photo and practically no cover lines on the front of the magazine.

"It was about finding a white space in the industry," Staple explained. "They wanted to own a white space in the magazine publishing world and address a basketball fan who was a bit older. We were literally creating white space on the cover. It was about creating a differentiating factor. We wanted it to be polarizing in a new and different way."

Dime had a unique look for a period of time, but the cover lines eventually multiplied on the front of the magazine like every other newsstand-dependent publication. "We ended up going back to bigger fonts," Staple conceded. "We had to make accommodations for the newsstand." *Dime* did not establish the same cultural footprint as *SLAM* but published for over a decade before ending their print magazine in 2013. Cassidy admits today he viewed *SLAM* as a competitor.

"That was our enemy," he said. "They were the big bad guy. They were owned by a publishing company with 50 titles under their umbrella. I was blowing through all my savings, having my buddy pay my rent in New York. There was an underdog mentality that made us angry for a long time."

To say the two magazines didn't get along was an understatement.

"I treated them with disdain," Osborne said. "It was personal at one point. You can never hate too much on people chasing a dream, but let's be real. They didn't have a concept. They just did what we were doing."

"We could not have been more different," Cassidy said. "They just wouldn't shut up, and I was a competitive guy. But we weren't innocent ourselves."

Page insists today *Dime* wasn't a competitor. "Our product was far superior," he said. "I never even considered them competition. It's the difference between Porsche and Ford."

As for Gervino? He managed the NBA's official publications shortly after they had airbrushed Iverson on the cover of *HOOP* and was optimistic about changing the magazine under his watch. He quit after three years.

"It was way less fun than *SLAM*," Gervino said. "I tried my best to be the bridge between the players and the league, but I was constantly frustrated by what the league thought was appropriate or not. In the end, you become just a guy in a giant machine."

DESTINY'S Child

It was the fall of 2000 when *ESPN the Magazine* NBA editor Jerry Bembry started brainstorming ideas for the NBA preview issue cover.

After graduating from Ohio Wesleyan University, Bembry landed his first job as a news reporter with *The Courier-News* in Bridgewater, New Jersey. He eventually accepted a night police reporting position at *The Sun* in Baltimore, allowing David Simon, creator of the television show *The Wire*, to move to the day shift. In 1993, Bembry became an NBA writer at the paper, covering the Washington Bullets. He joined ESPN in 1999.

It had been an eventful off-season.

Grant Hill and Tracy McGrady left Detroit and Toronto respectively to join the Orlando Magic as free agents. The Spurs re-signed Tim Duncan after he also flirted with the idea of joining the Magic and added guard Derek Anderson to their championship core. The Indiana Pacers, who lost to the Los Angeles Lakers in the NBA Finals, had a new head coach in Isiah Thomas, who replaced Larry Bird, and a new starting center, Jermaine O'Neal, who was traded from the Portland Trail Blazers. The Blazers, who came within a blown 15-point lead in Game 7 of the Western Conference Finals from possibly winning it all themselves, reshaped their roster as well, acquiring Shawn Kemp and Dale Davis to bolster their status as contenders. The Lakers appeared primed to start a dynasty with Shaquille O'Neal and Kobe Bryant.

There were plenty of cover subjects to choose from, but Bembry was intrigued by Steve Francis, the Houston Rockets guard who had won the Co-Rookie of the Year, sharing the honor with Chicago Bulls forward Elton Brand.

Born and raised in Takoma Park, Maryland, Francis stopped playing basketball after his sophomore year in high school, when his mother Brenda passed away from a heart attack while battling cancer. A standout performance at an AAU tournament landed him at San Jacinto Junior College in Texas. In his sophomore year, Francis transferred to Allegany College of Maryland to be closer to his grandmother, who was ill, joining the Maryland Terrapins a year later. He averaged 17.0 points and 4.5 assists in his junior season at Maryland and declared for the 1999 NBA Draft.

Francis did not hide his displeasure on draft night when the Vancouver Grizzlies selected him second overall. He pouted on national television. The idea of playing in another country for a team that finished a league-worst 8–42 the previous season was not appealing. Francis was traded to Houston in the off-season, spending his first NBA season playing with Charles Barkley and Hakeem Olajuwon, averaging 18.0 points and 6.6 assists in 77 starts.

The 6'3" guard played with a comfortable amount of confidence on the court. He surprised defenders with his quickness and hops. Francis had a killer crossover, a 43-inch vertical, and a willingness to trash-talk his opponents. He was described as someone with Allen Iverson's moves, Gary Payton's talent, and Gary Shandling's temperament. His playfulness and sense of humor endeared him to teammates.

The man nicknamed "The Franchise" was the successor in Houston as he entered his second season. Barkley was retired, and Olajuwon, who led the Rockets to back-to-back championships in 1994 and 1995, was in the twilight of his career. An R&B group from Houston, Texas, named Destiny's Child was creating plenty of buzz in the music industry at the same time, dominating airwaves with number one hits "Bills, Bills, Bills" and "Say My Name" from their second studio album, *The Writing's On the Wall*. Bembry decided to pitch the idea of pairing Francis and Destiny's Child together on the *ESPN the Magazine* cover.

The idea of sports and pop culture merging on the cover of a magazine had become commonplace on newsstands by the start of the 2000s. No combination was more popular than basketball players and rap artists, and no magazine provided a more authentic platform for this merger between hoops and hip-hop than *The Source*, who started their own sports magazine in 1998.

The origin story of *Source Sports* begins with the December 1992 issue of *The Source*, when Charles Barkley became the first NBA player to appear on the magazine's cover. The man nicknamed the "Round Mound of Rebound" talked trash to fans, butted heads with his coaches, and was known as not just the most dominant power forward in the league but the most outspoken. Having just returned from the Summer Olympics in Barcelona as a member of the gold medal–winning Dream Team, the Phoenix Suns forward was at the height of his popularity. Joining him on the cover was Spike Lee, the film director on a press tour for his upcoming film *Malcolm X*.

The two met at a Brooklyn studio for the photoshoot with photographers Keith Major and Chi Modu, and sat down with *The Source* to discuss the racial demographic at NBA arenas ("It's not that many Blacks at basketball games. That's the one thing that annoys me about the NBA. I would say, in basketball, about 95 percent of the fans are white."), being labeled outspoken by the mainstream media ("There's a certain image that Black athletes have been molded into. You're not supposed to speak out and stuff."), being Black in Hollywood ("We lost millions of dollars on *Do The Right Thing* because bullshit muhfukahs in the media telling white people that this movie was gonna cause riots."), and the media's role in creating a negative image of Black people ("The media has distorted Black people and white people. Most white people don't understand Black people, and most Black people don't understand white people. Most people believe everything they read in the paper and see on TV. Most people's perception of Black people is that we're all hoodlums.").

No traditional sports magazine consistently provided this kind of honest and unfiltered look on what it was like to be Black in America. *The Source* had inadvertently stumbled upon a blueprint for their sports magazine. The Barkley-Lee cover idea was conceived by Chris Wilder, who joined the magazine shortly after *The Source* moved from the campus of Harvard University to New York..

"They've never told me this, but I know it to be true. I was the first hire because they needed a Black person to legitimize the editorial staff," Wilder said.

The Source introduced a monthly sports column in 1995 with a feature interview with Dallas Cowboys cornerback Deion Sanders, who had released the rap album *Prime Time*. A 1996 NBA preview issue arrived on newsstands the following year, becoming the first issue published under the *Source Sports* name. Wilder became the editor-in-chief of *Source Sports* in 1998 when the spin-off magazine started publishing quarterly. He assembled a network of freelance sportswriters around the country. The network's racial makeup was reflective of the magazine's tagline: OUR ATHLETES. OUR VOICE.

"We had people like Jemele Hill and Stephen A. Smith helping us out while they were working their newspaper jobs," Wilder recalled. "I wanted our magazine to have the voice of hip-hop. It was important to me to have a variety of Black voices. Other people tend to view us as a monolith."

Source Sports had a different relationship with athletes than traditional sportswriters. The access led to a less conventional but more intimate way of profiling athletes. The magazine wouldn't arrive for a sit-down interview with a player after practice. They would call them up, go hang out with them for an evening, and write about it.

Wilder remembers a feature on Jerry Stackhouse starting at a listening party for New Jersey-based rapper Redman's new album at a midtown New York studio and ending several hours later at Justin's, a restaurant owned by Sean Combs, the founder of the hip-hop label Bad Boy Records.

Stackhouse spoke candidly in the feature about media members having "snitches inside the organization" and why he fought Jeff Hornacek during his rookie year. There was a level of trust and understanding between the players and the magazine.

"For the longest time, young Black athletes didn't have a place to express themselves," Stackhouse said. "When I was growing up, you wanted to be on *Sports Illustrated* and the Wheaties box. By the time

I came into the league, everyone was trying to get on *SLAM* and *The Source*."

Established in the music industry and respected in the sports world, *Source Sports* used their access to pair basketball players and rappers together on the cover of their magazine, including Stephon Marbury with Redman, Gary Payton with E-40, and Shaquille O'Neal with Master P.

"Every NBA player had a rapper they wanted to be paired up with," Wilder said. "They would come up to me and say, 'Why don't you pair me up with Nas?' Putting an athlete and an artist together was our base. If we saw something like that in another magazine, we'd say, 'What the fuck are they doing? That's our thing.'"

A year before Bembry came up with the idea of pairing a reigning NBA Rookie of the Year with an up-and-coming music act, Wilder had done the same, pairing Vince Carter on the cover of the magazine's 1999 NBA preview issue with Eve, whose debut studio album *Let There Be Eve… Ruff Ryders' First Lady* featuring the hit singles "Gotta Man" and "Love is Blind" sold 2 million copies.

ESPN the Magazine editors wanted to strike a balance in their voice between the more knowledgeable, sarcastic older brother who was really into sports and the person you would like to hang out with on a Sunday afternoon at the bar to watch a game with. ESPN blended their editorial room with a mix of voices, both young and old, emphasizing gender and racial diversity. But the decision-makers—including John Skipper, editor-in-chief John Papanek, and executive editor John Walsh—were old white men, requiring the magazine to walk a fine line between projecting a cool voice versus coming off like a try-hard.

The editorial team still cringes today when they think about an early Super Bowl preview cover featuring two scantily clad cheerleaders and the caption SUPA! It was reminiscent of a *30 Rock* scene where actor Steve Buscemi—wearing a "Music Band" t-shirt and backward baseball cap while carrying a skateboard—says, "How do you do, fellow kids?"

It also meant innovative cover ideas like Bembry's pitch that connected with a younger audience wasn't always understood in the editors' room. "People at the table weren't really embracing it," he recalled. "The only person who liked the idea was our senior photo editor Nancy Weisman. She was a little younger than the other people. She said, 'I think it's a really good idea, and you should pitch it again.'"

It wasn't just the cover. The Walt Disney Company, which owned ESPN, invested $100 million into the magazine's launch. There are inevitably editorial limitations for a publication backed by a powerful corporate conglomerate. Scoop Jackson still remembers when *ESPN the Magazine* editors tried to recruit him in 1998.

"There were two white male editors, and they came to my house," he recalled. "They didn't know anything about me. I remember they walked up to my house and said, 'Oh. You own this?' They thought it belonged to my parents because there was this public perception of me from this writing standpoint that I was this ghetto kid who could write.

"I took them down to my office and got everybody a beer. They sat down and saw my master's degree and said, 'Oh, you're going to be expensive.' I said, 'Of course.' Before we even started talking. I asked, 'Would I be able to write a story in your magazine about how Latrell Sprewell was right for choking P.J. Carlesimo?'"

The Golden State Warriors had a 1–13 record in 1997 when Carlesimo held a closed practice with his team. The head coach wasn't thrilled with

Sprewell's effort during a passing drill and reportedly told him to "put a little mustard on those passes." Neither has spoken about precisely what happened next, but when Carlesimo approached Sprewell, the Warriors guard responded by choking his head coach and was suspended for the remaining 68 games of the regular season. Sprewell hinted at the verbal spat between the two having crossed the line in a later interview, saying his family was disrespected in the exchange.

"You have to be careful about who you step to and how you step to them," Jackson said. "He stepped to Latrell in a very foul way. Especially as a Black human being, there's a slave-owner dynamic that still exists in a lot of workplaces. I think what I heard was he had called Latrell a 'boy.' Like, yo. That's it. It doesn't necessarily have to be the N-word. It was a situation where I'm not saying Latrell was right, but I understood."

The ESPN editors looked at each other and collectively said no to Jackson's pitch to write a story supporting Sprewell's actions in their magazine.

What they didn't know was Jackson already published the story.

It was in *Source Sports*.

"I said, 'Alright, the meeting's over,'" he recalled. "They were like, 'What do you mean?' I told them, 'I have the freedom at other places to do that. Why would I leave my freedom to come to a place where I've got handcuffs on?'"

Source Sports was a creative highpoint for Dave Mays and his editorial team. The magazine grew more ambitious with their feature ideas as their readership grew, organizing a roundtable discussion with Black NFL quarterbacks, and expanding their coverage to include wrestling, tennis, and major league baseball. *Source Sports* moved to a bi-monthly publishing schedule in 2000 and were on equal footing with *SLAM* and *ESPN the Magazine* when it came to their cultural footprint. They were engaging with a younger and hipper audience than traditional sports magazines.

"*Sports Illustrated* was so boring and had no flavor. They were your dad's magazine," Mays said. "When *ESPN the Magazine* came along and marketed themselves as this younger and cooler sports magazine, it validated my vision for *Source Sports*."

A series of poor business decisions at *The Source* led to the magazine's downfall just as they appeared primed to be *ESPN the Magazine*'s competitor for the next decade. Mays had taken out a $12 million loan in 1999 and invested a large amount of money into growing his company's digital presence.

"I was falling behind on my loan payments," he explained. "I was a 19-year-old who started a business without any investors or bank loans. I bootstrapped *The Source* from a one-page newsletter to a business that was doing $30 million in revenue every year by the late 1990s. But my biggest mistake was betting the farm on the dot com boom. I put the company in debt. That was the beginning of the end."

Mays called an impromptu meeting with Wilder in 2001 as he was preparing ideas for the next issue of *Source Sports*. "He was standing right there with an exit package for me," Wilder recalled. "He said, 'I fucked up, man. We have to shut down the magazine.' I was fired. It was completely out of nowhere." It was one thing for a magazine to shut down because it didn't have an audience. The news was especially crushing to Wilder and the rest of the editorial staff because they knew

Source Sports was just starting to grow. "I was devastated," Wilder said. "We were working toward something."

ESPN the Magazine's circulation grew to 2 million subscribers five years after their debut. *Source Sports* has been largely forgotten today.

"It was just bad timing," said Jackson. "Magazines are about three things: idea, execution, and timing. *Source Sports* was a great idea, and it was executed well. But you have to have all three. They only had two."

BEYONCÉ KNOWLES, MICHELLE WILLIAMS, and Kelly Rowland arrived at a Houston studio in the fall of 2000 for an *ESPN the Magazine* cover shoot. Bembry's idea was approved after a follow-up pitch. He supervised the shoot with his 11-year-old daughter Ashley, who got to spend three hours in the dressing room hanging out with her favorite R&B group. "She was so happy," Bembry recalled. "It was probably more amazing for her than it was for me."

When Francis finally arrived with teammate Cuttino Mobley, the photoshoot was delayed again. A Rockets team official had gotten lost on his way to the studio while bringing the jersey and shorts required for the cover photo. The Destiny's Child members waited patiently. "No one was looking at their watch," Bembry recalled. "Sometimes, at a photoshoot, the PR person will say, 'Alright, our time is almost up.' That never happened with them. Everybody was on the same page. This was also introducing them to a new audience, so I'm sure they were happy and willing to give us as much time as possible."

Photographer Marc Baptiste remembers seeing Francis' larger-than-life personality shrink in the presence of his fellow cover subjects. "Steve was shy," he recalled. "But you're going to get a little shy whenever you're around Beyoncé." Baptiste brought the cover subjects on set and handed Francis a basketball to pose with when everyone was finally ready. "His body language just changed once I put it in his hands," he said. "He was in his element. This was his world."

The vision for the cover photo was to portray Francis as a superhero and have Destiny's Child as his heroines.

Francis stood alongside Knowles, Williams, and Rowland on the cover of *ESPN the Magazine*'s 2000 NBA preview issue. The three R&B group members stood in matching white outfits with Francis as the standout in his Rockets jersey. The cover line, written in graffiti font, said DESTINY'S CHILD.

Today it is remembered as one of *ESPN the Magazine*'s most iconic magazine covers. It required Bembry's brilliant idea, Baptiste's execution, and the wonderful timing of Beyoncé appearing as a secondary cover subject next to Francis before she would go on to become a pop culture icon.

As they say: idea, execution, and timing.

The Chosen
ONE

The Cleveland Cavaliers led by one with three seconds left in the deciding game of their first round series against the Chicago Bulls in 1989, when head coach Doug Collins drew up a play for a 26-year-old Michael Jordan during a timeout. After catching the inbounds pass from teammate Brad Sellers, Jordan dribbled to his left toward the foul line, pulling up for the game-winning jumper as the clock hit zero. The ball swished through the net as he leaped into the air in celebration over a dejected Craig Ehlo and a stunned Richfield Coliseum home crowd. Collins ran on to the court with his hands in the air and joined a mob of teammates who had surrounded Jordan in celebration.

It became known as "The Shot."

Thirteen years later, a similar sequence unfolded, as a 38-year-old Jordan stood in the huddle inside Gund Arena in Cleveland, Ohio, watching Collins draw up a play for the game's final possession. The Washington Wizards, a .500 team in Jordan's first season in the NBA since he left the Bulls after six championships, faced a Cavaliers team with a 14–30 record. With 1.6 seconds left and his team trailing by one, Jordan shook his defender off a screen-action and caught the inbounds pass from teammate Popeye Jones at the top of the key just inside the three-point line, pulling up for the game-winning jumper as the clock hit zero. The ball swished through the net as Jordan walked toward center court, holding a fist pump in celebration. It was one more signature moment for the world's greatest player before his final retirement in 2003.

WATCHING IN THE STANDS WAS LEBRON JAMES, who was already considered an NBA-ready prospect as a 17-year-old high school junior. Born and raised by his mother, Gloria, in nearby Akron, Ohio, James moved around different neighborhood apartments growing up as his mom took on various jobs to provide for her son. He was introduced to basketball at the age of nine after moving in with youth football coach Frank Walker.

James made a pact as a kid with his AAU teammates Sian Cotton, Dru Joyce III, and Willie McGee to attend the same high school together. The quartet became known as "The Fab Four" at St. Vincent-St. Mary, a co-ed Catholic school in Akron, leading the school to a 27–0 record and a state championship in their freshman season. Teammate Romeo Travis would make it a "Fab Five." James was a man among boys who left scouts in awe with his mix of physicality, athleticism, and court vision. He was already receiving recruiting letters from hundreds of college coaches by his sophomore year. The buzz around James intensified in the summer before the start of his junior season, when he arrived at adidas's ABCD Basketball Camp in Teaneck, New Jersey. At this signature event for up-and-coming high school talent whose Most Valuable Player list included names like Stephon Marbury and Kobe Bryant, James dominated his one-on-one matchup with one of the country's top high school seniors, Lenny Cooke.

Sports Illustrated writer Grant Wahl watched Jordan's game-winner in the stands next to James. Born in Mission, Kansas, Wahl attended

Princeton University, where he covered the school's men's soccer team and fell in love with the sport. After graduating, he landed an internship at the *Miami Herald* before joining *Sports Illustrated* as a fact-checker in 1996, becoming a staff writer for the magazine a year later, covering soccer and college basketball.

Wahl took over as *Sports Illustrated*'s lead pro college basketball writer from Alexander Wolff in 2002. It was impossible to ignore the chatter about James, even though high schoolers were a bit outside of his usual purview. Wahl pitched the idea of a feature story on the high school junior and arrived in Akron on the morning of the Wizards-Cavaliers game. He is still amazed today by the time he got to spend with James.

"It was still the golden age of access in a sense," Wahl said. "The internet wasn't what it is today yet, and there was still a sense of this story being the introduction of LeBron James to a lot of people. I'm not sure if it could be replicated in today's media landscape."

It did take some convincing.

James appeared surprised when Wahl arrived at the school and introduced himself.

"To this day, I still don't know whether the athletic director told LeBron I was coming," he said. "When LeBron told me he was going to a Cavaliers game that night with his buddies, I remember pulling him aside in the locker room after practice and saying, 'Look, I'm sorry all of this happened really quickly, and I'm catching you off guard. But I think this could be a cover story, and I would love to take you guys to this game.' To his credit, he understood it. He said, 'Yeah, let's do it.' I'm eternally grateful for that."

Wahl arrived at his apartment later in the afternoon. He scanned the place for details to include in his story and noticed a *Sports Illustrated* cover framed above the television in the living room. The photoshopped cover with James as the cover subject had the caption IS HE THE NEXT MICHAEL JORDAN?

Wahl drove James and a group of his friends from Akron to Cleveland for the game, stopping by a McDonald's drive-thru on the way and listening to Jay-Z in the car. James had brought a notebook binder of CDs for the 45-minute ride. Wahl accompanied James to the Wizards locker room after the buzzer sounded and watched as the high schooler caught up with Jordan. An intense bidding war was already brewing between Nike and adidas to sign James to his first sneaker endorsement deal.

"This wasn't the first time LeBron had met him," Wahl explained. "Nike wanted to sign him, and Michael was clearly in recruitment mode."

Wahl tried to remain inconspicuous as the conversation unfolded, hoping to hide his *Sports Illustrated* media credential from Jordan.

"Michael still wasn't speaking to us in those days, so I was really trying not to get noticed," he recalled. "I thought I would get thrown out if he saw it."

Wahl drove the group back home, stopping for dinner at Applebee's before calling it a night. He ended up spending five days in Akron reporting for his feature. "I did a sit-down interview with LeBron after the first night," Wahl recalled. "I talked to his teammates, the athletic director, and Gloria. But I'll never forget the first day. Usually, when you fly in to write a feature, you don't do much on that first day. But it worked out so well. For all those things to have happened, it helped create a story that still stands out today."

The first draft of Wahl's feature landed on college basketball editor Greg Kelly's desk. Kelly immediately thought of Felipe Lopez, who he selected as the cover subject for *Sports Illustrated*'s 1994-95 college basketball preview issue.

A native of the Dominican Republic, Lopez moved to New York as a 14-year-old in eighth grade. He became the best high school point guard in the country—ranked ahead of Allen Iverson, who was in the same class—after leading Rice High School to a state championship. His decision to play for St. John's University became a national story. His first college practice was broadcast on ESPN. Local newspapers ran full-length features on the man nicknamed "The Dominican Michael Jordan." *Sports Illustrated* arranged a cover shoot and an image of Lopez jumping off a trampoline in mid-air in the Hudson River with the Statue of Liberty in the background appeared on the cover of the magazine's November 28, 1994, issue. The cover line said THE BIG EAST IS BACK. SUPER FRESHMAN FELIPE LOPEZ.

St. John's, who finished 12–17 the year before, was selected as one of *Sports Illustrated*'s top-25 teams in the country. Lopez averaged 17.8 points in his freshman year, but St. John's didn't make the NCAA tournament until his senior year. He was the 24th pick of the 1999 Draft and averaged 5.8 points over four seasons before retiring after a knee injury. Lopez called the *Sports Illustrated* cover a blessing for putting his community on the national stage but wished his college career started without those expectations. He runs a non-profit foundation today and is the president of a community center basketball team in the Dominican Republic.

The stories of the many basketball phenoms whose star faded after appearing on the *Sports Illustrated* cover were on Kelly's mind.

"As an editor, you always want to fight for your writers to have their story on the cover," he explained. "But we had seen that putting these kids on the cover could be damaging. I was hesitant about pushing for it because of all the criticism we had received."

Wahl's story played a significant role in changing his editor's mind. Kelly read the quotes from pro scouts in the feature and realized this wasn't just another high school phenom. James was headed to the NBA. The only question was if he could challenge the league's prep-to-pro rules and try to enter the draft before his senior year at St. Vincent-St. Mary.

"It was obvious that nothing we did was going to change the trajectory of his life," Kelly explained. "It was so clear from reading Grant's reporting. That's what swayed it for me."

He made the pitch to managing editor Bill Colson to put James on the cover and waited for his final call. Photographer Michael LeBrecht II was waiting too. A few weeks earlier he had met James at St. Vincent-St. Mary for a photoshoot to accompany Wahl's feature.

"He showed up by himself. His mom wasn't with him. His coach wasn't with him," LeBrecht recalled. "I'm from New York, so I brought a bunch of street mixtapes with me. LeBron told me his favorite rapper was Fat Joe, and I said, 'Alright, I got that.' He was willing to do whatever I asked. We started in the locker room. He had to practice for two hours. Then we shot for another two hours after that. I shot him wearing his warmups. Then we put his jersey on. It was a Catholic school, so we shot some portraits against these glass windows at this cathedral church inside the school. We did some shots of him dunking in the gym. It was a full day.

"I did the shoot and went to the Olympics not thinking anything of it. The snowboarding team was big news, and everyone assumed they would get the cover. I'll never forget the morning when the magazine came out. David Klutho, who I was assisting for at the time, just handed the issue to me and said, 'You made the cover.'"

The photo in front of the magazine was a close-up shot of James, posing in his high school uniform, holding a basketball in his right hand with an exaggerated expression on his brightly lit face against a black backdrop. "I was using two strip lights for a dramatic look," LeBrecht recalled. "I had his right hand reaching out to me, but it was creating this shadow on his face. I said, 'Let's switch it over. Let's go with the left hand and bend the right arm back. And let's get some expression.' I don't want typical screaming, but like a wooooo. He did the wooooo, and his hand in the photo is like going beyond the light, it's almost a silhouette, and you could see the jersey, the IRISH 23." The caption said THE CHOSEN ONE. It turned out to be a perfect cover line, taking the long view and correctly predicting a basketball phenom's impending stardom.

THE SPORTS ILLUSTRATED COVER SOLD OUT in Akron immediately, becoming a sought-after item among fans and collectors, reaching a point where James stopped autographing copies of it after signed versions started showing up for well above the magazine's original retail price on eBay. National newspapers and sports radio stations began to devote pages and airtime to the high school junior. St. Vincent-St. Mary hired a full-time public relations liaison to deal with reporters who started showing up to the school. Media members were prohibited from the premises during school hours.

SLAM had run a two-page feature on the high school phenom while he was a sophomore a year earlier. Ryan Jones remembers reporters around the country calling the *SLAM* Dome hoping to track down the new *Sports Illustrated* cover star.

"A photo editor from *The New Yorker* called and said they wanted to recreate this iconic photo of Lew Alcindor in high school with LeBron," Jones recalled. "I'll never forget talking to Gloria. She's like, '*The New Yorker?* Is that like *The New York Times* because we've already talked to them.' I said, 'No, it's this high-end, well-respected magazine.' She said, 'Nah. We're good.' I phoned *The New Yorker* back and told them, 'Nah, they're good.' Another time a reporter from the *Cleveland Plain Dealer* called our office trying to get a hold of LeBron. I was like, 'He's in your backyard, and you're calling us?' I said, 'No, I can't give you this kid's number.'"

Growing up during the Showtime Lakers era of the 1980s in Southern California, Jones joined *SLAM* after working at several newspaper jobs in Pennsylvania and New Jersey, including a part-time sportswriter position at the *Bergen Record*. "I did a lot of work for their arts and entertainment desk," he recalled. "It gave me a chance to do a lot of music writing. I was a hip-hop fan, so I wrote about that. It gave me a chance to cover sports and culture before I joined the magazine."

Jones became the magazine's go-to high school person and saw a sophomore from Akron on *USA Today*'s All-American First Team in 2001.

"It wasn't unusual to see a sophomore on the second team," Jones said. "But the fact that he was on the first team made us say, 'Okay, well, this kid must be legit.' We asked around, and the general feedback was, 'This guy is the real deal.'"

He convinced his editor Ben Osborne and editor-in-chief Russ Bengtson to let him travel to Akron and write a feature. The sign outside St. Vincent-St. Mary read WELCOME, SLAM! when Jones arrived.

"The coolest thing about *SLAM* was how excited people were when we showed up to any gym," he said. "Whether you were a high school kid or NBA star, it was a big deal to be featured in the magazine. To be the person who could walk into the gym and say you represented *SLAM*, it was an honor and a privilege and a cool thing to be a part of."

Jones hung out at the school and met James and his mom and friends at a local steakhouse in the evening for dinner. He conducted a sit-down interview and convinced James to write the magazine's high school diary the following year.

Atiba Jefferson was hired to travel to Akron for a subsequent photoshoot to accompany Jones' feature. He didn't think much about getting an assignment to shoot a high schooler. "Back then, you shot high school players, and then you graduated to shooting the NBA," he explained. "I had already shot players in the NBA, so when I got the assignment, I was like, 'Why am I going to a high school in Akron?' I scouted the high school and shot him in the gym and the locker room, and we ended up shooting outside as well."

The feature story and accompanying photos appeared inside *SLAM*'s September 2001 issue, with Shaquille O'Neal on the cover. Several months after *SLAM*'s profile of James arrived on newsstands, *Sports Illustrated* put the high school phenom on their cover as THE CHOSEN ONE. The editors at the *SLAM* Dome instantly lamented the decision to not push harder for James to be a cover story. Dennis

Page still regrets it today. "One of the biggest bummers of my career," he said.

"Every time I see Dennis, he brings it up," Jones said. "He always says, 'We blew it.' And I always tell him, 'Dennis, you never would have put a high school kid from Akron, Ohio, on the cover.' And he always says, 'Nah. We should have. We blew it.'"

Several months after the *Sports Illustrated* cover arrived on newsstands, *SLAM* decided to finally put James on their own cover. At the same time, Sebastian Telfair—the cousin of Marbury, who also attended Lincoln High School—was touted as the best high schooler in New York and the best junior in the country. The magazine decided to put the two most talked-about high schoolers together on the cover.

"We were trying to think of how we could flip it and make it seem like we were still ahead of the game after the *Sports Illustrated* cover," Jones recalled. "So we thought, 'The best junior and best senior. A New York kid and an Ohio Kid.' They were different players from different places and we would bring them together. That was our way of not following *Sports Illustrated*. We should have been the first on this, and we were going to find a way to do it a little different."

James and Telfair stood next to each other on the cover of *SLAM*'s August 2002 issue wearing their respective high school jerseys with adidas headbands matching their uniforms. Telfair posed with a basketball over his right shoulder, replicating Marbury's look in his first *SLAM* cover with Kevin Garnett. The main cover line said THE TAKEOVER. A second cover line, also referencing the Marbury and Garnett cover, said SEBASTIAN TELFAIR & LEBRON JAMES ARE ABOUT TO RULE THE WORLD. IMAGINE THAT.

JAMES HAD GONE FROM THE BEST high school prospect in decades to the number one story in sports, appearing on the cover of *Sports Illustrated*, *SLAM,* and *ESPN the Magazine* in a single calendar year before he appeared in an NBA game.

The *Cleveland Plain Dealer* spotted James driving a brand-new Hummer in January of 2003, starting a year-long controversy that would define his senior season at St. Vincent-St. Mary. The truck was an 18th birthday gift from his mom, who received a bank loan to make the purchase. Reporters did not buy the explanation, and speculated whether James and his family had instead violated his amateur status by accepting a payment from an agent to finance the car. Ohio High School Athletic Association commissioner Clair Muscaro absolved James of any wrongdoing after launching an investigation into the matter. Concerns over whether James was illegally receiving gifts didn't go away. Muscaro deemed James ineligible for the rest of his senior season after he accepted two throwback NBA jerseys for free from a local clothing store. James appealed the decision and was allowed to play the remainder of the season after serving a two-game suspension. He led St. Vincent-St. Mary to their third state championship in four years.

After the season, James declared for the 2003 NBA Draft. Jonathan Mannion flew to Akron a few days after the announcement for a *SLAM* cover shoot. Jones would write the cover story. The two arrived at the Spring Hill apartment complex where James lived.

"LeBron was on the top-floor balcony just waving down at us," Mannion recalled. "He said, 'Yo, I'm coming. I'll be right there.' He comes down, and he's just so excited. He knows he's entering the league. I always traveled with a portfolio of rappers and players I had photographed, just so it's like, 'Hey man, I just want you to know you're in good hands.' I showed him my book, and he was like, 'Wow, you did this? Oh man, what's Jay-Z like in person?' He was just this sweet, innocent kid in that very moment."

James came downstairs wearing a throwback Denver Nuggets Alex English jersey with a matching baseball cap. The Nuggets and Cavaliers had the best draft lottery odds to land the number one pick.

"He knew everyone wanted him to play in Cleveland," Mannion recalled, "and was like, 'Oh man, they're gonna love this.'"

James went back upstairs to change after the first part of the photoshoot was complete. He returned in a throwback Jordan jersey and a *SLAM* logo headband. "We had worked with this German sneaker brand named K1X. They gave us these headbands with our logo on them and we sent it to a bunch of high school guys, including LeBron," Jones said. "He already had an appreciation for *SLAM*, but I could have never dreamed of him wearing it for a cover."

On the cover of *SLAM*'s 71st issue, James stood against a white backdrop, with two chains dangling from his neck, a wristwatch on his left wrist. Palming a basketball in the same hand, wearing his throwback Jordan jersey with a matching white undershirt and a *SLAM* headband, the 18-year-old stared at the camera with the confidence of someone who tattooed "Chosen 1" on his back after making the *Sports Illustrated* cover. The cover line read KING JAMES. LEBRON IS READY TO RULE.

Cleveland selected him with the number one overall pick in June.

James would end the city's 52-year championship drought in 2016 and become the most popular cover subject in *SLAM* history.

PART 4

Postscript

AGAINST ALL ODDS/
Jeremy's World

Sports Illustrated writer Pablo Torre walked into Madison Square Garden on February 10, 2012, for a Friday night matchup between the Los Angeles Lakers and the New York Knicks. The best sports story in the world was taking place in New York and it featured a Taiwanese-American Ivy Leaguer who was crashing on the couch of his brother's Lower East Side apartment.

Twenty-three-year-old point guard Jeremy Lin had been waived twice earlier in the season, by Golden State and Houston, and had less than 400 career NBA minutes on his résumé at the start of the week. Lin sent DVDs with his own highlights to colleges around the country in hopes of landing a basketball scholarship as a senior at Palo Alto High School. He didn't receive a single offer despite leading his school to a state championship. Lin became a two-time First Team All-Ivy Leaguer at Harvard. He declared for the NBA Draft in 2010. All 30 teams passed. He went to Summer League and landed a two-year partially guaranteed contract with Golden State.

Lin didn't expect to be in New York long after the Knicks claimed him on waivers, so he crashed at his brother's place waiting to see if he would last more than a few weeks with the team. With Carmelo

Anthony out with a groin injury, Amar'e Stoudemire on personal leave after the death of his brother, and point guard Baron Davis injured, head coach Mike D'Antoni played Lin out of desperation as the Knicks took on the New Jersey Nets, having lost 11 out of their last 13 games. He scored a career-high 25 points in a win over the Nets. Lin set another career high two nights later with 28 points in a victory over the Utah Jazz and followed it up with 23 points and 10 assists in a win over the Washington Wizards. Now, he was set to face the Lakers on national television inside the most famous basketball arena in the world. Kobe Bryant wasn't playing along before the game, even though *Linsanity* was suddenly the biggest story in the NBA.

"Who is this kid?" he asked reporters. "I've heard about him and stuff like that, but what's he been doing? Is he getting like triple-doubles or some stuff? He's averaging 28 and eight? If he's playing well, I'll just have to deal with him."

Torre needed to interview Lin for his cover story and pleaded with Knicks vice president of public relations Jonathan Supranowitz before the game. In his most desperate moment, Torre offered to tutor Supranowitz's kids for free but was turned away. The Knicks guard scored a career-high 38 points in a 92–85 victory that evening, sending the Madison Square Garden crowd into a frenzy. Bryant scored 34 points in the loss. Torre left the arena with 48 hours until his deadline.

The *Sports Illustrated* writer finally persuaded Lin to call him over the weekend. Torre was kicking himself afterward because he forgot to ask the most important question. He wanted to know the color of the couch Lin was crashing on at his brother's apartment. Torre wanted to scoop everyone else as the couch became a national talking point, so he spent his entire Sunday afternoon texting Lin and got a response just before his deadline. A few days later, a photo of Lin driving to the basket with all five Lakers defenders surrounding him appeared on the cover of *Sports Illustrated*'s February 20, 2012, issue. The cover line said AGAINST ALL ODDS. The first paragraph of Torre's cover story referenced a brown couch.

THE *SPORTS ILLUSTRATED* COVER brought an immense amount of pride to Asian-Americans around the country.

"One of the things that we have dealt with from the outset of when we started immigrating to the United States are stereotypes," said Paul Okada, co-founder of the fan site JeremyLin.net. "Just to see an Asian-American on the cover of *Sports Illustrated*, it shows that we shouldn't be stereotyped, that Asian-Americans can do a lot of different things. It's not just math and science. That was meaningful."

ESPN the Magazine writer Ursula Liang remembers when Yao Ming appeared on the cover of ESPN's "NEXT" issue in 2001, but says Lin had a deeper connection with fans as a first-generation Asian-American.

"He represents so much of us," she said. "We always talk about Jeremy being the everyday Asian-American. There are so many firsts that are happening for Asian-Americans so late in the game. The cover was one of them."

Shanghai-based Los Angeles native Terence Lau, who met Lin when his family visited China for a league-sponsored tour before *Linsanity* ever happened, had a similar reaction.

"Everybody who went to college had a friend who went to church and played basketball," he said. "Even if I didn't know Jeremy, I still *knew* him."

American magazines were hard to track down in China, so Lau asked his friend Brian Yang back in the United States to get him a few copies. He was the perfect person to ask. Yang was an avid *Sports Illustrated* reader and was producing a Netflix documentary with Lin.

"It's the defining platform for sports journalism," he said. "To see Jeremy grace the cover, that's not something I could have dreamed of in my wildest dreams."

Torre was spending the weekend with *Sports Illustrated* senior writer David Epstein in Williamstown, Massachusetts, working on a feature story on transgender Olympic hammer thrower Keelin Godsey a few days after Lin's *Sports Illustrated* cover hit newsstands when his editor called.

Lin's run had continued. He hit a game-winning three against the Toronto Raptors earlier in the week, extending the team's win streak to six games, and followed it up with 28 points, 14 assists, and five steals in a victory over the Dallas Mavericks on a Sunday afternoon nationally televised game. *Sports Illustrated* wanted Torre to write another cover story.

Torre had less than 24 hours. He canceled his trip home and booked a hotel, flipping through every single contact on his phone, dialing anyone with even a tiny bit of connection to Lin, including Kenny Blakeney, an assistant coach at Harvard; Arne Duncan, the Secretary of Education and a Harvard alum; Ryan Fitzpatrick, an NFL quarterback and also a fellow Harvard alum; James Franco, Hollywood actor and Palo Alto High alum; and professional boxer Manny Pacquiao, who was the most high-profile Asian athlete besides Lin at the time.

The story was filed just in time. Lin appeared on the *Sports Illustrated* cover for a second straight week. On the cover of *Sports Illustrated*'s

February 27, 2012, issue was a photo of him fist-pumping in his Knicks home jersey was accompanied by the cover line FROM HARVARD TO THE GARDEN TO BEIJING. JEREMY'S WORLD. BIG SURPRISE. BIG MONEY. BIG HEART.

BACK-TO-BACK *SPORTS ILLUSTRATED* COVERS were generally reserved for cover subjects like Michael Jordan and for documenting historic championship runs across the major sports leagues. Lin's second consecutive appearance on the cover in the middle of the regular season was unprecedented. "Part of what made it feel okay was that there was such a feel-good nature to the story," said assistant managing editor Hank Hersch. "He was such an easy guy to get excited about."

The story had transformed from the number one sports story to the number one story in the world. "I don't have a child, but this was like being a parent and feeling pride for your kid who did something so well, like getting straight A's or becoming the president of the United States," Yang said. "It vaulted whatever feelings I had in the first week into overdrive. It was like, okay, now we're playing with house money. We already got our cover, and now it's happening again?"

Hua Hsu, a writer and associate professor of English at Vassar College, doesn't remember being excited about the *Sports Illustrated* covers because he was so wrapped up in the day-to-day experience of *Linsanity* living in New York. "It was like being drunk or high and not wanting to reflect on the moment too much and to sort of just live inside it," he said. Hsu was just as thrilled to see Torre, whose parents are from the Philippines, write the cover stories. "That really excited me," he added. "They got someone who had a thoughtful perspective on it."

Even Joseph Lin, Jeremy's younger brother and a freshman point guard at Hamilton College in Clinton, New York, couldn't believe what was unfolding. "It was crazy," he said. "It was indescribable. Everything was happening so fast. As a family, we were just like, 'Oh, my gosh.'"

LeBron James and the Miami Heat held Lin to eight points on 1-for-11 shooting a few days after the second cover. It was the beginning of the end for *Linsanity*. Lin's season ended after he suffered a meniscus tear in his left knee in March. He signed with the Rockets in the summer. Lin would play for six teams over the next seven seasons, landing with the Raptors in 2019, where he became the first Asian-American to win an NBA championship.

His two-week run in 2012 remains a cherished memory for Knicks fans and Asian-Americans around the country today.

"*Linsanity* is such a personal story to every Asian-American in a way that I think is special," Torre said. "Those two weeks, man. The most intense and satisfying of my entire career, easily."

The back-to-back *Sports Illustrated* covers are still remembered today.

"You just have to have a representation of what's possible, especially in the Asian-American community," Liang said. "Your parents need to see that it's possible. People don't need to know about sports to walk by a grocery store aisle and see Jeremy on a cover. That's a different type of visibility."

A third consecutive *Sports Illustrated* cover didn't happen. But when the magazine released their March 5, 2012, Major League Baseball preview issue with Ozzie Guillen and Jose Reyes of the Miami Marlins on the cover the following week, the cover line, sprawled across the middle in white, asked: MARLINSANITY?

OUTRO/ I'M COMING HOME

Chris Stone became the managing editor of *Sports Illustrated* in 2012. His first magazine cover assignment was the NBA season preview issue. The Los Angeles Lakers were championship favorites, having traded for Dwight Howard and signed Steve Nash in the off-season—adding two future Hall of Famers to a team already featuring Kobe Bryant and Pau Gasol. John Black was the team's vice president of media relations at the time. "Every person in the NBA was saying, 'Why bother with the season?'" he recalled. "Everyone thought we were winning the championship that year." It was no surprise when *Sports Illustrated* called to schedule a cover shoot. "We didn't have room in the practice facility that day," Black said, "so we shot it at the Hilton Garden hotel next door."

Howard and Nash appeared on the cover of *Sports Illustrated*'s October 29, 2012, NBA season preview issue wearing their Lakers uniforms, with exaggerated expressions on faces, their arms flailing out as if to welcome the entire world to the greatest show on Earth. The cover line said NOW THIS IS GOING TO BE FUN.

It was the opposite of Shaquille O'Neal pointing to his ring finger on the cover of *SLAM* before the Lakers went on to win three consecutive championships in the early 2000s.

The Lakers fired head coach Mike Brown after a 1–4 start and replaced him with Mike D'Antoni. Owner Jerry Buss passed away in February. Bryant tore his Achilles tendon in the last week of the season. The Lakers clinched a playoff spot on the final day of the regular season and were swept by the San Antonio Spurs in the first round. Howard signed with the Houston Rockets in the off-season.

Today, the magazine cover continues to be ridiculed and has become a popular internet meme. "I have no regrets," Stone said. "When you make predictions, you're going to be wrong pretty often. It's okay as long as you believe it."

A year later, Stone received a call from writer Franz Lidz.

"He told me there was an active NBA player who was thinking about sharing that he was gay," he recalled. "We didn't know who the athlete was, but we knew there was interest in sharing the story with *Sports Illustrated*. Franz had retired two years earlier, but I told him to pursue it."

Deputy managing editor Jon Wertheim and photographer Kwaku Alston flew to California and met the player. Back at the *Sports Illustrated* office, Stone consulted with Time Inc. editor-in-chief Martha Nelson about the cover on the Sunday evening before the magazine's deadline after receiving the photos.

"She always said, '60 percent of whether a person will purchase a magazine is the cover,'" he said. "Before we closed the magazine, she felt the cover choice was a bit flat, so I went back to the office at eleven at night to look at the photos. This was a historic moment, and we wanted to keep it understated to not get in the way of the actual story."

On the cover of *Sports Illustrated*'s May 6, 2013, issue was a close-up portrait photo of 12-year NBA veteran Jason Collins. He is smiling directly at the camera in a brightly lit room. There was a feeling of optimism and relief in his expression. The cover line said THE GAY ATHLETE. Below the cover line was an excerpt of his first-person cover story: "I didn't set out to be the first openly gay athlete in a major American team sport. But since I am, I'm happy to start the conversation."

"This wasn't sports history or cultural history," Stone said. "It was history."

Sports Illustrated moved to a twice-a-month publishing schedule in 2018. It's a monthly print publication today and releases a new digital daily cover story on their website from Monday to Friday each week.

DISPLAYED PROUDLY INSIDE THE HOME OFFICE of Lindsay Kagawa Colas are magazine covers featuring her many clients. "Magazine covers are a clear way to show what choices the media is making on who they are featuring as the hero," she explained. "It's telling the public who they should care about. There's a responsibility and power there."

On her desk is a framed photo of Brittney Griner's June 10, 2013, *ESPN the Magazine* cover. Griner had finished her college basketball career with Baylor, where she led the school to an NCAA champion-ship in her junior year, and wanted to share her personal experience of being a Black lesbian athlete with the world after being selected first overall by the Phoenix Mercury. Colas worked closely with ESPN to make sure someone told her story correctly.

"We were very protective of Brittney and how she developed her persona and her comfort with talking to the media openly about herself," she explained. "We wanted her to take control of her narrative about who she was. Even if she was still trying to figure it out, she was going to be honest."

Griner appeared on the cover of *ESPN the Magazine*'s 2013 "Taboo" issue, posing in a tank top with a yellow snake wrapped around her neck. The cover line said SNAKE-CHARMING, GENDER-BENDING, OUT-STANDING.

Colas grew up in the Bay Area and attended Stanford University on a student-athlete scholarship, where she became the captain of the school's volleyball team. A political science major, she realized how few of the athletes on campus understood how to use their stature and skill set to set themselves up for the real world. Colas helped her class-mates understand the value of networking and applied for internships for them. While obtaining a master's degree in organizational studies in her fifth year at Stanford, she founded a mentorship program for the university's athletes to teach local kids. Sports agent Bill Duffy hired Colas and asked her to assist his clients with their community involvement. Duffy would eventually give Colas an opportunity to start representing WNBA players herself.

Her first client was Diana Taurasi, who averaged 28.8 points and 12.9 rebounds in her senior season at Don Antonio Lugo High School in Chino, California, before winning three NCAA championships at the University of Connecticut. Selected first overall by the WNBA's Phoenix Mercury in 2004, Taurasi is generally considered the greatest women's basketball player of all-time. She has won three WNBA championships, two Finals Most Valuable Player Awards, an MVP, has been a nine-time All-Star, a 10-time All-WNBA First Team selection, and a five-time WNBA scoring champion, becoming the league's all-time leading scorer in 2017.

Taurasi has landed on only a handful of magazine covers in her career despite a résumé that would make her the greatest basketball player of our generation. "She would be the most famous athlete in the world if she were a man," Colas said. "There's no better interview. No one is funnier, and who has accomplished more than her? But because she's a woman, she has to be everything for everybody, and men are never held to that standard. Women have always had to be everything. To be the one they pick on the cover, you have to be not just conventionally beautiful. For the longest time, you had to appear to be straight. You had to be sexy to men in a conventional way."

Colas works for Wasserman Media Group today. Her client list includes WNBA pro Breanna Stewart, Olympic swimmer Simone Manuel, and fencer Ibtihaj Muhammad, the first American Muslim woman to wear a hijab in the Olympics. She has worked over the years with *ESPN the Magazine* to place her clients on the cover of their "Body" issue, an annual showcase of athlete bodies of different genders and shapes. The men and women appear nude on the cover in active poses.

"It was really important to me for all female athletes to feel respected for who they are as athletes," said Karen Frank, the magazine's director of photography. "We didn't in any way want to objectify any of the women who participated in the "Body" issue."

While agents and their athletes were skeptical of the idea at first, the "Body" issue eventually became one of the most coveted magazine covers in the industry.

ESPN promoted Alison Overholt to the magazine's editor-in-chief in 2016. Women started to appear more on the cover and inside the magazine. "When you have more women in decision-making roles, you start seeing different decisions getting made," Overholt said. "The idea that a women audience doesn't exist is the stuff of ancient history and old stereotypes. The issue is getting people to break out of their old ways of thinking. Humans are creatures of habit."

ESPN the Magazine ended the print version of their magazine in 2019 and continues today as a digital-only publication.

IN 2004, RUSS BENGTSON LEFT HIS ROLE as *SLAM*'s editor-in-chief, handing the job to Ryan Jones. After two years, he was replaced by Ben Osborne, who became the magazine's fifth editor-in-chief in 2006. Osborne was an editor at *SLAM* when *Sports Illustrated* beat them to putting LeBron James on the cover and still laments it today.

"It was a missed opportunity," he said. "It was a great cover and all that, but we had made an investment the year before to cover him when no one else outside of newspapers in Akron was doing it, and we get no credit for that. *SLAM* is forgotten altogether in that conversation, and that's too bad. But that first story helped us start a relationship with LeBron, which has since paid off for almost 20 years now."

Osborne decided in 2007 to turn the Cavaliers forward into the NBA logo on the cover for *SLAM*'s 106th issue. When photographer Atiba Jefferson flew to Cleveland to execute the idea, he was certain it would be a breeze. "I thought it would take five minutes," he said.

"But I realized it was impossible to capture a photo like that. You need someone to actually push them defensively, so they contort their upper body in a particular way. We never really got it right." Instead of having James replicate Jerry West's signature pose, Jefferson captured the Cavaliers forward in a series of different poses instead.

Creative director Melissa Brennan picked a photo of James posing with a basketball in his left hand in front of a blue-and-red backdrop, recreating the colors of the official NBA logo on the cover. The cover line read BRON IS THE ONE. Osborne calls it his favorite cover today, even if readers didn't pick up on the cover photo concept.

"It's one of our cleanest covers ever," he said. "LeBron was four years into his career, and he hadn't won anything yet. He hadn't even been to the Eastern Conference Finals. We said, 'Fuck all that, he's a god.'"

After winning his first NBA championship with the Miami Heat in 2012, James posted a photo on Instagram of a new *SLAM* cover of him celebrating the title win with the hashtag #SLAMIsFAM. The relationship between James and the magazine remains today and is reminiscent of what *Sports Illustrated* had with Michael Jordan.

JORDAN GRANTED UNPRECEDENTED EXCLUSIVE ACCESS to ESPN writer Wright Thompson when he turned 50 in 2013. The story remains the definitive feature of his post-playing career and one of the best pieces of sports journalism ever. Meanwhile, *Sports Illustrated* put the photo Walter Iooss Jr. took of Jordan from behind the stanchion at the 1988 Slam Dunk Contest on the cover of their February 18, 2013, issue. Phil Taylor contributed a cover story for the issue but lamented the lack of access to *Sports Illustrated*'s most popular cover subject of all-time.

"My story paled in comparison," he said. "Part of it was because I'm not Wright Thompson. Part of it was because I didn't get to hang out with him."

Jordan's silence toward *Sports Illustrated* entered its third decade as the magazine celebrated him on the cover for his 50th birthday.

THE NORTH CAROLINA TAR HEELS were in New York for the Holiday Festival tournament a few weeks after Jordan appeared on the cover of *Sports Illustrated*'s 1983–84 college basketball preview issue. Scott Smith waited at the team hotel and got Jordan and teammate Sam Perkins to sign the cover in the lobby.

Smith started collecting autographed *Sports Illustrated* covers in 1982. He estimates today the collection includes 95 percent of all the covers dating back to the first issue in 1954. Some of the cover subjects have passed away. Other cover subjects, including sports fans and models, have been difficult to track down. Smith is still optimistic he will one day have a complete collection of signed *Sports Illustrated* covers, but to do that he'll need to have Jordan autograph every one of his covers.

The two have developed a cordial relationship over the years. Smith still needed 20 of his covers signed after Jordan retired for the third and final time in 2003. He flew to the Bahamas for a celebrity golf tournament and found Jordan walking off the course with Spike Lee. Smith reached into his pocket, pulled out $10,000 in cash, and offered it as a charitable donation to Jordan's foundation.

"I need 20 covers signed for my collection," Smith told him. "You can personalize them if you want. They're not for sale."

"You've got enough in your collection," Jordan said.

"When you had three championship rings, was that enough?" Smith asked. "When you had $100 million in the bank, did you really need $200 million?"

Lee couldn't hold back his laughter.

Smith had a point.

Jordan grinned.

He held his stance and walked off the course without signing the covers.

Smith is still hoping to get those 20 autographs one day.

But he'll never have a *complete* collection.

There's one cover Jordan will never sign.

That's right.

It's the one with the BAG IT, MICHAEL! caption.

"Yeah, no way," Smith said. "He won't sign that one."

ADAM FIGMAN JOINED *SLAM* IN 2010 as an editorial intern and became the magazine's editor-in-chief six years later. He has recreated several classic *SLAM* covers since, including a Joel Embiid cover in 2017. He wore a Philadelphia 76ers jersey with the same cover line and a similar pose as Allen Iverson's iconic SOUL ON ICE cover. "We got some blowback for that in terms of whether Joel was able to carry the torch from a cultural perspective," Figman recalled. "The criticism was fair."

SLAM has reintroduced many of their classic magazine covers to a new generation of fans. Kevin Love, in a backward visor like Kevin Garnett, and Ricky Rubio, holding a basketball on his shoulder like Stephon Marbury, appeared on a 2012 cover with the caption SHOWBIZ & KL. RICKY RUBIO & KEVIN LOVE RULE EL

MUNDO. IMAGINE THAT. The 2014 rookie draft class, including Embiid, Jabari Parker, Andrew Wiggins, and others appeared in a gatefold cover posing against a brick wall backdrop with the caption READY OR NOT... HERE THEY COME! THE BEST ROOKIE CLASS SINCE... '03? '96?? '84??? Ben Simmons wore a throwback Jordan All-Star jersey on the cover in 2016 with a similar pose to when Jonathan Mannion shot James outside of his apartment with the caption BEN SIMMONS. HEIR TO THE THRONE.

Recreating classic magazine covers can be a challenge. In 2014, Doug McDermott was one of the best players in college basketball, leading the nation in scoring at 26.5 points per game and leading the Creighton Blue Jays to a 27–8 record in their first season in the Big East Conference. He evoked memories of another sweet-shooting forward named Larry Bird, who was a *Sports Illustrated* cover subject decades earlier during his college career. A cover shoot was scheduled inside Creighton's campus gymnasium. It was an honor for McDermott, who has three generations of family, including himself, who read the magazine growing up. When he arrived at the gym to meet photographer Al Tielemans, McDermott was slightly annoyed when asked to take off his undershirt. "I played every college game in my undershirt," he recalled. "I said, 'Shit, you could have let me know, I could have hit the weight room for an hour or something and gotten some biceps and triceps.'"

Tielemans wanted a specific look for the cover photo and asked McDermott to pose with team cheerleaders Kayleigh Begley and Kelsey Saddoris. "We had to be perfect in our stances," McDermott recalled. "I had to put my hands on my hips. It had to be a smirk and not a smile." At one point, Tielemans debated whether the crew should get nail polish remover to take off the colors on Begley and Saddoris's nails before realizing he could edit it out in post-production. The instructions to the cover subjects were exceptionally detailed because *Sports Illustrated* was recreating one of their all-time classic covers. In 1977, Bird appeared on the cover of the magazine's college preview issue, wearing his powder-blue Indiana State jersey with matching shorts, with two team cheerleaders, Sharon Senefeld and Marcia Staub, standing in front of him, their finger over their lips, making a shushing gesture, in reference to the cover line which read: COLLEGE BASKETBALL'S SECRET WEAPON.

On the cover of *Sports Illustrated*'s March 17, 2014, issue was a photo of McDermott standing between Begley and Saddoris with the same cover line from Bird's cover 37 years ago. The cover photo had the same backdrop, the same poses, the same shushing gesture from the cheerleaders, but it was not an exact replica. The color of the *Sports Illustrated* logo was changed from powder blue to royal blue to match McDermott's Creighton jersey. The cheerleader uniforms were also a different color. Bird was positioned below the magazine's logo, with the cheerleader's legs cropped from the cover photo. McDermott was placed higher, his head covering the logo and the cheerleader's bodies in full view. It was one of the best attempts at replicating an iconic magazine cover, and still, the differences were glaring. "As a photographer, you prefer to go out and make something on your own instead of duplicating something that's been done in the past," Tielemans explained. "There's no particular creative joy in recreating something that's already been done."

Figman recreates classic *SLAM* covers as a way to connect the present with the past. "It's a fun way to engage the new generation," he said. "The current players love it, the older players love it, and it helps kids learn about the history of the magazine."

MANY OF THE CHARACTERISTICS which made *SLAM* a pop-culture phenomenon in the 1990s have remained. They're still a favorite of basketball players around the world. CJ McCollum of the Portland Trail Blazers still remembers receiving the call from Figman—a fellow Lehigh University graduate—to schedule a cover shoot.

"I read *SLAM* growing up and remember all the covers and how much they meant to me," McCollum recalled. "It was our culture. It was sports culture and Black culture. They covered high school, college, and women's basketball. I remember how dope it was when they mentioned me during my freshman year in college. People were telling me, 'You're in *SLAM*!' That was the start of something for me."

McCollum appeared on the cover of *SLAM*'s 213th issue. "I made sure I had my hair lined up," he recalled. "I remember trying to figure out whether to smile or just give them a straight face."

The hip-hop influence has also remained.

Drake became the first rapper to appear on the *SLAM* cover in 2016. The pop culture icon, who also became the global ambassador of the Toronto Raptors, posed in a suit and tie, standing between Kyle Lowry and DeMar DeRozan with the caption 6 GODS. Figman was brainstorming cover ideas for the New Orleans Pelicans duo of Anthony Davis and DeMarcus Cousins two years later when he and senior editor Pete Walsh realized there was only one way to pay homage to The Big Easy.

A graphic design company named Pen & Pixel created an album cover aesthetic in the 1990s which defined hip-hop in the South. They became the in-house design firm for Master P's No Limit Records label, which originated on the West Coast before moving their operations to New Orleans in 1995. Pen & Pixel album covers were intentionally outrageous, but every decision was intentional. They consulted the artists for their specific visual requests and rejected anything racist. They also declined a request to put a pregnant woman holding a shotgun once.

"The number one purpose of the album cover is to sell the music," said Shawn Brauch, who founded the company with his brother Aaron. "The only way to do that is I have to stop you first. You have to be going through the store, you're browsing the cover, and you go, 'What the heck?' That's step one. I want you to hold that piece of artwork for seven seconds. That's when I can capture you. That's step two. You start looking at the details of the cover. You're like, 'Alright, I have to take it home and listen to it.' If you do all of that, I've done my job."

SLAM decided to recreate the Pen & Pixel look on their cover. Brauch received an email from creative director Alexis Cook and immediately responded with a preliminary sketch.

"I went Mardi Gras crazy," he recalled. "I had a marching band and clowns marching down Bourbon Street with beads. Alexis says, 'So we're not quite on the same page. It's a little festive, and we want it to be a little more sinister.' So I did a second sketch with both guys holding a basketball with an alligator. She said, 'I just want one basketball.' I did another sketch, and finally, it was what they were looking for."

A cover shoot was arranged with Davis and Cousins. The issue was set to hit the printers when Walsh looked at the cover and couldn't shake the feeling something was wrong. He realized the graphic had included a crocodile but it should have been an alligator instead.

Louisiana only had the latter and not the former. Walsh attributes his ability to spot the difference between the two to a Florida animal farm visit growing up. "Since that day, I've been able to spot the difference between alligators and crocodiles," he explained. "One has a more rounded snout. The other is more pointed." Figman reached out to a wildlife expert over Twitter to confirm the mistake. He asked Brauch for a last-minute revision.

On the 214th issue of *SLAM*, Davis and Cousins appeared on the cover, standing next to each other below a blinged-out *SLAM* logo. The cover line read 2 REAL. The alligator appeared at the bottom.

SLAM CONTINUES TO PUBLISH on newsstands today but has moved to a bi-monthly publishing schedule.

They have also embraced the digital era.

SLAM has one of the most elaborate social media presences of any magazine today. With each one covering a part of basketball and its culture, their multiple social accounts strategy has proven successful. League Fits, an Instagram page that documents the pregame and off-court outfits of players, has become one of the most popular pages on the internet. Accounts devoted to sneakers and high school basketball have gained a considerable following. The magazine also has a dedicated account to covering women's basketball.

After Maya Moore appeared on the *SLAM* cover in 2018, she was followed by A'ja Wilson and Liz Cambage of the WNBA's Las Vegas Aces the following year. Paige Bueckers became the first women's high schooler player to appear on the cover of *SLAM* in 2020. New York Liberty star Sabrina Ionescu appeared on the cover in 2021 with the cover line THE NEXT QUEEN OF NY. In the same year, Skylar

Diggins-Smith, Nneka Ogwumike, Sue Bird, and Taurasi appeared on a *SLAM* cover together to celebrate the WNBA's 25th season.

Susan Price Thomas is still the managing editor today. The magazine no longer works out of the original *SLAM* Dome. Thomas says the new office location still looks like a teenage boy's bedroom, but concedes it's a bit more professional-looking today.

Dennis Page remains the publisher of the magazine. Despite the publication's growing digital presence, he insists the *SLAM* cover is still the highest honor for any basketball player today. "The magazine cover is a piece of art," Page said. "You can't compare it to something on Instagram."

IT'S HARD TO SAY MAGAZINE COVERS don't mean anything anymore when I look at the cover stories in this chapter and think about what Jeremy Lin's back-to-back *Sports Illustrated* covers meant to many people around the world, but the digital era has eroded a magazine's ability to create a special relationship with their readers.

Many of our childhoods were shaped in part by a *Sports Illustrated* issue in our mailbox every Thursday, a new *SLAM* issue on newsstands every month, and a new issue of *The Source* we would find at the grocery store. The covers were a way for these magazines to start a conversation with their readers. These conversations are taking place online today and not in print. They take place through a *Players' Tribune* article, over a podcast interview, or with a feature documentary. Most people find out about *SLAM*'s new covers on Instagram and not the newsstand.

Can these conversations still take place inside a magazine?

Flagrant, a basketball and culture magazine with the tongue-in-cheek slogan "Digital Is Dead," believes so. The magazine, which was founded by four women, published their first issue in 2020. *Flagrant* has a broad focus on basketball and the sport's influence in the cultural space. They also have a strong online presence which has helped to cultivate a loyal audience.

Ashtyn Butuso, a Portland, Oregon, native, is the magazine's editor-in-chief. "Our magazine is about creating a sense of community," she explained. "Consuming print media versus digital media is a completely different experience. It's tangible. It's sensory. It's everlasting. I swear there is some kind of dopamine or serotonin released when a page is turned. There is a kind of magic in it. We are trying to remind people of that."

Magazines won't go away.

But they no longer feel necessary.

"Everything is immediate gratification now," said Jerry Bembry. "I remember when I got my mom to buy me a *Sports Illustrated* subscription when I was a kid in the 1970s. I would sometimes be waiting at the mailbox for the mailman. I was a huge boxing fan, so whenever Muhammad Ali fought, I needed to see those images in *Sports Illustrated*. It was the thrill back then of getting the magazine, going through the pictures first, then reading the stories. Now, you just pick up your phone, and it's right there. I can't remember the last time I picked up a copy of *Sports Illustrated*."

Bembry is right.

Here's one more cover story.

JAMES BROKE THE HEARTS OF CAVALIERS FANS in 2010 when he announced his intentions to sign with the Miami Heat in a one-hour television special hosted by Jim Gray called "The Decision" on ESPN. Despite raising over $2 million for the Boys & Girls Club, there was significant criticism toward how James made his announcement. He teamed up with Dwyane Wade and Chris Bosh in Miami and went to four consecutive NBA Finals, winning two championships.

Anticipation for a potential return to Cleveland intensified in 2014 when James opted out of his contract after Miami lost to the San Antonio Spurs in the NBA Finals. Fans followed James' every movement online and found the flight tracker to Cavaliers owner Dan Gilbert's private plane. The only media member who was privy to the information was *Sports Illustrated* writer Lee Jenkins, who had written previous cover stories of James, including his 2012 Sportsman of the Year feature. Several days before James made his decision, he asked Jenkins to fly to Las Vegas. After James finished attending a summer basketball camp, he revealed to Jenkins he was returning to Cleveland. A first-person essay was put together and sent to the *Sports Illustrated* office on a Friday morning. A half-dozen staffers were briefed on the situation and helped with editing and laying out the story for the magazine's website. The story went live two hours later at just past noon.

In an essay titled I'M COMING HOME as told to Jenkins, James explained his return to Cleveland, speaking candidly about his bond with the state of Ohio. The story received 3.7 million unique views in one day. The essay's online header featured a photo of James posing in a black suit with a championship ring visible on his right hand. It became the defining image of the story.

A photo of James' Cavaliers jersey hanging inside the home locker room at Quicken Loans Arena appeared on the cover of *Sports Illustrated*'s July 21, 2014, issue the following week.

It was an afterthought.

Acknowledgments

I want to start by thanking my parents for everything.

Thank to my eighth-grade homeroom teacher Francine Klein. You were formative in encouraging me to realize the power of writing and helped me see the possibilities of pursuing a creative path. It took a few decades but I'm here now.

For this specific project, I want to thank: Holly MacKenzie for the continuous feedback throughout the process, which was invaluable, Susan Price Thomas and Sammy Gunnell for helping to provide all the resources necessary to understand the history of *SLAM*, and Lauren Mitchell, who I want to be clear I am not sharing my million dollar(s) royalties with.

A special thanks to everyone who made the time to be interviewed for this book, especially Phil Taylor, Alexander Wolff, Russ Bengtson, Scoop Jackson, Dennis Page, Tony Gervino, and Rick Telander for the multiple phone calls and emails. This book wouldn't have been possible without you.

I want to thank all the writers, editors, and creatives who have given me an opportunity to build a career in sports media over the past decade and to everyone who has supported me along the way. I'll never forget all of the people who helped jumpstart my new career. A thank you to Ben Sin for opening the first door for me in this industry. I'll forever be appreciative.

Thank you to all the editors I've worked with over the years, including: Adam Figman, Ashley Fetters, Sarah Sprague, Eddie Maisonet,

Acknowledgments

David Roth, Gabe Guarente, Karizza Sanchez, Andrew Forbes, Matt Moore, Jared Dubin, Martin Rickman, Spencer Lund, Adi Joseph, Dan Toman, Mackenzie Liddell, Adam Francis, Shauntel Lowe, Elena Bergeron, Chris Gayomali, and Matt Moore. There are inevitably going to be people that I've missed and I apologize for it in advance.

Thanks to everyone at Triumph Books for making this project come to life.

Talk to you all soon.

SOURCES

Bibliography

Below is a list of books which were critical in the research process of this project.

25 Years of SLAM: The Covers. SLAM Media, 2019.

Babb, Kent. *Not a Game: The Incredible Rise and Unthinkable Fall of Allen Iverson*. Atria Books, 2015.

Birch, Ian. *Iconic Magazine Covers: The Inside Stories Told by the People Who Made Them*. Firefly Books, 2018.

Chang, Jeff. *Can't Stop Won't Stop: A History of the Hip-Hop Generation*. Picador, 2005.

Corbett, Sara. *Venus to the Hoop*. Anchor Books, 1997.

Croatto, Pete. *From Hang Time to Prime Time: Business, Entertainment, and the Birth of the Modern Day NBA*. Atria Books, 2020.

Deford, Frank. *Over Time: My Life as a Sportswriter*. Grover Press, 2013.

Draper, Robert. *Rolling Stone Magazine: The Uncensored History*. HarperCollins, 1991.

Erving, Julius, & Greenfeld, Karl Taro. *Dr. J: The Autobiography*. HarperCollins, 2013.

Garcia, Bobbito. *Where'd You Get Those: New York City's Sneaker Culture. 1960–1987*. Testify Books, 2006.

Halberstam, David. *Playing for Keeps: Michael Jordan & the World He Made*. Random House, 1999.

Jenkins, Sacha, & Wilson, Elliott, & Mao, Chairman, & Alvarez, Gabriel, & Rollins, Brent. *Ego Trip's Book of Rap Lists*. St. Martin's Griffin, 1999.

Jones, Ryan. *King James: Believe the Hype. The LeBron James Story*. St Martin's Griffin, 2005.

King, Stacey. *Magazine Design That Works: Secrets for Successful Magazine Design*. Rockport Publishers, 2001.

Sources

MacCambridge, Mike. *The Franchise: A History of Sports Illustrated Magazine.* Hyperion, 1997.

MacMullan, Jackie. *Shaq Uncut: My Story.* Grand Central Publishing, 2012.

McCallum, Jack. *Dream Team: How Michael, Magic, Larry, Charles, and the Greatest Team of All Time Conquered the World and Changed the Game of Basketball Forever.* Ballantine Books, 2013.

Miller, James Andrew, & Shales, Tom. *Those Guys Have All the Fun: Inside the World of ESPN.* Little, Brown, and Company, 2011.

Pearlman, Jeff. *Three Ring Circus: Kobe, Shaq, Phil, and the Crazy Years of the Lakers Dynasty.* Houghton Mifflin Harcourt, 2020.

Platt, Larry. *Only the Strong Survive: The Odyssey of Allen Iverson.* HarperCollins, 2003.

Pluto, Terry. *Loose Balls: The Short, Wild Life of the American Basketball Association.* Simon & Schuster, 2007.

Rhoden, William C. *Forty Million Dollar Slaves: The Rise, Fall, and Redemption of the Black Athlete.* Crown, 2007.

Rodman, Dennis, & Keown, Tim. *Bad as I Wanna Be.* Dell, 1996.

Rodman, Dennis, & Silver, Michael. *Walk on the Wild Side.* Delacorte Press, 1997.

Smith, Sam. *The Jordan Rules: The Inside Story of One Turbulent Season with Michael Jordan and the Chicago Bulls.* Pocket Books, 1993.

Sports Illustrated: The Covers. Sports Illustrated, 2010.

Windhorst, Brian. *LeBron Inc.: The Making of a Billion Dollar Athlete.* Grand Central Publishing, 2019.

Zirin, Dave. *Welcome to the Terrordome: The Pain, Politics, and Promise of Sports.* Haymarket Books, 2007.

Interviews

The following interviews were conducted for this book, including those who were quoted directly or whose knowledge and insight contributed to my reporting and research. They are listed in alphabetical order by last name (Asterisk denotes online/email correspondence).

Val Ackerman	Lois Elfman	Mike MacCambridge	Michael Silver
Evan Auerbach	Adam Figman	Jackie MacMullan	John Skipper
Seimone Augustus	Karen Frank	Dwight Manley	Brad Smith
Marc Baptiste	Tony Gervino	Jonathan Mannion	Scott Smith
Mike Barnett	Paul Gilbert	Dave Mays	Jerry Stackhouse
Shawn Brauch	Josh Gotthelf	Clay Patrick McBride	Jeff Staple
Gary Belsky	Sammy Gunnell	Jack McCallum	Chris Stone
Jerry Bembry	Peter Gunz	Katrina McClain	Phil Taylor
Russ Bengtson	Bill Hardekopf	CJ McCollum	Rick Telander
Ron Berler	Derrick Hawes	Doug McDermott	Susan Price Thomas
Andrew Bernstein	Hank Hersch	Terry McDonald	Al Tielemans
John Black	Steve Hoffman	John McDonough	Pablo Torre
Curt Bloom	Sue Hovey	Jim Moore	Tara VanDerveer
Lynn Bloom	Hua Hsu	Mark Mulvoy	Grant Wahl
Chris Bosh	Walter Iooss Jr.	Jonathan Nelson	Pete Walsh
Nathaniel Butler	Scoop Jackson	Paul Okada	Chin Wang
Ashtyn Butuso*	Atiba Jefferson	Ben Osborne	Jeff Weiss
Jim Callis	Cory Johnson	Alison Overholt	Rick Welts
Paul Cantor	Ryan Jones	Dennis Page	Lang Whitaker
Susan Casey	Larry Keith	Aron Phillips	Chris Wilder
Patrick Cassidy	Greg Kelly	Chris Pika	Alexander Wolff
Gary Cavalli	Terence Lau	Rick Reilly*	Steve Wulf
Keith Clinkscales	Michael LeBrecht II	Jalen Rose	Brian Yang
Lindsay Colas	Ursula Liang	Bob Ryan	Ronnie Zeidel
Anne Cribbs	Joseph Lin	Andy Serwer	
Lucy Danziger*	Terry Lyons	DJ Set Free	

References

INTRO/NORTH CAROLINA IS NO. 1

Keith, Larry. (2015, February 9). *SI Remembers: Writers and editors share their memories of Dean Smith*. Sports Illustrated. https://www.si.com/college/2015/02/09/si-remembers-dean-smith-sl-price-frank-deford-gary-smith-larry-keith

Brown, C.L. (2015, February 10). *Dean Smith wouldn't change his ways for today's freshmen*. ESPN. https://www.espn.com/blog/collegebasketballnation/post/_/id/103006/dean-smith-wouldnt-change-his-ways-for-todays-freshmen

Wolff, Alexander. (1997, December 22). Uncommon Man. *Sports Illustrated*. Retrieved from http://vault.si.com

Miller, Robert L. (1984, October 22). Letter From The Publisher. *Sports Illustrated*. Retrieved from http://vault.si.com

Kirkpatrick, Curry. (1980, December 1). College Basketball 1980-81: Cranking out the rankings. *Sports Illustrated* Retrieved from http://vault.si.com

A STAR IS BORN

Green, Ronald. (1979, August 2). Sports Illustrated — a happy 25th birthday. *The Charlotte News*. Retrieved from http://www.newspapers.com

Burpo, S.L. (1984, November 28). Is Rick Mount getting more of that 'special attention?' *The Reporter-Times*. Retrieved from http://www.newspapers.com

Quirk, Kevin (1984, June 20). Choosing Sides: No NBA Draft Surprises as Olajuwon Is 1st, Jordan 3rd. *The Charlotte Observer*. Retrieved from http://www.newspapers.com

Pearlman, Jeff. (2016, December 19). *Alexander Wolff Q&A*. Jeff Pearlman. https://jeffpearlman.com/2016/12/19/alexander-wolff/

Fluck, Adam. (2009, September 3). *Rod Thorn Drafted Michael Jordan at No. 3 In 1984*. NBA. https://www.nba.com/bulls/news/jordanhof_thorn_090908.html

Doyel, Gregg. (2016, December 2). *Purdue hero Rick Mount is mending fences*. Indy Star. https://www.indystar.com/story/sports/columnists/gregg-doyel/2016/12/02/doyel-purdue-hero-rick-mount-mending-fences/94682876/

Barrett, Mike. (2016, September 2). *Backroads Indiana - Sports Illustrated*. The Tribune. http://www.tribtown.com/2016/09/03/backroads_indiana__sports_illustrated/

Montieth, Mark. (2009). *Rick Mount Part 1*. Mark Montieth. https://markmontieth.com/one-on-one/rick-mount-part-1/

Deford, Frank. (1966, February 14). Brightest Star in Indiana. *Sports Illustrated*. Retrieved from http://vault.si.com

Cook, Kevin. (1986, December 22). A Grand And Heavy Legacy. *Sports Illustrated*. Retrieved from http://vault.si.com

Johnson, William. (1971, August 9). The Greatest Athletes In Yates Center, Kansas. *Sports Illustrated*. Retrieved from http://vault.si.com

Pearlman, Jeff. (1998, February 23). Mike Peterson, High School Phenom. *Sports Illustrated*. Retrieved from http://vault.si.com

Rushin, Steve. (2014, August 11). There And Back. *Sports Illustrated*. Retrieved from http://vault.si.com

Wolff, Alexander. (2002, January 21). Old Black Magic. *Sports Illustrated*. Retrieved from http://vault.si.com

Wolff, Alexander. (1984, December 10). In The Driver's Seat. *Sports Illustrated*. Retrieved from http://vault.si.com

YOUR SNEAKERS OR YOUR LIFE

Gilbert, Paul. (2006, June 11). He Loved This Game. *New York Times*. Retrieved from http://www.nytimes.com

Fury, Shawn. (2016, June 15). *How NBA Entertainment Helped Save the League and Spread a Renaissance*. VICE. https://www.vice.com/en/article/mgzgg3/how-nba-entertainment-helped-save-the-league-and-spread-a-renaissance

Tejada, Justin. (2015, May 14). *Your Sneakers or Your Life: Behind the Story That Shook Up the industry*. Sole Collector. https://solecollector.com/news/2015/05/sports-illustrated-sneakers-or-your-life

Lazarus, George. (1991, July 15). Splashy Gatorade bow set for Jordan. *Chicago Tribune*. Retrieved from http://www.newspapers.com

Berger, Warren. (1990, November 11). Selling the soul of Nike. *The Anniston Star*. Retrieved from http://www.newspapers.com

MacCambridge, Michael. (1994, August 16). 'SI:' Troubled words illustrate its evolution. *Austin American-Statesman*. Retrieved from http://www.newspapers.com

Warren, James (1987, April 15). Sports Illustrated goes the distance to win its bout with a deadline. *Chicago Tribune*. Retrieved from http://www.newspapers.com

Mulvoy, Mark. (1991, December 23). From The Publisher. *Sports Illustrated*. Retrieved from http://vault.si.com

Barr, Donald J. (1990, November 12). From The Publisher. *Sports Illustrated*. Retrieved from http://vault.si.com

The Education of Walter Iooss Jr. (2011, December 12). *Sports Illustrated*. Retrieved from http://vault.si.com

Telander, Rick. (1990, May 14). Senseless. *Sports Illustrated*. Retrieved from http://vault.si.com

THE DESIRE ISN'T THERE

O'Malley, John. (1991, December 18). Jordan to cherish Sportsman of Year. *The Times*. Retrieved from http://www.newspapers.com

NBA probes Jordan dealings with bail bondsman. (1992, March 21). Associated Press. Retrieved from http://www.newspapers.com

Jordan's Statement. (1993, August 20). *Tampa Bay Times*. Retrieved from http://www.newspapers.com

Nordgren, Sarah. (1993, October 8). What's next for Jordan? Relaxation. Associated Press. Retrieved from http://www.newspapers.com

Jordan: thankful and outraged. (1993, August 19). Associated Press. Retrieved from http://www.newspapers.com

Lopresti, Mike. (1993, August 14). Death shatters sense of security. *Statesman Journal*. Retrieved from http://www.newspapers.com

Muller, Bill, & Quillin, Martha. (1993, August 22). Jordan reveled in life as family man. *The News and Observer*. Retrieved from http://www.newspapers.com

Kamp, David. (1999, February 7). *The Tabloid Decade*. Vanity Fair. https://www.vanityfair.com/culture/1999/02/david-kamp-tabloid-decade

Breskin, David. (1989, March 1). *Michael Jordan, In His Own Orbit*. GQ. https://www.gq.com/story/michael-jordan-in-his-own-orbit-profile

References

Greenstein, Teddy. (2010, May 10). *Michael Jordan retired—for the 1st time — at a 'fiasco' of a news conference in 1993. Here's the oral history of that day at the Berto Center.* Chicago Tribune. https://www.chicagotribune.com/sports/bulls/ct-michael-jordan-retires-1993-last-dance-20200510-uaclf6oeb5arxlg2xednhvotcq-story.html

Brubaker, Bill. (1993, October 9). *Jordan Is Cleared In Probe.* The Washington Post. https://www.washingtonpost.com/archive/sports/1993/10/09/jordan-is-cleared-in-probe/2a03ccc3-ce38-4a4c-9d79-c21a3c2e6b9a/

McCallum, Jack. (1993, October 18). 'The Desire Isn't There.' *Sports Illustrated.* Retrieved from http://vault.si.com

Retro Basketball Highlights. (2014, June 30). *Michael Jordan/Ahmad Rashad Interview 1993 Finals Game 1.* YouTube. https://www.youtube.com/watch?v=1iXHS5Ri73g

BAG IT, MICHAEL!

Berkow, Ira. (1994, April 9). Jordan's First Crack As a Baron An Event. *The New York Times.* Retrieved from http://www.nytimes.com

Chass, Murray. (1994, February 8). Swish Just Won't Cut It In Jordan's New Sport. *The New York Times.* Retrieved from http://www.nytimes.com

Jordan Turns Down All-Star Invitation. (1994, June 30). *The New York Times.* Retrieved from http://www.nytimes.com

Street, Jim. (1994, February 26). Seattle pitcher tires of talk. *Seattle Post-Intelligencer.* Retrieved from http://www.newspapers.com

Jay Bell figures Jordan hasn't earned right to autograph a baseball. (1994, March 8). *The Akron Beacon Journal.* Retrieved from http://www.newspapers.com

Sox sign Jordan—to minor leagues. (1994, February 7). Associated Press. Retrieved from http://www.newspapers.com

Bus rides await Jordan in minors. (1994, March 22). Associated Press. Retrieved from http://www.newspapers.com

Jordan responds to tough article. (1994, March 10). Associated Press. Retrieved from http://www.newspapers.com

Craig, Jack. (1995, December 31). An indelible Mark at SI. *The Boston Globe.* Retrieved from http://www.newspapers.com

Fegan, James. (2020, May 10). *Thanks to 1994, Michael Jordan will always be the most famous Birmingham Baron.* The Athletic. https://theathletic.com/1803492/2020/05/10/thanks-to-1994-michael-jordan-will-always-be-the-most-famous-birmingham-baron/

Simpson, Allan. (2005, January 1). *How Baseball America Began.* Baseball America. https://www.baseballamerica.com/stories/how-baseball-america-began/

Ruda, Mark. (1994, March). *Scouting Michael Jordan: Can His Airness Make It In Baseball?* Baseball America. https://www.baseballamerica.com/stories/scouting-michael-jordan-can-his-airness-make-it-in-baseball/

Dodson, Aaron. (2017, July 11). *That time Michael Jordan left the Bulls, went to baseball's minors, and chased his childhood dream.* ESPN the Undefeated. https://theundefeated.com/features/cover-stories-michael-jordan-baseball-america/

Robinson, Eric. (2015). *The Peculiar Professional Baseball Career of Eddie Gaedel.* Society for American Baseball Research. https://sabr.org/journal/article/the-peculiar-professional-baseball-career-of-eddie-gaedel/

McCallum, Jack. (2014, August 11). Ripping Into A Big Rift. *Sports Illustrated.* Retrieved from http://vault.si.com

Sutton, Kelso F. (1979, September 3). Letter From The Publisher. *Sports Illustrated.* Retrieved from http://vault.si.com

COVER STORY

McDonell, Terry. (2003, November 10). The Cover Story: Why Getting Covered By SI Is Complicated. *Sports Illustrated*. Retrieved from http://vault.si.com

Halberstam, David. (1991, December 23). A Hero For The Wired World. *Sports Illustrated*. Retrieved from http://vault.si.com

Wulf, Steve. (1994, March 7). Cinderella Story. *Sports Illustrated*. Retrieved from http://vault.si.com

Wulf, Steve. (1994, March 14). Err Jordan. *Sports Illustrated*. Retrieved from http://vault.si.com

Popovich, J.M. (1994, April). Disliked Mike. *Baseball America*.

RARE BIRD

Hoban, Phoebe. (1997, September 7). Behind The Velvet Ropes. *The New York Times*. Retrieved from http://www.nytimes.com

Covitz, Randy. (2003, March 30). The early 'Worm.' *The Kansas City Star*. Retrieved from http://www.newspapers.com

Haight, Robert. (1993, February 28). 'The Worm' digs himself a hole. *The Reporter*. Retrieved from http://www.newspapers.com

Dennis is still a menace. (1993, November 19). Gannett News Service. Retrieved from http://www.newspapers.com

Maddon, Michael. (1996, May 7). Circus shots from Rodman. *The Boston Globe*. Retrieved from http://www.newspapers.com

Vorva, Jeff. (1996, May 2). Stern backs refs, not Rodman. *Northwest Herald*. Retrieved from http://www.newspapers.com

Rodman just a sideshow. (1995, May 16). *El Paso Times wire reports*. Retrieved from http://www.newspapers.com

Spurs win game without Rodman. (1995, March 21). Associated Press. Retrieved from http://www.newspapers.com

Adande, J.A. (1994, November 2). *Rodman Suspended Indefinitely By Spurs*. The Washington Post. https://www.washingtonpost.com/archive/sports/1994/11/02/rodman-suspended-indefinitely-by-spurs/2d7c8481-60ce-42a6-9bba-e532d505b7b1/

Telander, Rick. (1993, November 8). Demolition Man. *Sports Illustrated*. Retrieved from http://vault.si.com

Silver, Michael. (1995, May 29). Rodman Unchained. *Sports Illustrated*. Retrieved from http://vault.si.com

Silver, Michael. (1999, June 21). Prince of the City. *Sports Illustrated*. Retrieved from http://vault.si.com

DON'T BAG IT, MICHAEL

Pogrebin, Robin. (1998, January 19). ESPN Rivals Set for Fight as Magazine Debut Nears. *The New York Times*. Retrieved from http://www.nytimes.com

Wise, Mike (1999, January 14). The Final Word From Jordan. *The New York Times*. Retrieved from http://www.nytimes.com

NBA Champion Bulls Take TV Ratings Title, Too. (1998, June 17). Associated Press. Retrieved from http://www.newspapers.com

Bulls' 'last dance' brings out the fans, ushers in speculation. (1998, June 17). Associated Press. Retrieved from http://www.newspapers.com

Hillyer, John. (1995, March 21). Higgins had an inkling that Jordan's fire was still burning. *The San Francisco Examiner*. Retrieved from http://www.newspapers.com

Hofmann, Rich. (1994, June 17). NHL will never slam-dunk NBA. *Philadelphia Daily News*. Retrieved from http://www.newspapers.com

Isaacson, Melissa. (1995, March 11). Sox's loss Bulls' gain? *Chicago Tribune*. Retrieved from http://www.newspapers.com

References

Silverstein, Jack M. (2020, March). *'I'm Back': The 45 days that drove MJ back to basketball*. NBC Sports Chicago. https://www.nbcsports.com/chicago/bulls/michael-jordan-im-back-fax-1995-nba

Montieth, Mark. (2015, March 23). *Jordan's Return Created Unprecedented Spectacle*. NBA. https://www.nba.com/pacers/news/jordans-return-created-unprecedented-spectacle

MacMullan, Jackie. (2020, April 17). *The Michael Jordan I knew is about to be revealed to the world in 'The Last Dance.'* ESPN. https://www.espn.com/nba/story/_/id/29041173/the-michael-jordan-knew-be-revealed-world

Armour, Terry. (1995, October 14). *Rodman Plays In Peoria*. Chicago Tribune. https://www.chicagotribune.com/news/ct-xpm-1995-10-14-9510140168-story.html

Telander, Rick. (1998, April 6). Michael Jordan on Phil Jackson, Jerry Krause and the one NBA player he couldn't stand the most. *ESPN the Magazine*. Retrieved from http://www.espn.com

Taylor, Phil. (1998, February 16). Hang in There. *Sports Illustrated*. Retrieved from http://vault.si.com

"YOU WANNA HEAR A FRESH RHYME..."

Kelley, Tiny. (2003, June 10). Art Cooper, Who Transformed GQ Magazine, Is Dead at 65. *New York Times*. Retrieved from http://www.nytimes.com

Carmody, Deirdre. (1992, September 14). Hip-Hop Dances to the Newsstands. *New York Times*. Retrieved from http://www.nytimes.com

Carmody, Deirdre. (1992, September 21). 'Vibe' arises from hip-hop. *New York Times*. Retrieved from http://www.nytimes.com

Cooper, Barry. (1992, May 20). Shaq playing waiting game in Los Angeles. *The Orlando Sentinel*. Retrieved from http://www.newspapers.com

Coble, Don (1993, February 21). Land of the Giant. *Star-Gazette*. Retrieved from http://www.newspapers.com

Horovitz, Bruce. (1992, December 6). A matchup for center of attention. *The Cincinnati Enquirer*. Retrieved from http://www.newspapers.com

DeCaro, Frank. (1987, April 29). Guides for trendy spenders. *Detroit Free Press*. Retrieved from http://www.newspapers.com

Matange, Yash. (2020, November 6). *This Date in NBA History (Nov 6): Shaquille O'Neal begins his legendary NBA career with impressive double-double*. NBA. https://ca.nba.com/news/this-date-in-nba-history-nov-6-shaquille-oneal-begins-his-legendary-nba-career-with-impressive-double-double

Murphy, Keith, & Walters, Stephanie. (2016, September 15). *'Shaq Diesel' An oral history of professional sports' only platinum album*. ESPN the Undefeated. https://theundefeated.com/features/oral-history-shaq-shaquille-oneal-shaq-diesel-the-making-of-rap-hip-hop/

Frisch, Ian. (2015, October 14). *Shaq's Next Act: Behind the Turntables*. VICE. https://www.vice.com/en/article/3dg8q3/shaqs-next-act-behind-the-turntables

Callas, Brad. (2018, November 29). *The 20 Greatest Years in Hip-Hop History, Part 4: 5-1*. DJ Booth. https://djbooth.net/features/2018-11-29-hip-hop-greatest-years-part-four

Kimble, Julian. (2020, October 27). *Rewind: Ahmad Rashad on 30 Years of 'NBA Inside Stuff.'* The Ringer. https://www.theringer.com/nba/2020/10/27/21535316/nba-inside-stuff-ahmad-rashad

Thompson, Derek. (2015, May 8). *1991: The Most Important Year in Pop-Music History*. The Atlantic. https://www.theatlantic.com/culture/archive/2015/05/1991-the-most-important-year-in-music/392642/

Connell, Christopher. (1992, September 22). *Quayle Demands That Rap Record Be Yanked*. Associated Press. https://apnews.com/article/a249c215c523dbd528710412cb91b193

Charnas, Dan. (2018, September 27). *'We Changed Culture': An Oral History of Vibe Magazine*. Billboard. https://www.billboard.com/articles/columns/hip-hop/8477004/vibe-magazine-oral-history

Adande, J.A. (2011, March 12). *Fab Five changed the game forever*. ESPN. https://www.espn.com/nba/columns/story?columnist=adande_ja&page=fabfive-110312

Light, Alan. (1992, August 20). *The Rolling Stone Interview: Ice-T*. Rolling Stone. https://www.rollingstone.com/feature/ice-t-1992-cover-cop-killer-interview-247663/

Allen, Harry. (December 1994–January 1995). Time Bomb: Clocking the history of hip hop 15 years after "Rapper's Delight." *Vibe*. Retrieved from http://books.google.ca

THE IN YOUR FACE BASKETBALL MAGAZINE

Greene, Andy. (2017, January 6). *Rolling Stone at 50: Making the First Issue*. Rolling Stone. https://www.rollingstone.com/music/music-features/rolling-stone-at-50-making-the-first-issue-193707/

Cohen, Rich. (2017, December). *The Rise and Fall of Rolling Stone*. The Atlantic. https://www.theatlantic.com/magazine/archive/2017/12/rolling-stone-jann-wenner/544107/

Tolinski, Brad. (2021, January). *A history of Guitar World: the good, the bad and the ridiculous*. Guitar World. https://www.guitarworld.com/features/a-history-of-guitar-world-the-good-the-bad-and-the-ridiculous

SCOOP & A.I.

Shabazz, Sherron. (2010, April 15). *Scoop Jackson: Backboards & Basslines Part 1*. HiphopDX. https://hiphopdx.com/interviews/id.1526/title.scoop-jackson-backboards-basslines-part-1#

Jackson, Scoop. (1996, January). No Questions Asked. *SLAM*.

Jackson, Scoop. (1997, September). White Man's Burden. *SLAM*.

READY OR NOT... HERE THEY COME!

Remme, Mark. (2013, July 30). *Rookie Transition Program Helps Players Adjust To NBA Life*. NBA. https://www.nba.com/timberwolves/news/rookie-transition-program-helps-players-adjust-nba-life

Wang, Oliver. (2008, April 18). *Chatting With the Chairman: An Interview ego trip's Jeff Mao*. UCLA Asia Pacific Center. https://www.international.ucla.edu/asia/article/90797

Squadron, Alex. (2020, November 17). Oral History of the Legendary SLAM 15 Cover Shoot. *SLAM*. Retrieved from http://www.slamonline.com

THE *SLAM* DOME INTERLUDE

Konigsberg, Eric. (2002, February 3). The Slam Team. *The New Yorker*. Retrieved from http://www.newyorker.com

Ricapito, Maria. (1998, May 10). Basketball: Walk it, Wear it, Read It. Retrieved from http://www.nytimes.com

Mixon, Imani, & Cuevas, Jaz, & Kenner, Rob. (2013, October 17). *The Stories Behind The First Covers of Famous Rap Magazines*. Complex. https://www.complex.com/style/2013/10/stoires-behind-frst-covers-of-famous-rap-magzines/

Alvarez, Gabriel. (2016, February 22). *The 1996 Project: Looking Back at the Year Hip-Hop Embraced Success*. Complex. https://www.complex.com/music/2016/02/the-1996-project-looking-back-at-the-year-hip-hop-embraced-success

Hotchkiss, Wheat. (2020, May 7). *"I Almost Fell Over": An Oral History of Reggie Miller's 8 Points in 9 Seconds*. NBA. https://www.nba.com/pacers/news/i-almost-fell-over-oral-history-reggie-miller-8-points-9-seconds

247HH.com. (2020, April 13). *Robert "Scoop" Jackson—How XXL Came To Be & Funny Argument With Timbaland (247HH EXCL)*. YouTube. https://www.youtube.com/watch?v=gAzQJHsLBZE

SHOWBIZ & KG

Chalifoux, Jordan. (2007, June 17). *Jonathan Mannion Q&A*. Format Mag. http://formatmag.com/features/jonathan-mannion/

Pereira, Julian. (2012, March 22). *Jonathan Mannion Tells All: The Stories Behind His 25 Favorite Album Covers*. Complex. https://www.complex.com/music/2012/03/jonathan-mannion-tells-all-the-stories-behind-his-25-favorite-album-covers/

References

Bristout, Ralph. (2018, June 25). *The oral history of Jay Z's 'Reasonable Doubt' cover*. Revolt. https://www.revolt.tv/2018/6/25/20823243/the-oral-history-of-jay-z-s-reasonable-doubt-cover

Farber, Michael. (1997, January 20). Feel the Warmth. *Sports Illustrated*. Retrieved from http://vault.si.com

Johnson, Cory. (November 1994). The Future. *Vibe*. Retrieved from http://books.google.ca

Montville, Leigh. (1999, May 3). Howlin' Wolf. *Sports Illustrated*. Retrieved from http://vault.si.com

THE BEST POINT GUARD IN THE WORLD (YOU'VE NEVER HEARD OF)

Mallozzi, Vincent. (1990, November 11). Legend of the Playground. *The New York Times*. Retrieved from http://www.nytimes.com

Slotnik, Daniel. (2017, April 25). Greg Marius, Impresario of Harlem Street Ball, Dies at 59. *The New York Times*. Retrieved from http://www.nytimes.com

Bondy, Stefan. (2018, September 2). *Meet Joe Hammond, the greatest street baller that ever lived, before a life in the drug world took it all away*. New York Daily News. https://www.nydailynews.com/sports/basketball/ny-sports-endzone-hammond-20180830-story.html

Buckheit, Mary. (2008, February 7). *From American gangster to crossover legend*. ESPN. https://www.espn.com/espn/blackhistory2008/columns/story?page=buckheit/080207

Bengtson, Russ. (n.d.). *A history of Rucker Park: The True Mecca of Basketball*. Complex. https://www.complex.com/sports/history-of-rucker-park-true-basketball-mecca

Lambert, Charisse. (2017, April 29). *Greg Marius married hoops and hip-hop to revive the Rucker summer league*. ESPN the Undefeated. https://theundefeated.com/features/an-appreciation-greg-marius-rucker-summer-league/

Flores, Ronnie. (2011, August 23). *Rafer Alston globalized streetball*. ESPN. https://www.espn.com/high-school/boys-basketball/story/_/id/7943650/rafer-alston-globalized-streetball

Christian, Olivia. (2018, December 21). *DJ Set Free On The Origin And Legacy Of The AND1 Mixtape*. WBUR. https://www.wbur.org/onlyagame/2018/12/21/and1-mixtapes-basketball

Lambert, Rashaad. (2020, October 7). *The Crossover: How Hip-Hop Culture Was Set Free In The NBA*. Forbes. https://www.forbes.com/sites/forbestheculture/2020/10/07/the-crossover-how-hip-hop-culture-was-set-free-in-the-nba/?sh=758763557603

Sepkowitz, Leo. (2019, February 12). *How The NBA Got its Handles*. Bleacher Report. https://bleacherreport.com/articles/2820399-how-the-nba-got-its-handles

Telander, Rick. (1973, November 12). They Always Go Home Again. *Sports Illustrated*. Retrieved from http://vault.si.com

McCarron, Anthony. (1997, December). Rafer Madness. *SLAM*.

GENERATION NETS

Carty, Jim. (1995, February 5). Are NBA's misfits misunderstood? *The Courier-News*. Retrieved from http://www.newspapers.com

Halls, Bill. (1995, January 29). Magic's Anderson lends helping hand. *Detroit Free Press*. Retrieved from http://www.newspapers.com

New Jersey Americans. (n.d.). Remembering the ABA. http://www.remembertheaba.com/new-jersey-americans.html

Dowd, Tom. (2019, September 10). *Nets History Timeline: From 1967 To Today*. NBA. https://www.nba.com/nets/news/feature/2019/09/10/nets-history-timeline-from-1967-to-today

Politi, Steve. (2019, March 30). *Who knows what Nets could have been if Dr. J stayed?* The Star-Ledger. https://www.nj.com/nets/2012/04/politi_who_knows_what_nets_cou.html

D'Alessandro, Dave. (2012, April 22). *The best and worst of Nets basketball in New Jersey*. The Star-Ledger. https://www.nj.com/nets/2012/04/post_11.html

Wilbon, Michael. (1994, November 11). *Beard's Working Hard, But Little Net Gain So Far.* The Washington Post. https://www.washingtonpost.com/archive/sports/1994/11/11/beards-working-hard-but-little-net-gain-so-far/762c93c7-d70f-4cf4-b922-9e957386159a/

Taylor, Phil. (1995, January 30). Bad Actors. *Sports Illustrated.* Retrieved from http://vault.si.com

MacMullan, Jackie. (1999, March 8). Inside The NBA. *Sports Illustrated.* Retrieved from http://vault.si.com

SOUL ON ICE

Girard, Fred. (1973, January 22). Black… Not So Beautiful On Paper. *St. Petersburg Times.* Retrieved from http://news.google.com

Gilmer, Lance. (1971, March 15). New Magazine on Black Athletes. *The San Francisco Examiner.* Retrieved from http://www.newspapers.com

Iverson stuns Knicks with 35. (1996, November 13). Associated Press. Retrieved from http://www.newspapers.com

Lee, Lorraine. (1996, November 16). NBA's Rites Of Passage. *St. Louis Post-Dispatch.* Retrieved from http://www.newspapers.com

Aschburner, Steve. (1996, November 17). NBA notebook. *Star Tribune.* Retrieved from http://www.newspapers.com

Smallwood, John. (1997, February 10). Attack on Iverson is relentless. *Philadelphia Daily News.* Retrieved from http://www.newspapers.com

Heath, Thomas. (1997, February 10). Iverson's entourage a concern. *The Washington Post.* Retrieved from http://www.newspapers.com

Telander, Rick. (2000, May 11). Image-mad NBA creates coverup. *Chicago Sun-Times.* Retrieved from http://www.newspapers.com

Smith, Stephen A. (2000, May 9). Altered Iverson photo drawing controversy. *The Philadelphia Inquirer.* Retrieved from http://www.newspapers.com

Jones, Ryan. (2019, April 23). *An Oral History of the Iconic Allen Iverson SLAM Cover.* SLAM. https://www.slamonline.com/nba/an-oral-history-of-the-iconic-allen-iverson-slam-cover/

Lukas, Paul. (2020, December 10). *History Lesson: 'Black Sports' and 'Our Sports' Magazines.* Uni Watch. https://uni-watch.com/2020/12/10/history-lesson-black-sports-and-our-sports-magazines/

Hudson, Jill. (2017, May 31). *Muhammad Ali's 1968 'Esquire' cover is one of the greatest of all-time.* ESPN the Undefeated. https://theundefeated.com/features/muhammad-ali-1968-esquire-cover/

Gotthardt, Alexxa. (2018, November 7). *The Photograph That Made a Martyr out of Muhammad Ali.* Artsy. https://www.artsy.net/article/artsy-editorial-photograph-made-martyr-muhammad-ali

Walks, Matt. (2016, May 7). *The little-known story behind Allen Iverson's 'practice' rant.* ESPN. https://www.espn.com/nba/story/_/id/29143112/the-little-known-story-allen-iverson-practice-rant

CHAMIQUE

McDonald, Soraya Nadia. (2020, March 10). *Cheryl Miller's career as a baller may have been cut short, but her story is big.* ESPN the Undefeated. https://theundefeated.com/features/cheryl-millers-women-of-troy/

de la Cretaz, Britni. (2019, May). *An Audience of Athletes: The Rise and Fall of Feminist Sports.* Longreads. https://longreads.com/2019/05/22/an-audience-of-athletes-the-rise-and-fall-of-feminist-sports/

McDermott, Barry. (1982, April 5). The Rich Get Richer, High-Tech Style. *Sports Illustrated.* Retrieved from http://vault.si.com

THE SUMMER OF WOMEN

Pogrebin, Robin. (1997, September 21). Adding Sweat and Muscle To a Familiar Formula. *The New York Times.* Retrieved from http://www.nytimes.com

Elliott, Stuart. (1996, July 15). Sports Illustrated and Nike hope girls just want to read about women's sports and female athletes. *The New York Times.* Retrieved from http://www.nytimes.com

References

Carr, David. (2002, October 17). Time Inc. Is Closing Sports Illustrated Women. *The New York Times*. Retrieved from http://www.nytimes.com

Goad, Kimberly (1996, February 1). Hoops Not Just a Game For Top Women Pros. *Dallas Morning News*. Retrieved from http://www.newspapers.com

Berlet, Bruce. (1997, October 28). An Eye On The ABL. *Hartford Courant*. Retrieved from http://www.newspapers.com

Kelly, Keith. (1999, January 7). *Sports Illustrated Relaunching Women's Title*. New York Post. https://nypost.com/1999/01/07/sports-illustrated-relaunching-womens-title/

Newberry, Paul. (2020, August 13). *Summer of Women: Females stole the show at 1996 Olympics*. Associated Press. https://apnews.com/article/ct-state-wire-international-soccer-basketball-ca-state-wire-softball-0729beb591c94cef3bd8a0ed5357a898

Seeds of USA Basketball Women's Olympic Gold Medal Streak Sown 20 Years Ago. (2015, May 25). USA Basketball. https://www.usab.com/news-events/news/2015/05/20-year-anniversary-of-95-96-wnt-being-named.aspx

1995-96 USA Basketball Women's Senior National Team. (2010, June 10). USA Basketball. https://www.usab.com/history/national-team-womens/1995-96-usa-basketball-womens-senior-national-team.aspx

Bashaw, Michelle. (2016, May 16). *By the numbers: cover photo shoot for the WNBA 20-themed magazine issue*. ESPN. https://www.espn.com/wnba/story/_/id/15563119/by-numbers-wnba-20-magazine-cover-photo-shoot

Berg, Aimee. (2016, July 14). *Flash back 20 years to the Atlanta 1996 Olympics—when women reigned supreme*. ESPN. https://www.espn.com/espnw/sports/story/_/id/17078201/flash-back-20-years-atlanta-1996-olympics-women-reigned-supreme

Messer, Kate. (1997, August 15). *WNBA: The "We Got Next" Generation*. The Austin Chronicle. https://www.austinchronicle.com/screens/1997-08-15/wnba-the-we-got-next-generation/

Kelly, Keith. (2000, June 28). *Get Off The Court!—Conde Nast Folds Women's Sports Mag*. New York Post. https://nypost.com/2000/06/28/get-off-the-court-conde-nast-folds-womens-sports-mag/

Sherwin, Bob. (1997, December 14). *The State of the ABL—There Is Life Below The Rim—ABL Has the Talent but WNBA Has TV, Marketing Muscle*. Seattle Times. https://archive.seattletimes.com/archive/?date=19971214&slug=2578144

Knight, Athelia. (1998, January 2). *In Its Second Season, ABL Is Above Average*. The Washington Post. https://www.washingtonpost.com/archive/sports/1998/01/02/in-its-second-season-abl-is-above-average/ba5d50b8-e830-4402-807a-73f0672ef015/

Martin, Susan. (1998, December 23). *Bankrupt ABL Folds At Halftime Of Third Season*. The Buffalo News. https://buffalonews.com/news/bankrupt-abl-folds-at-halftime-of-third-season/article_37336578-ab55-5744-b2ee-9196dd53f2f7.html

Wolff, Alexander. (1996, July 22). The U.S. Women. *Sports Illustrated*. Retrieved from http://vault.si.com

Lopez, Steve. (1997, June 30). They Got Next. *Sports Illustrated*. Retrieved from http://vault.si.com

Wolff, Alexander. (Spring 1997). United No More. *Sports Illustrated Women/Sport*.

Leath, Virginia M, & Lumpkin, Angela. (1992). An Analysis of Sportswomen on the Covers and in the Feature Articles of Women's Sports and Fitness Magazine, 1975-1989. *Journal of Sport and Social Issues, 16(2), 121-126*. https://kuscholarworks.ku.edu/bitstream/handle/1808/11739/Lumpkin_Analysis_of_Sportswomen.pdf

Sheaffer, Lisa. (2005). Identity Crisis: Why Do General Women's Sports Magazines Fail? *University of Florida*. https://ufdcimages.uflib.ufl.edu/UF/E0/01/18/31/00001/sheaffer_l.pdf

THE AIR APPARENT

Roberts, Selena. (1998, February 9). Jordan Stars One Last Time (Probably). *The New York Times*. Retrieved from http://www.nytimes.com

Smith, Theresa. (1995, November 15). Rookie Stackhouse flashes into the NBA in great style. *The Sacramento Bee*. Retrieved from http://www.newspapers.com

Patton, Robes. (1992, August 20). Morris has no Israel deal—or Heat guarantee. *South Florida Sun Sentinel*. Retrieved from http://www.newspapers.com

Heisler, Mark. (2000, March 9). As Carter's star glows, so does The Comparison. *Los Angeles Times*. Retrieved from http://www.newspapers.com

Johnson, L.C. (1999, March 9). Hurdling The Competition. *The Orlando Sentinel*. Retrieved from http://www.newspapers.com

Carter, Ivan. (2002, June 13). Shaq puts LA on short list of three-peat NBA legends. *The Kansas City Star*. Retrieved from http://www.newspapers.com

Bliss, Marjo Rankin. (1999, March 14). SI for Women something for everyone. *The Charlotte Observer*. Retrieved from http://www.newspapers.com

Pennington, Bill. (1984, December 16). Jordan vs. the Doc: NBA debate rages. *The Record*. Retrieved from http://www.newspapers.com

Hyde, Dave. (1992, June 25). Heat's choice plain as nose on your. *South Florida Sun Sentinel*. Retrieved from http://www.newspapers.com

Powell, Shaun. (1992, June 25). Like Mike? Heat hopes so. *The Miami Herald*. Retrieved from http://www.newspapers.com

Vorva, Jeff. (1993, January 9). Hardaway makes it look all too easy. *Northwest Herald*. Retrieved from http://www.newspapers.com

Reeves, Jim. (1993, May 27). If you find Hardaway, bag him fast. *Fort Worth Star-Telegram*. Retrieved from http://www.newspapers.com

Arace, Michael. (1993, November 4). With Jordan, Bird and Magic gone, the NBA's remaining stars find themselves in a league of their own. *Hartford Courant*. Retrieved from http://www.newspapers.com

Bowen, Les (1994, November 15). Jordan heir: Already, Grant Hill poised to be next star on and off the court. *Philadelphia Daily News*. Retrieved from http://www.newspapers.com

O'Connor, Ian. (1994, November 3). Heir Jordan: Grant Hill has the stuff to be just like Mike. *New York Daily News*. Retrieved from http://www.newspapers.com

McGraw, Mike. (2000, March 13). Raptors' Carter can't escape comparisons to MJ. *The Daily Herald*. Retrieved from http://www.newspapers.com

Rowe, John. (2000, March 26). Kobe has that certain air. *The Record*. Retrieved from http://www.newspapers.com

Presenting the new, improved Kobe Bryant. (1997, October 8). Associated Press. Retrieved from http://www.newspapers.com

Howard-Cooper, Scott. (1997, October 6). Harris, Bryant Maintain Confidence. *The Los Angeles Times*. Retrieved from http://www.newspapers.com

Bembry, Jerry. (1998, February 8). Bryant: visions of Jordan. *The Baltimore Sun*. Retrieved from http://www.newspapers.com

Sheridan, Chrs. (1998, February 9). Jordan asserts his MVP status again. Associated Press. Retrieved from http://www.newspapers.com

Price, Dwain. (2002, June 11). Lakers benefit big as Bryant matures. *Fort Worth Star-Telegram*. Retrieved from http://www.newspapers.com

Ding, Kevin. (2002, May 21). Big Shaq contributes with smaller deeds. *The Orange County Register*. Retrieved from http://www.newspapers.com

Top NBA Finals moments: Kobe takes over in Game 4 of 2000 Finals. (2017, May 17). NBA. https://www.nba.com/top-nba-finals-moments-kobe-bryant-delivers-game-4-2000-finals

Medina, Mark. (2016, January 15). *Kobe Bryant's 'airball game' in 1997 was a defining moment in his career*. Los Angeles Daily News. https://www.dailynews.com/2016/01/15/kobe-bryants-airball-game-in-1997-was-as-defining-moment-in-his-career/

Davis, Seth. (2014, July 7). Harold Miner. *Sports Illustrated*. Retrieved from http://vault.si.com

Coker, Cheo Hodari. (1998, March). Manchild In The Promised Land. *SLAM*.

References

DESTINY'S CHILD

Whitt, Richie. (2000, October 29). Previewing The West: Sweet Talker. *Fort Worth Star-Telegram*. Retrieved from http://www.newspapers.com

Grizzlies trade Francis in three-way deal. (1999, August 28). Associated Press. Retrieved from http://www.newspapers.com

Valdes-Rodriguez, Alisa. (2000, April 8). What Does the Future Hold for Revamped Destiny's Child? *The Los Angeles Times*. Retrieved from http://www.newspapers.com

Boucher, Geoff. (2003, June 29). Destiny's Child just gettin' stronger. *The Los Angeles Times*. Retrieved from http://www.newspapers.com

Menconi, David. (2005, July 22). Destiny's blessed child. *The News and Observer*. Retrieved from http://www.newspapers.com

Tan, Cheryl Lu-Lien. (2000, September 19). Manifest Destiny. *The Baltimore Sun*. Retrieved from http://www.newspapers.com

Whitt, Greg. (2016, August 4). 'The Source,' December 1992. ESPN the Undefeated. https://theundefeated.com/features/cover-stories-the-source-spike-lee-charles-barkley-magazine/

Bembry, Jerry. (n.d.). *Houston postcard: Mr. Destiny*. ESPN. http://www.espn.com/magazine/1102coverpost.html

Smith, Danyel. (2000, May 7). *Free to be Spree*. Time. http://content.time.com/time/magazine/article/0,9171,44526-2,00.html

Wilder, Chris. (1992, December). Nineties N------. *The Source*.

Riley, Chris (1999, December). Real Playas Do Real Things. *Source Sports*.

THE CHOSEN ONE

One-time New York basketball king Felipe Lopez shares story of perseverance. (2019, April 29). New York Post. https://nypost.com/2019/04/29/one-time-new-york-basketball-king-felipe-lopez-shares-story-of-perseverance/

Armstrong, Kevin. (2014, May 29). *New York hoops legend Felipe Lopez still an inspiration as mentor to South Bronx youth.* New York Daily News. https://www.nydailynews.com/sports/basketball/zone-ny-hoops-legend-felipe-lopez-article-1.1738959

Powers leads U.S medals sweep in halfpipe. (2002, February 11). ESPN. https://www.espn.com/olympics/winter02/snowboard/news?id=1327572

Davis, Seth. (2001, July 23). Inside College Basketball. *Sports Illustrated*. Retrieved from http://vault.si.com

Jones, Ryan. (2001, September). Ohio Player. *SLAM*.

Jones, Ryan. (2003, August). Super Lotto. *SLAM*.

Wahl, Grant. (2002, February 18). Ahead Of His Class. *Sports Illustrated*. Retrieved from http://vault.si.com

AGAINST ALL ODDS/JEREMY'S WORLD

Torre, Pablo. (2012, February 20). From Couch To Clutch. *Sports Illustrated*. Retrieved from http://vault.si.com

Torre, Pablo (2012, February 27). A Run Like No Other. *Sports Illustrated*. Retrieved from http://vault.si.com

OUTRO/I'M COMING HOME

Katz, Michael. (1983, December 28). St John's Wins; Tar Heels Romp. *The New York Times*. Retrieved by http://www.nytimes.com

Fagan, Kate. (2013, May 29). *Owning The Middle*. ESPN. https://www.espn.com/espn/feature/story/_/id/9316697/owning-middle

Thompson, Wright. (2013, February 22). *Michael Jordan Has Not Left The Building*. ESPN. http://www.espn.com/espn/feature/story/_/page/Michael-Jordan/michael-jordan-not-left-building

Farhi, Paul. (2014, July 11). *How Sports Illustrated landed the LeBron James 'I'm Coming Home' scoop.* The Washington Post. https://www.washingtonpost.com/lifestyle/style/how-sports-illustrated-landed-the-lebron-james-im-coming-home-scoop/2014/07/11/a1f18202-093a-11e4-a0dd-f2b22a257353_story.html

Silverman, Justin Rocket. (2013, October 7). *Scott Smith is all in on Sports Illustrated, with autographs from Michael Jordan, Roberto Clemente and 95% of the cover subjects.* New York Daily News. https://www.nydailynews.com/life-style/superfan-sports-illustrated-covered-article-1.1476558

Meet Shawn and Aaron Brauch of Pen and Pixel Graphics. (2018, June 27). Voyage Houston. http://voyagehouston.com/interview/meet-shawn-brauch-aaron-brauch-pen-pixel-graphics-inc-north-east/

Bushnell, Henry. (2021, March 3). *Changed The Game: Meet the radical agent-activist behind sports' most inspiring stories.* Yahoo! Sports. https://ca.sports.yahoo.com/news/womens-history-wnba-agent-lindsay-kagawa-colas-changemaker-180510760.html